DOING BUSINESS IN THE NEW VIETNAM

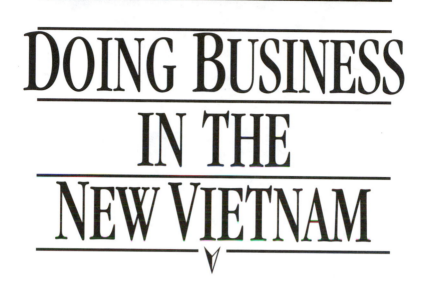

Christopher Engholm

PRENTICE HALL
Englewood Cliffs, New Jersey 07632

Prentice-Hall International (UK) Limited, *London*
Prentice-Hall of Australia Pty. Limited, *Sydney*
Prentice-Hall Canada, Inc., *Toronto*
Prentice-Hall Hispanoamericana, S.A., *Mexico*
Prentice-Hall of India Private Limited, *New Delhi*
Prentice-Hall of Japan, Inc., *Tokyo*
Simon & Schuster Asia Pte. Ltd., *Singapore*
Editora Prentice-Hall do Brasil, Ltda., *Rio de Janeiro*

©1995 *by*
PRENTICE HALL

10 9 8 7 6 5 4 3 2 1

Library of Congress Cataloging-in Publication Data

Engholm, Christopher.
   Doing business in the new Vietnam : for investors, marketers,
and entrepreneurs / by Christopher Engholm.
      p.   cm.—(Prentice Hall emerging world market series)
   Includes index.
   ISBN 0-13-325853-X (cloth)
   1. Export marketing. 2. Export marketing—Vietnam.
3. International business enterprises—Vietnam. 4. Investments,
Foreign—Vietnam. 5. Corporate culture—Vietnam. 6. Vietnam—
Economic conditions. I. Title. II. Series.
HF1416.E544   1995   95-22992
658.8'48'09597—dc20   CIP

ISBN 0-13-325853-X

PRENTICE HALL
Career & Personal Development
Englewood Cliffs, New Jersey 07632
A Simon & Schuster Company

Printed in the United States of America

DEDICATION

This book is for Richard Carter—
mentor, encourager, visionary

ACKNOWLEDGMENTS

Writing a book about Vietnam's emerging business scene is like shooting an arrow from a moving train and trying to hit a target on a passing jet. The pace of change in the country is staggering. Many people helped me stay abreast and keep my sanity along the way. In particular, I am indebted to Tamara Richardson at the Graduate School of International Relations and Pacific Studies in San Diego for her expert research assistance both in the United States and during a two-month stay in Vietnam. You did a fantastic job!

I would also like to express my appreciation to all of the people who graciously donated time to share their insights and opinions about doing business in Vietnam, without whom writing this book would simply not have been possible. They are (in alphabetical order): Kenneth M. Atkinson of PCS International Ltd.; Joe Bangert, President of Bangert Associates, Inc.; Fred Burke, Attorney at Law with Baker & McKenzie; Benilda Custodio, Certified Public Accountant with Ernst & Young; David F. Day, Attorney at Law; Germano De Marco, Quality Control manager with Lotto; Al DeMatteis of DeMatteis Vietnam; Jean Pierre Fouche, Representative of Societe Generale; Mark Gillin, Chief Representative for MBf Indochina Ltd.; Christopher Heerin, Operations Manager for Gateway Pharmaceuticals Australia; Gerald Herman, Managing Director of Lotus Communications; Bui Mai Hien, an artist with Painter Family Gallery; Sally Higgins, Partner with BDT & Associates; Andrew Homan, editor for *Vietnam Investment Review*; William J. Howell, Business Development Consultant to IBM; Wendy Huynh, Marketing Manager with Phu Qui Far East Company; Mel Jackson, Administration Manager with Red River Oil Company; Luu H. Le, Vice President and Indochina Representative for Bank of America; Mark R. Mitchell, Director of VATICO; Henry Ng, Chief Representative of DHL Worldwide Express; Nguyen Xuan Oanh,

President, N.X. Oanh Associates; Huu Quang Pham, Account Executive with Vietnam Advertising; Jason Phua, Project Director with CTS International PTE LTD; Robert J. Remnant, Chief Representative, Jardine Pacific (Vietnam); James Rockwell, Managing Director of VATICO; Stewart D. Stemple, Managing Director in Vietnam for BBI Investment Group, Chartered; Jeff Swiatek, Hanoi Manager for MBf Indochina Ltd.; Ngo Van Diem, Director of SCCI Office of the State Committee for Cooperation and Investment; Dinh Thai Vinh, Chief of Marketing with CMT, Xerox Division; and Chris Wijnberg, Director of Vietnam Fund Management Company Limited.

In the United States, a number of people were of great help in this effort as well, including researcher and writer David Fletcher, Director of Marketing at the Engholm Group; Scott Grimes, M.A., who helped with the early conception of the book; my wife Jeanie Engholm; and my indefatigable agent, Julie Castiglia.

Prentice Hall's Emerging World Markets Series

As part of the Clinton Administration's National Export Strategy, the U.S. Department of Commerce recently issued a report about the so-called Big Emerging Markets. It was found that although the large industrialized nations of the world economy "will continue to be the largest U.S. markets for decades to come," the *emerging* economies of the world hold "far more promise for large incremental gains in U.S. exports."

In short, growth in exports toward the century's end will be seen in countries such as China, Indonesia, South Korea, Mexico, Argentina, Brazil, South Africa, Poland, and Turkey—the "A" list of Big Emerging Markets, or BEMs, chosen from over 130 of the world's developing economies.

American companies are a perfect match to supply the needed production equipment, business services, engineering expertise, computer hardware and software, health products, and—once wages climb in them—consumer goods to these emerging nations. Our effort is warranted because by 2010, the top ten BEMs will import more than the European Union and Japan combined. BEMs already purchase about one-quarter of America's exports, well over $100 billion worth each year.

Yet there is nothing fast or easy about dealing with countries that share positive as well as negative commercial characteristics. These are countries in transition, both economically and politically. They are undergoing structural reforms of their commercial and legal systems, which are tectonic in scope. Naturally, the risks are manifold. But taking a wait-and-see approach may be even riskier, given the tangible advantages that earlycomers gain in emerging economies like Brazil, Poland, and Vietnam.

The purpose of the Prentice-Hall Emerging World Markets Series is to both encourage companies to make an early commitment to entering these markets, and to assist them in adroitly navigating their way toward prospering in them.

ABOUT THE AUTHOR

Christopher Engholm is founder of The Engholm Group in Del Mar, California, which specializes in market research and company representation in Asia and Latin America. He has conducted international business consulting and seminars for firms such as Hughes, Chevron, and Science Applications International Corporation, and is a frequent speaker on the topic of emerging markets, business culture, and protocol.

He has authored six other books, including *WHEN BUSINESS EAST MEETS BUSINESS WEST: A GUIDE TO PRACTICE AND PROTOCOL IN THE PACIFIC RIM, THE ASIA AND JAPAN BUSINESS INFORMATION SOURCEBOOK,* and *DOING BUSINESS IN ASIA'S BOOMING "CHINA TRIANGLE."*

CONTENTS

PART FOUR: WORKING WITH THE VIETNAMESE

INTRODUCTION:
Asia's Alighting Dragon

Though I was of a younger generation than so many Americans who visited Vietnam in recent times under different circumstances, I could not help but feel a strange sense of nostalgia as the China Airlines 747 jet I was sitting in bumped out of the cloud cover and presented me with a view of a place I had seen so often in Hollywood movies. Below, the Mekong River was in the process of killing hundreds of villagers, whose deluged abodes with their shiny tin roofs winked from beneath a canopy of dense jungle. In the green distance fin-backed mountains rose like a backdrop for an Oliver Stone helicopter ballet. Saigon airport is not much more than a huge cement slab, but it was once the U.S. army base located in South Vietnam. As we taxied to a stop, I noticed a cement storage shed with a fading peace sign painted upon it. Eugene Matthews, one of the most successful American business people working in the country, has said that "Vietnam is a country, not a war." That is true, but the reminders of the American presence in Vietnam and our history there rise up to greet the visitor at every turn.

Later in the day I visited the Ben Thanh Market in the heart of Saigon. A man carrying a tray of postcards for sale asked me if I was from America. I said that I was. He asked if I knew a gentleman called Bill whom he was best friends with 26 years ago during the war. I asked him if Bill had a last name, but he didn't know it. He called himself Bill, also. He said that he and Bill were best friends during the war and they had had more fun than at anytime during his life. He implored me to help him find Bill in the United States, but I told him that would be impossible without a last name. He was the first Vietnamese citizen whom I met in the country.

The second was a woman who called herself Kat and worked at the state-owned jewelry store in my hotel. She lives in Cholon and is Chinese, but worked as a secretary for the

Americans during the war. The American troops that she worked with had called her "Pussy Cat" and now she calls herself Catalina—"Kat" for short, because it means union in Chinese. When the Vietcong arrived in 1975, she had worried about being carted off to a re-education camp because she had worked for the Americans. The Vietcong had taken her grocery shop, but had allowed her to stay in Saigon. Nowadays she spends most of her days adding complex English words to her dictionary; she spoke English almost perfectly. She said she was a Buddhist, but also read in the Bible. Buddhism had taught her to trust in destiny, while Christianity, seemingly, had taught her to believe in doomsday, which she predicted for the year 2000. The flood of the Mekong was a sign of things to come. "You can't fight destiny," she said. "Look at you. You were born in America, and I was born in a poor communist country."

But things are changing in Vietnam, as the country redefines its destiny with *doi moi,* economic renovation initiated in 1986. The new Vietnam is wooing the world. Every aid organization, international lending institution, and company that considers itself a player in the emerging markets of the postcommunist world, has representatives who fill the lobbies of every (fully-booked) hotel in Saigon and Hanoi.

Vietnam, with its hard-working population of 74 million, has emerged as the hottest new business frontier on the Pacific Rim. Even before President Clinton lifted the U.S. embargo on Vietnam in February, 1994, scores of major American companies had conducted discussions in Vietnam for future deals and/or signed deals through foreign subsidiaries. All the excitement is understandable. After Indonesia, Vietnam is the most populated country in Southeast Asia. Its economic reform program has prompted an explosion of private business activity and record rates of economic growth; Gross National Product grew by 8 percent in 1993 and 8.8 percent in 1994. Vietnam's growth has encouraged a stampede of foreign investment. As of December 1992, there were 556 foreign projects in operation in Vietnam, representing a total value of $4.63 billion in contracts. By mid-1994 total pledged foreign direct investment (FDI) climbed to an admirable U.S. $9.5 billion, near the total combined FDI of Hungary, Slovenia, Poland, and the New Czech Republic.

Strategically, Vietnam is a window into the still untapped natural resources and unsatiated consumer markets of Laos, Cambodia, and even Myanmar.

Since the relaxation of the U.S. trade restrictions in December 1994 and full normalization of relations between the U.S. and Vietnam in July 1995, a slew of U.S. firms have applied to open offices in Vietnam, while hundreds more have opened negotiations with their Vietnamese counterparts. Ho Chi Minh City (formerly Saigon) has exploded with new hotels, offices, and investment zones. Over 500,000 business people now travel to Vietnam every year.

WHO ARE THE VIETNAMESE?

The Vietnamese are entirely unique in Asia, culturally and in their approach to foreign companies. With the influence of the French, Chinese, and the Americans, the Vietnamese are cosmopolitan where the Mainland Chinese are xenophobic. They have a hard-core work ethic where the Thai and Malays are rather laid-back. They are pragmatic pseudo-Buddhists while the Indonesians are staunch and inflexible Muslims.

Even though officially a communist country, the government adopted market principles in the 1992 constitution and had actually been experimenting with economic reforms as early as 1979. Finally, in 1986 the Vietnamese government decided to embrace market reforms. "*Doi moi*," or "economic renovation," has dramatically changed the economic environment. Stabilization policies have been adopted, prices deregulated, official foreign exchange rates have been brought in line with black market rates, and a host of other reforms have been undertaken.

As a result, Vietnam today has essentially a free market economy, though it's still in its infancy (the perfect juncture at which to get involved). The most important thing to note is that the Vietnamese aren't socialists. While the last 20 years have definitely left an impression on those educated with Marxist ideology, there is widespread belief that the economic changes of the last 4 years are positive and correct. Capitalism has been welcomed with open arms and many Vietnamese have proven to be entrepreneurial and innovative. Thomas L. Friedman, who lives in Hanoi, has watched as the Vietnamese have responded to the call of capitalism . . . from the woman with her scale who charges to weigh you in the local market, to the Foreign Ministry Press Officer who charges $25 to make you an appointment with officials. Everybody seems to be in business. As Friedman says, "the Ministry of Health sponsors ballroom dancing on Friday nights to raise cash. The Hanoi Golf and Country Club is built on land leased from the army. If the Ho Chi Minh Trail existed today it would be a toll road." Mark Gillon, one of the top foreign consultants in the country, suggests that the potential of Vietnam is tremendous, that the country will do better than Thailand or Malaysia. "Hong Kong and Singapore were in first and way ahead, while China is big, but Vietnam is going to grow in a major way. The Vietnamese know exactly what they want and many know how to get it." They were exposed to U.S. capitalism during the war and they have seen the success of the overseas Vietnamese. Their economy is dollar-based already, and their language is romanized.

For other Americans, Vietnam unfortunately conjures up memories of America's military defeat there. In many boardrooms across America, the decision not to get involved in the country has been made because of emotional luggage that many of us carry inside. Indeed, the destiny of our two countries seem inextricably linked. Now, however, that link is made not for the purpose of communist containment, but for mutual prosperity.

GLOSSARY

100% FOREIGN-OWNED: A form of investment usually limited to major projects where no Vietnamese presence is required within the project.

BUILD OPERATE TRANSFER (BOT): A form of investment whereby the foreign party builds and operates a project with an agreed duration, at the end of which the project is transferred back to the Vietnamese free of charge.

BUSINESS COOPERATION CONTRACT (BCC): A contract between a foreign investor and a Vietnamese party to undertake a project. A legal entity is not created.

JOINT VENTURE (JV): A separate legal entity created when a foreign investor and Vietnamese enact a project. JVs are the most common form of investment in Vietnam.

MEMORANDUM OF UNDERSTANDING (MOU): Agreement between a foreign company and a Vietnamese organization to cooperate at some time in the future. Generally regarded as the first step in securing a JV, it is not legally binding, is rarely exclusive, and is non-enforceable.

PROFESSIONAL LICENSE: Though not yet formally embedded in the system by statute, these are reserved for professional organizations (lawyers, accountants, construction contractors), and have the same status and conditions as Rep Offices. Authorization to open an office is granted by the relevant ministry.

REPRESENTATIVE OFFICE LICENSE (REP OFFICE): Issued by the Ministry of Trade & Tourism (or by the State Bank in the case of foreign banks), Rep Offices are forbidden to undertake any business in Vietnam, but exist only to represent the overseas parent company. Rep offices are usually the first step in the investment process and are utilized to research the market and establish relationships.

STATE COMMITTEE FOR COOPERATION & INVESTMENT (SCCI): The central body through which applications for foreign investment must be passed. It has the power to approve, reject, extend, suspend, review, or revoke investment licenses.

LEGAL TERMS USED BY THE VIETNAMESE

LAWS: The highest form of legal instrument in Vietnam, passed only by the National Assembly.

ORDINANCES: When the National Assembly is not in session, ordinances are passed by its Standing Committee.

DECREES: These include more detailed regulations and are passed by the government entity implementing laws or ordinances.

CIRCULARS: Issued by individual ministries, circulars will usually provide guidance on how a particular ordinance, law, or decree is to be interpreted and administered.

GUIDELINES: Though not legal instruments, guidelines outline policies issued by the Prime Minister and determine what committees are to be convened to handle particular issues.

ACRONYMS

ASEAN   Association of Southeast Asian Nations; currently comprised of Brunei, Indonesia, Malaysia, Philippines, Singapore, Thailand, and Vietnam.

CMEA   Council for Mutual Economic Assistance; or COMECON (defunct since 1992)

BOT   Build, Operate, Transfer

EPZ   Export Processing Zone

FIE   Foreign-Invested Enterprise

JV   Joint Venture

LFI   Law on Foreign Investment

MOF   Ministry of Finance

MFN   Most Favored Nation

MIA   Missing in Action

MOSTE Ministry of Science, Technology and Environment

MOTT   Ministry of Trade and Tourism

SBV   State Bank of Vietnam

SCCI   State Committee for Cooperation and Investment

SOE   State-owned Enterprise

SRV   Socialist Republic of Vietnam

UBCV   Unified Buddhist Church of Vietnam

VCCI   Vietnam Chamber of Commerce and Industry

VCP   Vietnam Communist Party

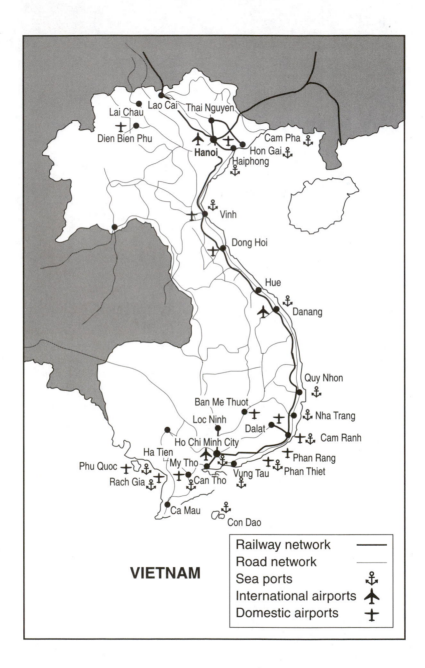

Lai Chau
Lao Cai
Thai Nguyen
Dien Bien Phu
Cam Pha
Hanoi
Hon Gai
Haiphong
Vinh
Dong Hoi
Hue
Danang
Quy Nhon
Ban Me Thuot
Nha Trang
Loc Ninh
Dalat
Cam Ranh
Ho Chi Minh City
Phan Rang
Ha Tien
My Tho
Phan Thiet
Phu Quoc
Vung Tau
Rach Gia
Can Tho
Ca Mau
Con Dao

Railway network
Road network
Sea ports
International airports
Domestic airports

VIETNAM

PART ONE

Country Profile

Over mountains and rivers of the South reigns the Emperor of the South.

As it stands written forever in the Book of Heaven.

How is it then that you strangers dare to invade our land?

Your armies, without pity, shall be annihilated.

MOUNTAINS AND RIVERS OF THE EMPIRE OF THE SOUTH
BY LY THUONG KIET (1019-1105)

Hue today is a cuisine, not a battle; TET is a New Year's celebration, not an offensive; Haiphong is a harbor, not something to be bombed at Christmas; and Highway One is where they run the Hanoi marathon, not the military artery of an enemy nation.

THOMAS L. FRIEDMAN,
WRITING FOR THE NEW YORK TIMES NEWS SERVICE

Vietnam at a Glance

General

Language:	Vietnamese
Currency:	Dong
Religions:	Buddhist (80%), Catholic, Taoist

Population

Total:		73.6 million
Density:		214 persons/km:
Growth rate:		2.2%
Distribution:	Urban:	20%
	Rural:	80%
Under 25 years:		58.9%
Proportion of females:		51.3%

Health

Infant mortality rate (1991):	43/1,000
Life expectancy (1992)	
Male:	64 years
Female:	69 years
Malnutrition (under 5 years):	42%

Education

Adult literacy rate (1992):	
Average	89%
Female	84%
Male	93%

Employment

Labor pool:	38 million (1993)
Employment:	33 million (1993)
State sector:	9.3% (1992)

Economy

GDP growth (1993):	8.0%
GDP avg.growth (1990–93):	6.8%
GDP avg.growth (1986–90):	3.9%
GNP per capita:	USD 220 (1992)
GDP growth by sector (1993):	
Agriculture:	3.1%
Industry:	9.2%
Services:	10.5%

Share of GDP by main sectors (1993):
Exports: USD 3.0 billion (22% growth)
Imports: USD 3.3 billion (31% growth)
Exchange rate: USD 1 = Dong 10,981

Principal exports (1993):	
Crude oil:	6.2 million tons (USD 370 m)
Rice:	1.7 million tons
Marine products:	USD 350 m
Garments:	USD 350 m

Infrastructure

Roads:	87,500 km 12% paved, 40% poor condition
Railways:	3,260 km
Telephones:	260,000
Electricity:	10,000 Kwh

CHAPTER 1

THE VIETNAMESE PEOPLE

*E*ven within the diverse group of countries that comprise Southeast Asia, Vietnam can undoubtedly be considered unique. Historically, excluding a thousand-year Chinese occupation, Vietnam was colonized a great deal later and much more quickly than those countries colonized by the British or Dutch. More importantly, Vietnam has found itself entangled in struggles against foreign powers more often than any other country in the region. In fact, while the Asian Miracles were allowed to concentrate on economic development in the 1960s and 1970s, Vietnam was still embroiled in one of the more tragic wars of the twentieth century.

A COUNTRY OF DISTINCTION

Culturally, the overriding influence of China has strongly shaped social and political values. Confucian thought has long been a predominant feature of Vietnamese society and continues to manifest itself today in human relations and politics. But unlike several neighboring countries, such Indian religions as Islam and Hinduism did not take hold, though Buddhism has a large following. Politically and economically, Vietnam is really the only country among Southeast Asian nations that adopted socialism and held onto it for such a duration of time. Consequently, Vietnam is also the only Southeast Asian country, aside from the Philippines and Burma, that didn't experience marked economic growth from the early 1960s through mid-1980s. One positive feature of socialism, however, was its emphasis on social equality, which is given more weight in Vietnam than in many countries in the region. Perhaps Vietnam's most unique feature is that the country is divided by several cleavages, yet seems to maintain a common purpose and sense of unity in the face of these divisive factors. Whether it be regional, ethnic, political, or economical differences, the Vietnamese have managed to overcome natural splits in their society in order to defeat foreign intruders, retain independence, and achieve some measure of internal cohesiveness. Of course, that is not to say that Vietnamese society is one of complete harmony. More often than not, individual Vietnamese will pursue the same objective, but take different paths, as the war with the United States so clearly demonstrated. In the absence of an external threat and with rapid economic development, it will be interesting to see how this dynamic plays out among the Vietnamese.

What are the geographical and climatic differences between regions in Vietnam?

Vietnam has been called the "Jewel of the South China Sea," and rightfully so. The S-shaped country is situated along the same parallel as Central America in the Western hemisphere. The country's land mass is roughly that of the state of New Mexico—125,000 square miles stretching 1,100 miles along the eastern seaboard of the Indochina peninsula, at one point only 50 kilometers wide. Vietnam's 1,150 kilometer northern border is shared with China; the western mountainous region borders both Laos and Cambodia. The Troung Son Mountains, which cover three-quarters of the country, make up Vietnam's Central Highlands. The highest peak in the country is Phang Si Pan (3,143 meters) in the Hoang Lien Mountain range located in the country's extreme northwestern corner.

Two alluvial river deltas are formed by the Red River in the north and the fabled Mekong River in the South. These huge deltas equal nearly one fifth (75,000 square km) of Vietnam's land mass and comprise its productive agricultural zones. Before it forms its large fertile delta, the Red River cuts a wide valley from northwest to southwest along its 210 kilometer trek starting at the Chinese border and ending at the South China Sea. The Mekong and the Red Rivers both find their source in Yunnan and the Tibetan highlands.

Nestled on the coast between the northern and southern urban delta regions lies the central region (Trung Bo). This area covers about 125 miles of beautiful white sand beaches lapped by the warm South China Sea. This is the Quang Tri province with its principle port city of Da Nang, near the coastal area that Americans dubbed "China Beach" during the war.

The South (Nam Bo) is tropical and regularly drenched by heavy rains throughout the monsoon season from May through November. By contrast, the North (Bac Bo) is subtropical and cool; frosty winters near the Chinese border are not uncommon.

What are the differences between Northern and Southern Vietnam?

Looking at the map, one can see that the Northern and Southern parts of Vietnam are larger, distinct regions divided by a very narrow central coastal plain area. Americans may think that differences in the two regions only go back to war-time with the influence of U.S. and Soviet culture dividing the North and South. This view has a bit of truth to it, but differences in the regions have always existed and can be traced to such basic elements as the geography and climate. In the northern region, a large area of the mountainous and midland areas are plagued by low fertility, defor- estation, and soil erosion, while the most fertile areas are subject to population pressures. The area between Hanoi and the central region lies in the typhoon belt and is subject to strong winds and torrential rains. In short, the whole Northern region suffers from much harsher weather than the South. Humidity in particular poses great problems for agriculture and natural disasters occur more often. All of these climatic factors have meant that northerners have always had to work harder to cultivate food and support their families. One consequence of this is a tendency for those in the north to be more thrifty and save more "for a rainy day."

The South enjoys a much better climate and soil quality for rice cultivation and industrial crops. In fact, the Mekong Delta is the largest rice-producing area of the country and currently accounts for 45 percent of Vietnam's annual total rice production. In contrast to the experience of the North, southerners have consistently enjoyed higher agricultural yields without the constant threat of natural disasters. As a result, southern Vietnamese have been able to take advantage of more free time and spend money without the worry of future crop damage.

GETTING TO KNOW THE VIETNAMESE PEOPLE

What groups of people live in Vietnam, what are their origins, and where do they reside?

Vietnam has fifty-six different ethnic groups, with the ethnic Vietnamese (called *Viet* or *Kinh*) comprising roughly 87 percent of the total population. The origin of the Vietnamese people is still disputed, but the general consensus is that they descend from people who lived in the Red River Delta between 500 and 200 B.C. Although the Vietnamese language is tonal and therefore closer to the Sino-Tibetan languages spoken by Chinese peoples, physiographically, the Vietnamese are believed to be a mixture of Austaliod, Mongoloid, and Indonesian people that migrated to the area. Ethnic Vietnamese live in the lowlands, primarily in the alluvial deltas and the coastal plains.

As for the minorities, five groups make up two-thirds of Vietnam's minority population. They are as follows:

Group	% of Minority Population
Tay	13%
Thai	12%
Hoa	11.7%
Khmer	10.6%
Muong	10.5%
Nung	8.4%

Most minority groups live in the highlands. However, they are not dispersed proportionally. Most of the minorities, about 68 percent, live in the North, while the rest live primarily in the South. Those minorities who live in the mountainous areas are known as "Montagnards." The Tay and the Nung are Sino-Tibetan peoples who now live in the mountains north of the Red River Delta and most are rice or swidden farmers. In the mountain highlands adjacent to the Red River Delta live the Thai, who migrated from southern Chinese provinces over the last several centuries. Almost all of the Khmer live in the provinces south of Ho Chi Minh City, the lower provinces of the Mekong Delta, and are primarily rice farmers. They are the descendants of Cambodian people whose empire fell to Vietnamese southern expansion in the seventeenth century. The Khmer have managed to maintain their own language, customs, and religion, Theravada Buddhism. Although closely related to the Vietnamese, the Muong inhabit the mountains near Hoa Binh.

Traditionally, the hill tribes have had little contact with the ethnic Vietnamese due to suspicion and resentment of tribal territory encroachment. As a result, they've been able to maintain separate religious and cultural traditions. From the Viet perspective, the hill tribes are unsophisticated and in need of economic and educational assistance. In fact, twelve of the ethnic groups have no university graduates and the rest have no members with postgraduate degrees. Many of the hill tribes have traditionally practiced slash and burn agricultural techniques, which are posing a serious problem for the government in terms of deforestation. As a result, the government is implementing policies that provide land leases and credit for tribes to purchase seeds or animals and engage in reforestation, agriculture, and animal husbandry. Given the location of most minority groups and their level of development, they will play little or no role in foreign investment projects. In reality, the foreign businessperson will be dealing almost entirely with the ethnic Vietnamese and the ethnic Chinese, especially in the South.

What are the major demographic trends in Vietnam?

Vietnam is the twelfth most populous country in the world and the second most populous in Southeast Asia, with an estimated population of nearly 74 million people. At an annual growth rate of about 1.9 percent, Vietnam's population should easily reach 80 million by the turn of the century. While this growth proves to increase

Vietnam's already abundant human resources, it also poses one of the greatest challenges to Vietnam's future. Environmental degradation and rampant unemployment are only two of the dire consequences awaiting Vietnam if measures are not taken to curtail population growth. As a result, the Vietnamese Government has made family planning a priority. Despite non-governmental organizations and governmental efforts, the results are not promising and the population is not likely to decline in the near future.

Another way to overcome the negative impact of population growth is redistribution. Accordingly, the government has moved more than 3 million people in the last 14 years and plans to redistribute another 2 million by the year 2000. New Economic Zones have been established for the resettlement of city dwellers and those living in the crowded delta areas. However, this resettlement campaign has not been entirely successful due to the reluctance of Vietnamese to leave the family and the government's stalling on delivering incentives.

As for the current distribution of the population, about 72 percent reside in rural areas with the remainder living in the urban areas. Among the largest cities, Ho Chi Minh City (formerly Saigon) has a population of approximately 4 million, Hanoi 3 million, Hai Phong 1.5 million, Da Nang 500,000, and Nha Trang and Hue 250,000 each. Hanoi and Ho Chi Minh City are two of the most densely populated urban centers in Asia; the density in parts of Ho Chi Minh City is greater than in Hong Kong.

More than one-third of Vietnam's population is under the age of 15, and according to projected growth rates, the number of people entering the workforce will continue to rise until the year 2020. After that time, the percentage of elderly will begin to increase. This implies that absorption of the labor force into industry may take much longer than needed to reach a level of economic development close to that of neighbors that followed similar expansion strategies.

What is the status and role of Vietnam's Chinese population?

Perhaps the most important minority group, particularly in terms of business, are the *Hoa*, or ethnic Chinese. Today, 80 percent of the approximately 960,000 ethnic Chinese live in the South, with 340,000 living in Ho Chi Minh City. Only about 10,000 reside

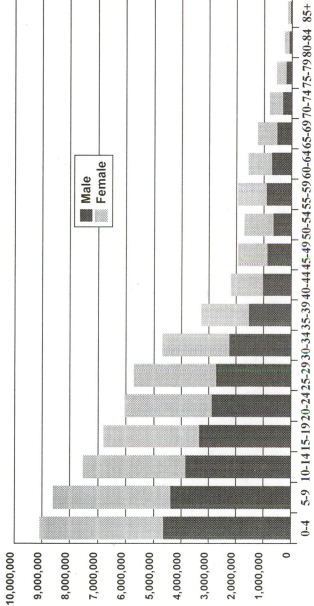

**Vietnam's Population
(By Gender and Age, 1989)**

Male
Female

Source: Statistical Publishing House, Hanoi.

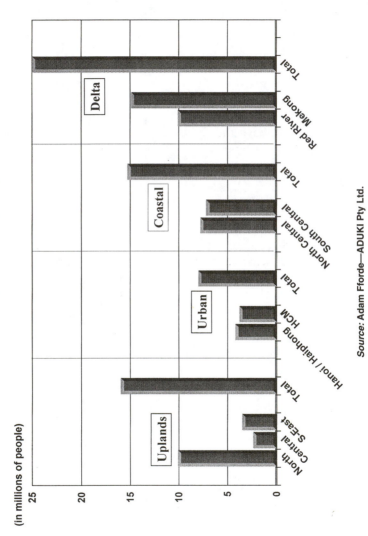

Vietnam's Population by Region

(in millions of people)

Source: Adam Fforde—ADUKI Pty Ltd.

in Hanoi. Relative to other minorities, the Chinese came to Vietnam fairly recently, having migrated in the seventeenth and eighteenth centuries from the coastal provinces of Fukien and Guangdong, or from the island of Hainan, in search of commerce and refuge from the Manchu conquest. Thus, they speak Cantonese, the language of South China and Hong Kong. Unlike most other Vietnamese minority groups, the Hoa reside in the lowland urban centers of the North and South. Traditionally, they have dominated urban private commerce, and until the end of the war in 1975, Chinese distinctiveness was tolerated much more than in most other Southeast Asian countries. The Chinese were allowed to live in separate communities (*bang*), have their own schools, engage in private commerce, and retain Chinese nationality. Some estimates show that prior to reunification, the Hoa in Saigon controlled 90 percent of the wholesale trade, 80 percent of industry, 50 percent of banking and financial services, and about 50 percent of the retail trade.

After the country was reunified in 1975, wealthy merchants became subject to scrutiny and property confiscation. A few were even publicly executed. "The Chinese tycoons were the first to go after 1975," a 47-year-old Chinese woman told me, whose family grocery business was taken over by the State in the early 1980s. "Then the monied class, and then the middle class." Regulations were issued that abolished large-scale private commerce, Chinese schools and hospitals were seized and many Chinese feared a forcible integration campaign. In reaction to the government's policies, scores of Vietnamese people fled their country, to become commonly known as "boat people." Two-thirds of those who left were Chinese. Since the introduction of *doi moi* conditions have improved for the Hoa and they have made their way back into commerce, particularly in the South. The Chinese enclave in Ho Chi Minh City is called Cholon, though the difference between this "Chinatown" and the rest of Saigon is not as striking as it can be elsewhere; you don't see red and gold signs covered with Chinese characters and different forms of dress. The Cholon district doesn't stand apart all that much from the rest of the city.

What religions are predominant, and what role do they play in Vietnamese society?

Several different religions are practiced in Vietnam, but most Vietnamese consider themselves Buddhists (80 percent), followed by Taoists (12 percent), and Roman Catholics (7 percent). Every Vietnamese family, however, will also venerate their ancestors and most homes have a family altar where prayers are made and incense burned. Mahayana, as opposed to Indian Theravada Buddhism, is the Chinese version of Buddhism and was adopted by most Vietnamese, especially in the North. In 1990, Vietnam had 4,743 active Buddhist pagodas, schools and monasteries, along with 17,000 practicing monks and nuns. Prior to the expansion of Buddhism, Vietnam was fundamentally a Confucian society. However, traditional practices combined folklore, Confucianism, Taoism, and animism in a ceremonious fashion. Catholicism also acquired a substantial following during French colonial rule and is the second largest practiced religion in Vietnam. After the Philippines, Vietnam's 2 million Catholics make up the largest percentage of Catholics in Southeast Asia. Due to migration after 1954, the South has twice as many Catholics as the North. Other religions include Cao Dai, a synthesis of Christianity, Confucianism, and Buddhism, and Hoa Hao, a modified version of Buddhism, both of which have much smaller followings.

One does not see the same number of orange- and brown-robed Buddhists in Vietnam that are visible everywhere in Thailand. While most homes and public places (such as shops and restaurants) do have incense burning upon an altar to honor ancestors, religion is not as pervasive as in other Southeast Asian countries. Instead, the Vietnamese seem to operate more on Confucian ideals, putting emphasis on the character of individuals. To what extent this is attributable to the imposition of communist ideology after 1975 is not clear. Religion is somewhat of a controversial issue for Vietnam and has become closely linked with human rights issues.

The Constitution of the Socialist Republic of Vietnam states that "citizens enjoy freedom of worship, and may practice or not practice a religion." However, this is qualified by the fact that no religious group may undermine the socialist goals of the state. Since 1991 when the Vietnamese Communist Party's Seventh General Congress issued an unprecedented positive affirmation of the value of the religion, Catholics at least have enjoyed more freedom. Prior to that time, religious oppression left churches and cathedrals in disrepair and theological training was conducted in secret. However, in recent years, the Communist party has allowed the reopening of seminaries, approved the printing of Bibles, and released some prominent clergy from prison. The difference can be seen in the flood of people attending Sunday services. While most of these changes are most likely politically motivated because of relations with Western countries, Catholics are at least benefitting from the reform. Unfortunately, Buddhists don't enjoy the ties with Western countries that Catholics do, and as a result are still suffering from religious persecution. The Vietnamese government has tried to co-opt the Unified Buddhist Church of Vietnam (UBCV) by forcing it to join with the State-sponsored Vietnamese Buddhist Church, which it has refused to do. (The Vietnam Buddhist Church is the only Buddhist church officially recognized by Hanoi.) Though the government has stated that "there is absolutely no suppression against religion in general and Buddhism in particular," there have been recent arrests of senior monks from the UBCV, which was once the Buddhist authority in former South Vietnam, and which continues to claim to be the legitimate church body in Vietnam today.

CHARACTER FORGED BY A BITTER HISTORY

As the historical sketch below will reveal clearly, the most important feature of Vietnam's heritage is its struggle against foreign aggression. Wars not only dispersed resources, but also deprived the country of many economic achievements. On the positive side, long years of fighting against foreign intruders also served to unify the country, fostering a sense of nationalism and pride.

What are the key events in Vietnam's violent history?

In 939 A.D., the Chinese were driven out of Vietnam after nearly 1,000 years of rule. Subsequent attempts at reclamation were also thwarted by the Vietnamese, with the defeat of Kublai Khan's armies in 1288 marking the end of Chinese expansionism into Vietnam. The next time a foreign intruder assumed control of Vietnam, it took the Vietnamese much less time to expel it. Having seized Vietnam in 1884, France left Vietnam only 70 years later after its defeat at Dien Bien Phu in 1954. In its drive to establish the Greater Co-Prosperity Sphere, Japan entered Vietnam in 1940 and appointed a government headed by Bao Dai, the former Annamese emperor. However, the resulting nationalism only served to undermine Japan's intentions. During this time, the Viet Minh Independence League mobilized under the direction of communist guerilla leader Ho Chi Minh and eventually forced out the head of the Japanese-appointed regime in August 1945. One month later, Ho declared independence and established the Democratic Republic of Vietnam (DRV).

From 1946 to 1954, France fought to reassert control with financial assistance from the United States, while the Viet Minh were backed by China and the Soviet Union. France's defeat ended in the 1955 Geneva Accords, where Vietnam was divided at the 17th parallel, with a French-installed government in the South. From that point on, the United States stepped up its military support of South Vietnam. In 1964, the United States began to launch a series of devastating air strikes on the North, which continued on and off through January 1973 when peace talks were finally concluded. Two years later, the North surprised the South with a massive offensive, which brought down Saigon on April 30, 1975 and reunified the country as the Socialist Republic of Vietnam.

How has a history of repelling foreign aggressors shaped the Vietnamese character?

For nearly 2,000 years, the Vietnamese have been driving would-be conquerors out of their territory. Having successfully kept four foreign powers from controlling their country, pride and nationalism are strong components of the country's psyche. These attitudes have been perpetuated by a socialist education, which focused on the nationalist struggle, the victories of the Vietnamese people, and the correctness of the ideology they adopted. While the educational system is fighting to modernize itself, young people throughout the country are still subject to Marxist theory and biased accounts of history. However, even if Vietnamese youth are not being exposed formally to an academic critique of their country's performance record, they live in conditions that are a constant reminder of the bankruptcy of the socialist model, at least in economic terms.

Nationalism has perhaps been the most important source of the country's unity. It has its roots in times long before the arrival of the French and will likely continue into the future. However, Vietnam no longer has an enemy to provide fuel for nationalist sentiment. More than likely, this sentiment will eventually manifest itself in the form of economic competition with other developing countries in the region.

Years of war have also made the Vietnamese a resilient, determined, and hardworking people. While some of their "work ethic" was negated by the perverse incentives of socialism, the Vietnamese are rebounding and are as busy as ever. Visitors to Vietnam are struck by the level of activity taking place in shops, in alleyways, and on the streets. In spite of the country's poverty, it is easy to imagine Vietnam succeeding simply because the country's people refuse to give up in any endeavor to which they commit. Vietnam's historical record indicates that the people can prevail even when the odds are decidedly stacked against them.

What are the cultural and political differences between North and South?

Northerners and Southerners make glaring generalizations about each other. While some of these generalizations hold a great deal of merit, others are clearly exaggerations. Physically, you can't tell the Northern and Southern Vietnamese apart. Everyone looks the same. But the dialects differ between the two regions. For example, in the North an "r" might be pronounced as a "z," while in the South it will sound like an "r." Likewise, "gi" is pronounced like a "z" in the North and with a "ch" sound in the South. The Southerners speak more nasally than the Northerners; this is said (by Northerners) to be irritating on the ears. Southern Vietnamese consider Northerners to be less sophisticated and creative, and more regimented, stubborn, and cold. In contrast, Northern Vietnamese often complain about the flashy, arrogant, informal behavior of Southerners. As already mentioned, Vietnamese in the south are not distinguished for their ability to save money relative to those in the north. Instead, they are said to flaunt their wealth by wasting money on unnecessary, extravagant goods, or at least to spend their money quickly on consumer goods. While this is admittedly a characterization by Northerners, it is not entirely false.

People in the South are generally more open to new ideas and foreign practices, and willing to take risks. Of course, this tendency can be traced to the capitalist roots of the South and the strong influence of the United States prior to 1975. The typical Southerner didn't experience the war directly and yet experienced the "re-education" process more directly. Northerners suffered years of bombing while the South did not. The South has always been able to feed itself; the North has suffered periods of famine.

The South is richer, yet the North is more educated. The South is entrepreneurial, the North is more governmental; in the South, you might see a statue of Ho Chi Minh, but in the North you see statues of Lenin.

While Southerners may be outwardly more friendly, that doesn't necessarily mean they are more trustworthy. Northerners can be more blunt, but at least it's easier to understand their position. Southerners will be more cunning and insincere in order to cloud their position. In business, there is clearly more of a corruption problem in the South. For the most part, the corrupt practices of the South are due to its distance from central oversight and the relative autonomy of officials there. It goes without saying that this is a sweeping generalization and certainly cannot be applied across the board.

Predictably, Northerners are far more supportive or tolerant of the Communist Party than those in the South. While even northern Vietnamese are starting to get a lot more critical of politics, they still do not openly attribute as much fault to the leadership as those in the south. Long before *doi moi* became an official policy, capitalism was thriving in the South, where collectivization never fully took hold and the parallel markets thrived. As opposed to Northerners, who have noticed an appreciable improvement in their standard of living since the adoption of *doi moi* and largely credit the government, Southerners see the government as a deterrent to real progress. Though not everyone would share this view, the majority of southern Vietnamese would probably support a more democratic form of government. Once most Vietnamese reach a certain standard of living, it is probable that the luxury of political activism will become more affordable and the political differences between the North and the South will be less visible.

In terms of the economies of the North and South, the South is definitely in better shape. Ho Chi Minh City and the surrounding areas have received the lion's share of foreign investment projects. Southerners simply had a head start in business training because of the region's history. The North has been under the physical and psychological constraints of socialism twenty years longer, and the shackles are taking more time to break, but they *are* breaking. All over Southeast Asia, the overseas Chinese community is known for its skills in commerce, and there may be some correlation between the preponderance of ethnic Chinese living in the South, but chances are that the South's bustling economy is more a result of its distance from Hanoi and its capitalist history.

CHAPTER 2

THE ECONOMIC

LANDSCAPE

Vietnam's current economic policies might seem eclectic, and for good reason. The country is borrowing pieces of modernization policy from throughout its region. It is imitating China in allowing swift economic changes, but remaining intolerant of critics of one-party rule by the Communist party. It is setting up export processing zones and industrial parks much along the lines of Taiwan in order to attract foreign investors to set up export-oriented manufacturing factories. From South Korea, it has borrowed the notion of guiding selected industries, such as automobiles and consumer electronics, and protecting key companies from foreign competition. Like Singapore, Vietnam has enacted a body of liberal foreign investment law, which has already resulted in over $10 billion of pledged foreign investment. From Japan, it has borrowed the idea of an industrial master plan; Mitsubishi designed such a plan for Vietnam's automobie industry in the early 1990s.

A TIGER ON A BICYCLE

Vietnam has been nicknamed "a tiger on a bicycle" because its immense vitality and productive potential are being realized in the face of huge obstacles, not the least of which is the severely insufficient state of its industrial infrastructure. Vietnam has also encountered potholes in privatizing its state-owned companies, though most of its state-owned companies are relatively small and do not account for the dragon's share of the economy. Its leaders have been at great pains to further develop a legal framework to accommodate foreign investment, and its banking system is a long way from being reformed along Western lines. Perhaps most foreboding is that inflation has jumped to 14 percent in 1994, up from 5.2 percent in 1993.

But even atop a rickety two-wheeler, Vietnam's economy has climbed to unpredicted heights. Since 1989, when economic reforms picked up steam, the economy has basically been operating according to market principles, and experiencing an annual growth rate of approximately 8 percent per year. While the national economy grew 8.8 percent in 1994, Saigon's GDP increased by 14.5 percent. In 1994, Hanoi increased its annual industrial gross output by 18 percent; the figure for Hai Phong was 32.5 percent, and for Quang Nam Da Nang, 19 percent. The official per capita income for Saigon residents is now set at $810, well over two times the national average. Incoming foreign investment in 1994 hit a record, with $3.7 billon pledged by foreign companies, bringing total pledged foreign investment since 1988 to nearly $11 billion. Foreign aid agencies committed $2 billion to be spent in 1995, up from $1.8 billion in 1993. Already, Asia's languishing backwater capitol—Hanoi—is home to the corporate offices of over 400 companies from 35 different countries.

What is Doi Moi?

While economic reforms were attempted as early as 1979, most policies had concentrated on the agricultural sector to spur production, as the proper economic incentives always involved a slight relinquishment of governmental control. In order to maintain its delicate political balance, the Vietnam Communist Party never allowed liberalizing reforms to last for long. Instead, there have

Gross Domestic Product, by Activity

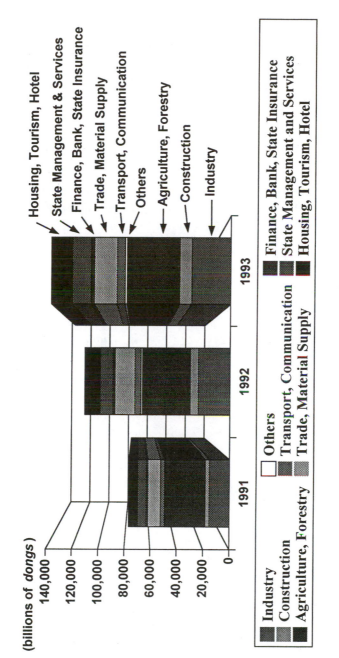

(billions of *dongs*)

Housing, Tourism, Hotel
State Management & Services
Finance, Bank, State Insurance
Trade, Material Supply
Transport, Communication
Others
Agriculture, Forestry
Construction
Industry

Legend:
Industry
Construction
Agriculture, Forestry
Others
Transport, Communication
Trade, Material Supply
Finance, Bank, State Insurance
State Management and Services
Housing, Tourism, Hotel

Source: Statistical Publishing House, Hanoi.

been cycles of reform and retrenchment since the early 1980s. By 1986, Vietnam's economic outlook was so desolate that the government had no choice but to adopt dramatic reforms in order to somehow retain its own legitimacy. The Sixth Communist Party Congress of 1986 marked a departure from the Soviet style of economic planning. In order to remedy the severe economic crisis that Vietnam was facing, *doi moi*, or "economic renovation," was officially endorsed and a host of dramatic reforms were launched.

Doi moi was officially endorsed in 1986 at the Sixth Party Congress of the VCP in the face of triple-digit inflation, declining aid from Comecon countries, unmanageable debt, and an overall unsustainable, inefficient economy. In its original form, *doi moi* encompassed a wide range of economic reforms. Under the program a number of changes were made:

- the rural collective system was replaced by a long-term lease system based on family farming;
- price controls were lifted;
- the exchange rate of the *dong* was unified, its value to be determined henceforth by market forces alone;
- interest rates were raised to control inflation;
- state subsidies for state enterprises were reduced and eliminated, and tax reform generated increased revenue for the government;
- fiscal reforms brought the national deficit down from 8.4 percent of GDP in 1989 to only 1.7 percent by 1992;
- private enterprise was given official sanction through commercial laws and encouragement;
- foreign investment laws were ratified to open the door to foreign capital;
- the government loosened its foreign trade regime, replacing a system of import quotas with import licenses and tariffs, giving Vietnam's state and private companies more access to imports and to foreign markets; and
- over a million soldiers were discharged from the military and/or have returned from conflicts outside Vietnam, while the government set a number of programs for citizen retraining to deal with the growing problem of unemployment.

REFORM OF VIETNAMESE ENTERPRISE

Reform of state enterprises has proceeded with two objectives: first, to reduce subsidies and level the playing field between the state and private sectors; and second, to "privatize" firms in the state sector and thereby transfer state assets into private hands. Fortunately for Vietnam, the country's state sector is much smaller as a percentage of its economy than other transitional economies in Asia, East Europe, and the former Soviet Union. State-owned enterprises accounted for 25 percent of the GDP, while in most other transitional economies the figure would range from 50 to 75 percent. The state's share of rural output is extremely limited. The agricultural sector accounts for one-third of the country's GNP, yet agricultural state enterprises make up only 0.8 percent of total output as of 1989. (Poland, for example, set about on its transition to a market economy with 82 percent of its economy in the hands of the state sector. For Hungary the figure was 65 percent, and for China, 99 percent.)

Does the State sector still control the industrial economy?

For 11 years after the reunification of Vietnam in 1975, the State's involvement in the Vietnamese economy was predictably pervasive. Drawing on the Soviet model, the government became involved in every facet of the economy. However, since 1986 the Vietnamese government has assumed a diminished role in industry. The purpose of the *Stipulations On Renovation Policies of Planning and Socialist Business Accounting Policies for State Enterprises* was to provide those enterprises more autonomy to subcontract with other enterprises, upgrade their machinery, sell or lease unused assets, determine the prices for their production, select their own banks, recruit labor; and it provided limited independence of decision-making as to their production plans.

In practice, however, the central government maintains very heavy control over the finances and profits of enterprises. While state enterprises were being given freer reign with the right hand, with the left the government pursued objectives that limited an enterprise in practicing its new autonomy. Under the state enterprise regulations decreed in 1991, the government will maintain its role in defining what particular business activities a state-owned firm will engage in, assign it necessary capital, and expect it to follow its direction in terms of duties and responsibilities, especially as they pertain to social welfare and national defense. It is doubtful that the government will relinquish control anytime soon of such lucrative sectors as transportation, utilities, and those related to national security.

Though state enterprises are now responsible for covering their own costs, they still enjoy better access to credit and lower tax rates. Moreover, the government encourages foreign investors to enter into J.V.s with public sector firms, and most foreign investors opt for a state enterprise in order to reduce risk. Oddly, of the 12,000 remaining SOEs, less than 10 percent are considered to be profitable. Instead of forcing bankruptcy and closures on inefficient firms, the government is about to undertake a dubious plan to form conglomerates out of all SOEs, thereby combining the losers with the winners. The ultimate amalgamation of the public sector now hinges on the Prime Minister's decision, but is unlikely to be thwarted given the interests of the Party members in the directorships of most SOEs. (A Party member is prohibited by law from becoming a manager of a private business, and because all state enterprise managers are Party members, it figures that there is absolutely no incentive for the card-carrying managers of state-run companies to shut them down, before finding another place for themselves in the system. Thus, rather than close their companies, they opt to merge them together with other losing firms run by similarly motivated managers, such that no one loses their job.)

Legally, the private sector receives the same treatment as state enterprises and cooperatives, though politically the public sector is still the priority. (Most so-called cooperatives were formed in rural areas in the agricultural sector. Since the initiation of *doi moi*, they have been decollectivized, with their members receiving land. Nowadays when one speaks about sectors of Vietnam's economy, one refers to either the state sector or the private sector.)

Is Vietnam's state-controlled economy disappearing as reform takes hold and private enterprises start up?

State enterprises in Vietnam should not be underestimated, for they still dominate in important industrial sectors. Virtually all

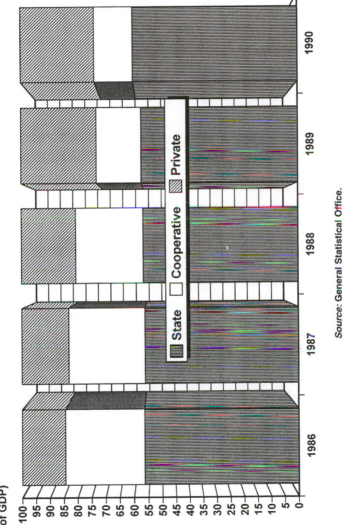

Economic Output by Type of Enterprise

(% of GDP)

State Cooperative Private

1986 1987 1988 1989 1990

Source: General Statistical Office.

heavy industrial and large-scale light industrial companies in Vietnam are owned by the state, even though the state sector accounts for only 55 percent of total industrial production. All major construction enterprises are state-owned, as are transport firms and the banking system; meanwhile, handicraft production, garment-making, assembly, and food processing are areas increasingly in the hands of private companies. The major exporting companies, including petroleum, marine products, and processed rubber, are in state hands as well, though the primary production of rice, shrimp, fruit, and coffee for export are primarily owned by private rural-based companies.

The task of privatizing state-owned firms, called *equitization* in Vietnam, has been slow and arduous. Of the twenty-one state-owned companies selected for the pilot program, only nine were deemed suitable for privatization by government officials. In 1993, two companies became shareholding companies: The Union of Transportation Agencies, and the Refrigeration Electric Engineering company (REE). Hiep An Shoes and Legamex are in the share-issuing phase of the process. Five others—the Thaoh Nan Brick Factory, the Llai Phong Bus Joint Stock Company, the Binh Minh Plastic Factory, the Long Export Processing Enterprise, and the Construction Factory No.3—have completed their asset evaluation and are about to sell shares.

The actual process involved is complicated. Once the state-owned enterprise is deemed a candidate for equitization, a company board is formed. This board is comprised of a enterprise director or vice director as board chief. The enterprise submits prepared documents to the various government boards and committees involved. Then it goes through an asset evaluation and review of its previous 3 years of accounting documents by a committee appointed by the Ministry of Finance (MOF). The MOF submits its report to the Prime Minister for final approval and the responsible People's Committee sets the date for privatization.

A major problem is a lack of capitalization due to the public's reluctance to invest in equitized companies. Even though state bonds and bank term bonds are being issued in Vietnam, few understand the concept of shareholding. Moreover, senior Communist party members and government officials cannot agree about equitization policy. Many believe that privatization of state-owned firms is harmful to the country's economy and security, guaranteeing that enterprises involved in telecommunications, infrastructure construction, irrigation, electricity, and pivotal economic sectors, such as petroleum and gas, beer, tobacco, cement, and steel, will not be equitized. At this juncture, priority is being given to small- to medium-sized businesses, such as those dealing in tourism, transportation, services, and consumer goods.

Most state managers fail to see the wisdom of equitizing themselves out of a prestigious job, and you can't blame them. The original nine state enterprises selected for equitization all eventually opted out of the program, except for Legamex. Managers of state-owned enterprises who have, for example, "equitized" their firm by hocking parts of it off to family relatives, are fair game for white-crime fighters. As one of the State firms selected to be privatized, Legamex was touted as a great financial success, even by many foreign reporters. The managing director, Nguyen Thi Son, lacked experience to run a capitalist firm, however, and soon buried the company in debt. She was arrested by Saigon police in 1994 and charged with "intentionally infringing on the government's regulations on economic management, with severe consequences." Her former deputy was arrested as well. She allegedly used most of the borrowed money to set up outside companies to be run by her family members. Nguyen Xuan Oanh, one of the architects of doi moi, and acting Prime Minister of the country in 1965 to 1966, said to me about Legamex: "The management was not trained to do that job. The gal who was made director of the company, she doesn't know a thing about [running a publicly-traded company]. She had brothers and sisters and they bought [parts of the company] at a low price."

There appears to be little motive for the typical manager to privatize his or her firm. The state might own the enterprise, but the manager controls its revenues. By placing the firm's income into special accounts and funds—reserve funds, expansion funds, bonus, and welfare funds—pretty soon they don't have to pay much at all to the state. "The government has selected seven companies for equitization and four have already dropped out for the simple reason that [their managers] know that if the ownership of the company belongs to the shareholders that [the managers are going to be replaced]," says Mr. Oanh.

What effect has economic reform had on the Vietnamese laborer?

Official unemployment stands at 25 percent, but unofficially, it's probably closer to 45 percent. An estimated 70 percent of the figure occurred in the agricultural sector, which helps explain the tendency for rural unemployed people, especially males, to move to urban areas in search of work. Roughly seven out of ten Vietnamese work in agriculture, as opposed to industry, and this figure has remained relatively constant in recent years. By the year 2000 Vietnam's population is expected to expand to 80 million, with an estimated 45 million people entering the labor market. Vietnam's crisis of unemployment gained momentum when the number of state enterprises was reduced from 12,000 to 6,000 in the late 1980s. These enterprises were not privatized—they were closed down or joined with others and many of their employees were cut loose. Luckily for Vietnamese workers, however, only 6 percent of the country's labor force was employed in state enterprises (the figure was as high as 77 percent in the Soviet Union). Second, the government has been scaling back its military personnel and demobilizing soldiers after conflicts in Cambodia and with China. In addition, workers from Vietnam who have been in Eastern Europe are now returning, as are Vietnamese refugees from Hong Kong. The government is looking to microenterprises in manufacturing and services, as well as the agricultural sector, to help re-employ a growing legion of jobless and the underemployed. A huge informal economy re-employs many, whether the "job" is selling one's possessions on a street corner without a license, exchanging *dong*s for dollars at slightly better than the official rate, or providing streetside haircuts and manicures.

Is there economic tension between the Chinese and the Vietnamese communities?

In addition to economic change, *doi moi* has also brought about a change in the government's attitude toward the *Hoa*. Since 1987, the Chinese have been entitled to restoration of citizenship and participation in commercial activities. Consequently, Hoa have again begun operations in light industry, mainly food processing, textiles, and electronic equipment assembly. In fact, the *Far Eastern Economic Review* reported in 1991 that the eth-

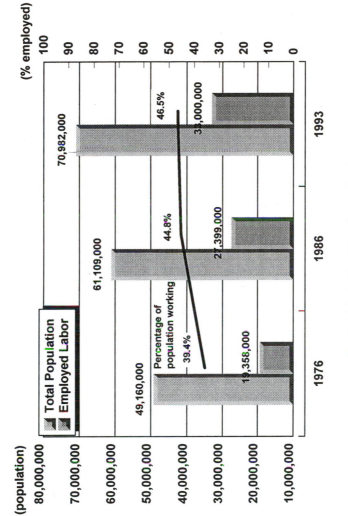

Total Population and Employed Labor

(population)

(% employed)

Total Population
Employed Labor

70,982,000

61,109,000

49,160,000

46.5%

44.8%

39.4%

Percentage of
population working

33,000,000

27,399,000

19,358,000

1976   1986   1993

Source: Statistical Publishing House, Hanoi.

nic Chinese in Ho Chi Minh City controlled two-thirds of the small-scale industrial sector and one-third of all commercial activities.

Many ethnic Vietnamese, however, don't care for the Chinese, though the ill-feeling is hardly as overt as that between the ethnic Malay and the Chinese in Indonesia or Singapore. But there is a caveat here: in other Southeast Asian countries where ethnic Chinese play an important economic role, the Chinese clearly dominate economically because collectively, as entrepreneurs, they are superior to local Thais, Malays, or Filipinos. These groups tend to accept the fact that the Chinese are commercially more astute than they are, and thus, as indigenous ethnic groups, they tend to maintain control over the workings of government while letting the Chinese minority run the business and financial community. It's a sort of truce, an understanding, a cultural detente. But in Vietnam, the Chinese dominate commercially only in the South, and not in the North. And here, the Vietnamese are top-notch entrepreneurs just as the Chinese are. So the relationship is much more competitive economically, and thus perhaps more explosive.

How large is the Vietnamese diaspora, and what economic role does it play in the country?

Some 2 million ethnic Vietnamese people live outside of Vietnam, mainly in North America, Europe, and Australia. The term *Viet Kieu* refers to Vietnamese living overseas, not just in America but anywhere outside Vietnam. Most of these people left their home country either as evacuees before the fall of Saigon or as political exiles and refugees afterward. The $1 billion in remittances that they send to relatives still in Vietnam has been a significant factor in the country's economic progress. When Vietnam first opened, there were few privileges given to Viet Kieu, but because the government so desperately desires overseas Vietnamese to return with their funds and their skills, preferential treatment is now offered. Concessions include various tax breaks and the right to set up foreign joint ventures in the country as if they were local Vietnamese. Overseas Vietnamese have invested in a total of fifty-one projects since 1988, for a total invested capital of $90 million.

Many Viet Kieu have returned to get their families' land back. Wendy Huynh, whose father is a successful overseas Vietnamese living in Guam, has returned with her family to Saigon to reclaim land held by her wealthy grandfather before 1975, the year he lost everything. She told me that the family is getting back the land piece-by-piece, and that one must have connections with current or former cadres to do so because so many claims are being made. "The government builds all it can on your land before it sells it back to you," she says. "They build four walls and call it a building, claiming it had a roof and had water and electricity and that although they took out all these things, you still have to pay for them."

What is the role of women in Vietnamese society, and in the economy?

Unfortunately, Vietnam's economic "renovation" may not have been the best prescription for women. Although *doi moi* has certainly created opportunities for women with foreign-invested firms, rural women are suffering the consequences of market reforms. Le Thi Quy, a sociologist at Hanoi's Center for Family and Women's Studies, points to growing incidents of prostitution and domestic violence as negative side effects of economic opening. Vietnam's government estimates that over 200,000 female prostitutes now work in the business and tourist centers including Ho Chi Minh City, Vung Tau, Nha Trang, and Hai Phong, where the dancing bars and brothels prevalent during the 'American war' have made a dramatic comeback.

Roughly 80 percent of Vietnam's agricultural labor force is comprised of women, and *doi moi* has given these women little incentive to stay in the fields. One reason is that many men have migrated into the cities for part-time employment, leaving the women to perform extremely taxing duties at home. Another problem is that the pre-*doi moi* cooperative social structure has been severely minimized. Free basic medical care and education are no longer assured. As a result, female illiteracy is on the rise. Sadly, families that are forced to pay for their children's education will give priority to the sons.

Based on the practices of most Asian countries, one would guess that Vietnamese women are probably relegated to a lower status, while men are considered the superior gender. Fortunately, this really isn't the case in Vietnam. While Vietnamese society is stratified such that men and women engage in distinct activities, respect is not given according to gender. In the workplace, there is ample opportunity for female advancement, and it is certainly not unheard of to have a woman in a high ministerial or managerial position.

According to precommunist, Confucian ideals, women were expected to strive for the four female virtues—cooking, beauty, silence, and faithfulness. While Vietnamese women today certainly do cook, appear to be faithful, and can be very beautiful, silent would not be a very apt description of a typical Vietnamese woman. It is not surprising to meet a very outspoken, aggressive woman in Vietnam. In fact, such women are the norm. Walking down any busy street in Hanoi or Ho Chi Minh City, one is struck by the amount of work the women seem to be doing relative to the men. Pass any coffeehouse and the number of men taking a break to enjoy coffee, tea, and conversation far exceeds the number of women. (However, don't expect a Vietnamese man to tell you the same story.) In all fairness to Vietnamese men, it is true that men take care of the majority of household expenses, but as the table below indicates, the women do most everything else in the house and in family businesses.

DIVISION OF HOUSEHOLD LABOR BETWEEN HUSBANDS AND WIVES

	Percent of work provided by:		
	Wife	Husband	Both
Housework	90	3	2
Childcare	71.1	6.5	19.4
Major expenses	12.6	60.4	24.3
Sale of products	70.1	8.2	18.0

Source: Institute of Female Studies

Compared to most other East Asian countries, the respect given to Vietnamese women is impressive. The favorable position of women in Vietnamese society has its roots in history, tradition, and socialist ideology. From a historical perspective, the Vietnamese have female revolutionary heroes, such as the Trung Sisters, who led an insurrection against the Chinese in 40 to 43 B.C., that are still held in very high regard. Almost every major town and city in Vietnam has a main street named Hai Ba Trung which means "the two Trung Sisters." Socialism only helped solidify the status of women in Vietnam by stressing gender equality and bringing more women into the workplace.

Moreover, women came to hold high-ranking positions on the basis of merit, though meritocracy is nothing new to Vietnam. The female manager of the Refrigeration Electric Engineering company, once a state-owned firm that has been converted to a joint stock company, won Entrepreneur of the Month in a recent issue of *Vietnam Economic Times*. Interviewing her, we found her level of managerial expertise to be extremely high. The Secretary General of Vietnam's Chamber of Commerce and Industry, Phan Chi Lan, is a woman. Often a woman, whose ostensible role is that of the "secretary" or "translator," is the real power behind the males at the negotiation table. Women's organizations also came to play an important part in Vietnamese society, with women's labor unions mobilizing a substantial amount of support. Today, Vietnamese women account for 46 percent of Vietnam's teachers, 32 percent of its researchers, 14 percent of its industrial and business workforce, and 8 percent of state managers. Foreign ventures have a preference for hiring Vietnamese women as staff, and many Vietnamese men openly complain about this. Women are generally more informed than men in Vietnam, and it seems that more of them speak English.

Sexism is surging with the opening up of society, however. Increasingly, Vietnamese women complain that Vietnamese men operate under the double standard that they can cheat on their wives, but find it unthinkable that their wives would cheat on them. Vietnamese men commonly quip: Man cannot live by rice alone, but also must have *fu*. Fu refers to noodles, but is also a homonyn for a slang word for "prostitute." In the fast-growing number of nightclubs, males routinely order "beiyu ohm"; that is, beer with hostess, and many Vietnamese businessmen include the offer of a woman for the evening to their foreign counterpart as part of meeting protocol. Indeed, the foreign businessman could deal with someone who expects the same favor in return.

Women vs. Men in the Workforce

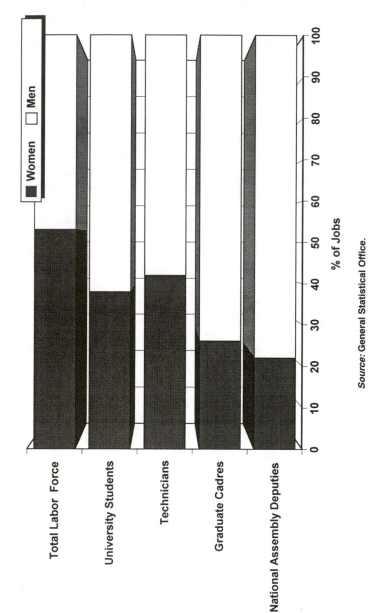

Source: **General Statistical Office.**

THE POLITICAL

LANDSCAPE

*I*n its political structure, Vietnam is a mini-dragon, mirroring the policies of its big brother to the north. Like China, its bureaucracy is inherited from the Soviet ministerial system. Its industry is centrally governed by central and local arms of those ministries. The Communist Party is charged with moral and political indoctrination and social education.

How is Vietnam's government administration organized?

A cursory glance at the Vietnamese governmental structure would lead one to believe that the National Assembly is the most important organ. Constitutionally, the National Assembly is the highest legislative authority in Vietnam. Elected by universal suffrage to serve five-year terms, its members convene two times every year; one-third of the members form the continuously functioning lawmaking body, the Standing Committee of the National Assembly, which is chaired by the Prime Minister.

In practice, the National Assembly and its Standing Committee only act as a rubber stamp for Politburo decisions, (though since the adoption of the 1992 constitution, the National Assembly has become more outspoken and influential in the policy-making process). Legislation actually originates in party bodies or the Government, formerly called the Council of Ministers, which is Vietnam's top executive and administrative body. The Government issues its legislation in the forms of decrees and directives, circulars and guidelines, which are then passed by the National Assembly in order to become law, and implemented by ministries, state committees, and departments. (See the organizational chart below.) The seat of power within the Government is its Cabinet, comprised of twenty ministers, the governor of the central bank, the Chairman of State Committees, various ministers with portfolios, and the head of a group of general departments.

The entire bureaucracy, in addition to the armed forces, is subordinate to the authority of the Communist Party of Vietnam (CPV). The Party's executive body is the thirteen-member Politburo, elected by its Central Committee during annual National Party Congresses. The Party secretariat issues directives to Party members and to the officialdom.

The head of state and of the armed forces is the President, currently Le Duc Anh.

PLAYERS IN THE BUREAUCRACY

Head of State:	President Le Duc Anh
Main Members of the Cabinet:	
Prime Minister	Vo Van Kiet
Deputy Prime Ministers	Nguyen Khanh
	Tran Duc Luong
	Phan Van Khai
Ministers	
Agriculture & Food Industry	Nguyen Cong Tan
Commerce & Tourism	Le Van Triet
Communications & Transport	Bui Danh Luu
Construction	Nho Xuan Loc
Culture, Information, & Sports	Tran Hoan
Education & Training	Tran Hong Quan
Energy	Thai Phung Ne

Finance	Ho Te
Foreign Affairs	Nguyen Manh Cam
Heavy Industry	Tran Lum
Interior	Bui Thien Ngo
Justice	Nguyen Dinh Loc
Labour, War Invalids & Social Welfare	Tran Dinh Hoan
Light Industry	Dan Vu Chu
National Defence	General Doan Khue
Population & Family Planning	Mai Ky
Science, Technology, & Environment	Dang Huu

Government Structure

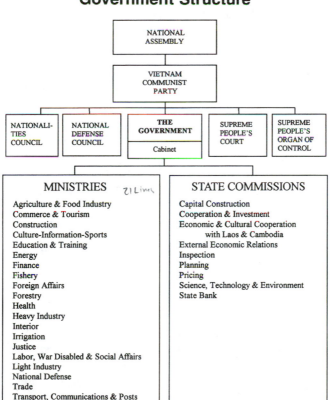

What is the function of the Communist Party?

With 2.2 million members, Vietnam's communist party celebrated its 65th anniversary in February 1995, and remains the "driving force of the population," says Vice Chairman of the Ideology Commission of the Party's Central Committee, Pham Quang Nghi. The party enjoyed an increase of 60,000 members in 1994, a 13 percent increase over 1993. Vietnam's Communist Party reaffirms its stance against the formation of a multiparty system, and will not allow the dilution of the Party's leadership in the style of the Soviet program Perestroika, which it views as a huge political mistake. The Party is its most outspoken apologist as well as critic. In January 1995, Party General Secretary Do Muoi, the 78-year-old Party Chief, who wears a high-collared Mao jacket, admitted, "bureaucracy, abusive power and corruption have surfaced among not a small section of officials in the party and state apparatus." He conceded that the party needed fresh blood from outside. And that is what happened when the Vietnamese elected 177 independent and nonparty members in local elections in November 1994 to become members of provincial, district, and commune level People's Councils throughout the country. But Do Muoi also indicated that "the Communist Party shall not in whatever circumstance share its leadership of Ho Chi Minh's Vietnam with anybody." In its 1994 national conference the Party committed itself to building a "Socialist state of the people, by the people and for the people" under the sole leadership of the Communist Party along the principle of "democratic centralization." Though economic reforms were launched in 1986, the Party remains committed to forging a market economy under "state management."

How are decisions made in the government bureaucracy?

Vietnam's bureaucratic centralism model of decision-making implies that policies will be formulated at the central level and implemented accordingly at the provincial level. In practice, the direction of authority between the central and provincial government bodies is not so evident. Policies implemented by provincial authorities may only approximate the State's original policy and in some cases will diverge significantly. Oftentimes, the State sanctions local adaptation of centrally promulgated policies, or the policies themselves may be so general as to necessitate provincial engineering. As a result, implementation styles usually differ by province and locality. Depending upon the province, local authorities can wield a substantial amount of power and establish policies independent of the central government as long as they do not radically defy the principles of existing laws. *Doi moi* has only contributed to the autonomy of provinces by further decentralizing the decision-making process and cutting off local authorities from central subsidies.

National decisions are made at the central level and authority is delegated to provincial bodies to implement policies in accordance with the localities' special characteristics. While it may appear that the direction of authority runs downward, from central to provincial, this is not necessarily the case. In many ways, provincial People's Committees can wield much more power than ministries. One reason for this is that People's Committees control land permits. Foreign investors, therefore, rely on good relations with the People's Committee to see their projects through in a timely manner.

How is Vietnam's leadership changing?

Many of the recent political and economic reforms can be attributed to generational changes in the leadership. New blood has been allowed to enter the decision-making process. Hanoi's aging leadership will eventually be circulated out, just as in China, but we've seen how long that can take. Since 1986, more Southerners have obtained high-level positions, which has had a major impact on the nature of economic policies. In fact, bureaucrats don't divide into an Old Guard and Young Turks as they do in China. They divide along the lines of north and south. When they started *doi moi*, officials in the North invited economists in the South to join the effort, officials who had been booted out of the leadership ranks after Liberation. During the past few years, therefore, increasing numbers of progressive Southerners have entered the highest echelons of the government.

Many people in their thirties who have been trained abroad, and who are more progressive in their thinking, are moving into positions of leadership. Many government officials are jumping ship to take up positions in private industry; others are dying off.

Elections of lower-level officials generate a significant degree of turnover, which, combined with the removal of officials on corruption charges, ensures that new blood is circulated through the corridors of government. Within a decade the complexion of Vietnam's leadership will be rejuvenated.

Is economic reform to be accompanied by political reform, and to what extent?

Much debate these days is focused on the effects of economic liberalization on politics, particularly under authoritarian regimes. Without diving into theory, suffice it to say that once people start experiencing a higher standard of living and receiving better education, expectations rise. Economic liberalization eventually leads to a political transformation, though not necessarily to democracy, as other East Asian examples would indicate. In the case of Vietnam, the VCP has managed to achieve a substantial amount of economic reform while still maintaining power and political stability. Part of the reason for this is that most Vietnamese people are much better off than they were even four years ago. However, few are at the point where they have the luxury to be politically active. The unemployed are not mobilized and the rest of the country seems to be so busy trying to make money that they don't have time for political resistance.

Even so, politics are not static, and as Vietnam grows, its people promise to become more politically active. The VCP has taken its own corrective measures to eradicate corruption by skillfully announcing each incident and the perpetrator's punishment. Common sense tells us that corruption is still in every echelon of Vietnamese government, but by attacking itself and sacrificing a few individuals, the government is hedging against future political unrest.

Somewhat like Japan, Vietnam has imported a great deal of social practices, but has always succeeded in assimilating those imports and injecting indigenous values to create something uniquely Vietnamese. Politics is no exception. Historically, the Vietnamese were conditioned by Chinese Confucian principles, which stressed a strong political center surrounded by semiautonomous, but loyal, villages and subjects. Officials were chosen on the basis of meritocracy rather than nepotism. In order to command the respect of the people, rulers were expected to be virtuous, compassionate, and moral. This mentality is still quite relevant today. Although some officials are benefiting from reforms through corrupt practices, the government is at the same time striving to maintain legitimacy by appearing to eradicate corruption.

One of the interesting aspects of Vietnamese politics is that the VCP has avoided the Maoist- or Stalinist-style personality cults that usually characterize communist regimes. Since the death of Ho Chi Minh in 1969, no single leader has dominated the political scene. This has facilitated the economic transformation by allowing a host of leaders to participate in the decision-making process. However, politics are complicated by tensions between local and central governments and varying degrees of commitment to economic reform. Despite divergent opinions about the extent to which *doi moi* should be pursued, one thing is clear: leaders are not willing to entertain the idea of political pluralism, a multiparty system, or the advent of opposition parties. While refusal to open up the political process is predicated on the idea that economic reform would be undermined by political instability, it is also evident that Party leaders are not ready to relinquish control of a system that is providing them economic sustenance. This is hardly ironic given that Ho Chi Minh once said that "bureaucratic disease" would be the future enemy of Vietnam, a prediction that has since come to fruition. The law of diminishing returns has once again proven to be correct: too much bureaucracy in Vietnam has severely diminished the administrative capacity of the government. While bureaucrats are very adept at setting targets and measuring production levels, they have little ability to think outside of the plan, although this is changing.

How do people feel about the government and the changes brought by doi moi?

The Vietnamese are generally happier than they were five years ago, and thus they are supportive of the government and the ruling Communist Party. Families that were once starving can now put food on the table. Scores of people can now accumulate the once unfathomable sum of $1,800 to purchase a motorbike. In truth, the figure of $200 per capita GNP doesn't take into account the enormous grey economy, hidden wealth, and the payments from relatives abroad. Many people thank the Party for this improvement in their lives. Many are anticorruption, but unlike the case in China, corruption is not perceived as synonymous with the Communist Party. This is an important distinction between the way Vietnamese feel about the Party and how the overseas Vietnamese feel about the Party. Inside the country, rampant corruption has not yet tarnished the image of communism as it has outside the country. It is thought that there are *individuals* in the bureaucracy who are corrupt and that those people should be eradicated, but it is generally believed that the system of socialism is a good one for the country. Of course, many intellectuals in Vietnam believe that officials in the Party are corrupt by nature and corruption goes with the territory of communist bureaucracy. But members of this segment of the population, who are also vocal with their opinions, comprise perhaps 1–2 percent of the total citizenry. While the people in this group are more akin to overseas Vietnamese in mentality and aspirations for their country, they are also the most politically vulnerable group in the country.

The higher echelon realizes that *doi moi* reform is not enough, in terms of political reform, to keep the population mollified forever. Without improvement in the economy, the Party has no political legitimacy. It no longer has a political revolution that the people have to uphold and carry forward; there is no common foe. The Party has no way of uniting the people behind it other than improvement of their lives. Hearts and minds are won not through ideology, but by food on the table. The only reason the Vietnamese people have not yet lashed out at the government is that they are better off than they were four years ago. They also realize there is little they can do constructively, so they are focusing on bettering their lives economically. Political activism, it is felt, is a luxury that comes after economic ascendency.

How concerned are Vietnamese citizens with political issues?

As Article three of the Constitution of the Socialist Republic of Vietnam states: "the State . . . severely punishes all acts violating the interests of the motherland and of the people." But despite the looming shadow of the State in Vietnamese life, the

Vietnamese people are very concerned with political issues and their implications. For at least the last 20 years, most Vietnamese have been educated with Marxist theory and have been subjected to a flood of political propaganda. As a result, it is difficult to separate politics from everyday life, especially in this new environment of openness.

However, Vietnamese do not yet have the luxury of weighing political concerns more highly than economic ones. Before 1987, the Vietnamese had extremely poor living conditions and little opportunities for improvement; but since the Sixth Party Congress, the standard of living has improved for most sectors of society and the people now have avenues for advancement. Accordingly, a great deal of energy can be felt everywhere as Vietnamese rush to make money. For right now, it appears that the pursuit of wealth is more important than political change. Once the Vietnamese have attained a certain level of comfort, it is plausible that political issues will be at the forefront of social activity. Another factor inhibiting Vietnamese political action is the historical acceptance of institutions and respect for leaders. However, respect is something that must be deserved—it is not automatically obtained. Therefore, if government leaders continue to steer the economy correctly and critique their own shortcomings, or at least appear to be taking measures against corruption, the Vietnamese people will have little incentive to engage in politics more than economics.

Do the Vietnamese speak openly about the policies of their government?

Upon arrival in Vietnam and even after some time there, one is not struck by the presence of an intrusive police state. Nevertheless, it is still there. While many government officials would happily jump to the private sector for better pay, they certainly do not advertise that fact. In addition, if you ask these same officials (provided they are not Party members) if they would want to join the Party, don't expect to get a straight answer. Of course, the political pressure for government officials is far greater than that for the general public. Even so, people watch their backs if they feel they're saying something a little too critical. Suspicion is a big factor in human relations in Vietnam.

If a person does not know well the person with whom he is speaking, he will undoubtedly be extra cautious.

You will come across opinionated Vietnamese always ready to tonguelash the government, but most people will not speak openly about politics. After the fall of Saigon, the government tightened lips, perhaps forever, by implementing a Soviet-style "informant" system wherein people were forced to reveal secrets about the political activities of their neighbors. Fear of informants and submerged resentments are the root cause of another core personality trait of the Vietnamese business person—an unwillingness to trust those outside his or her family.

Vietnamese people have definite opinions about their government and politics, probably more so than Americans, but they may not be as anxious to share them. The informant society that permeated every day life for much of the 1950s, 1960s, 1970s, and even the 1980s has yet to vanish. As a result, political discussions rarely take place on the street. Instead, such discussions are often heard among friends and family members in the home.

When the Vietnamese do discuss politics, they are critical. Since the introduction of *doi moi*, people are more outspoken and groups such as students and intellectuals have been able to exert some influence on the government. For example, during 1988 to 1989, a host of student protests over outdated textbooks, poor living conditions, and restricted admission policies led the government to placate the students by introducing new curricula, improving living conditions, and disassociating a person's political background with admission requirements.

Is the press censored in Vietnam?

In 1987, media control was loosened and the press was encouraged by the government to be the voice of the masses in exposing complaints about corruption and bureaucracy. "Generally, the press here is quite free. Where the impression of the foreigner is that Vietnam is a communist state," says Andrew Homan, an editor for *Vietnam Investment Review* in Saigon, "restrictions on the Vietnamese press are quite relaxed and relaxing still." Moreover, the cessation of state subsidies forced publications to cater more to public interest for the sake of profit. The number of publications increased quickly, some were not legally sanctioned, and some began to cover morally questionable topics. But perhaps the most pressing problem for the government was the rapidity with which the press and the public had taken to criticism of the government. In order to rein in this trend, the government imposed new censorship regulations and shut down several newspapers and magazines in 1989. Throughout 1991 and 1992, the Party moved to increase its control over the media and pressed for "guided information" to avoid the negative effects of pessimistic articles on society. Political pressure, like many things in Vietnam, is not making a linear progression downwards; rather, it oscillates between light and heavy depending on the security of the government and the VCP.

Are violations of human rights part of Vietnamese society today?

International human rights organizations have reported no recent political killings or torture in Vietnam, though they have accused Vietnam's government of intolerance and inhumane treatment of prisoners. Vietnam's response to a U.S. State Department annual report on these issues, in February 1995, was curt. A foreign ministry spokesman said: "We think that no state has the right to judge and impose its own opinion on the human rights situation in other countries."

In the United States, we hear quite a lot about the violations of human rights, press censorship, repression of religion, and imprisonment of dissidents at the hands of Communist officials. In Vietnam, however, you hear nothing at all of these things. People tell you: "We aren't political...we don't care about politics." People generally want to raise their standard of living and eagerly seek to train themselves to do so. As an expat from France says, "Going into a long-term gripe with the government is not one of the perceived paths to improving one's prospects." The message of *doi moi* is clear: Keep your nose clean and prosper.

No one would deny that there is a human rights problem in Vietnam, but it's clearly not, as some Viet Kieu would have you believe, as egregious as that in China, or Indonesia, or even Thailand. Most Viet Kieu haven't been to Vietnam in twenty years. But whenever a Vietnamese delegation comes to the United States to promote the country's business opportunities to American business people, out come the Viet Kieu protesters. Many American companies drop out of business conferences at the last minute when protests are mounted, fearing negative publicity. To the protesters, the Vietnamese official visitors are purebred communists who victimized their families, stole their businesses, and continue to persecute anybody who speaks out against the government. Fear of protest has even kept American universities from holding Vietnam conferences. The University of California at San Diego is one school that will think twice before sponsoring another Vietnam conference like the one it did on May 17, 1994. Two Viet Kieu protesters gained entry into the conference and began asking visiting officials hostile questions about the current government in Vietnam, from prepared lists of questions typed on the stationery of a well-known Viet Kieu political group. They sat on either side of the room and wouldn't let up in attempting to disrupt the proceedings.

What issues are going to be contentious between the United States and Vietnam in the coming years?

With diplomatic relations on the way to being normalized, and the MIA issue partly delinked from trade, Vietnam's bid for MFN is currently the looming issue between the two nations. When the trade embargo was lifted in February 1994, the reaction among Americans was mute; like his move to restore diplomatic relations with Vietnam, the action didn't win or lose President Clinton many points. Thus, it doesn't hurt President Clinton to stall on the issue of granting Vietnam MFN status. The only people who might get behind the MFN issue are a few intrepid importers...and they are largely Viet Kieu. While the Vietnamese want MFN status granted immediately, the United States is withholding such status until full diplomatic relations are initiated, the timetable for which is unclear as of this writing.

United States–Vietnam relations pivot on a number of different current issues. While the Vietnamese claim that no more POWs remain alive and that the issue should no longer be a top priority in discussions, the American view is that more information is available, but is not being turned over, and that 2–5 more years will be necessary to obtain records and investigate crash sites. While the Vietnamese feel that their 1992 National Constitution provides for steady progress in human rights, America is demanding the release of political critics, the ratification of penal reforms, and constitutional amendments providing for increased political pluralism and religious freedoms in Vietnam. While the Vietnamese urge the United States to increase aid to its own veterans who were exposed to Agent Orange, the American view is opposed to "reconstruction" aid but open to efforts to detoxify Vietnam's affected environment. While the Vietnamese want to sign a new tax treaty with the United States in order to generate U.S. investment, the American side wants to do so only after diplomatic ties are in place. While the Vietnamese want overseas Vietnamese, who did not renounce their citizenship before leaving Vietnam, to ask for permission to do so; the Americans consider Vietnamese Americans to be U.S. citizens and believe that Vietnam should recognize their dual citizenship. While the Vietnamese want the United States to assist them in removing mines and explosives, the United States claims it has done all that is required of it by the 1973 Paris Peace Agreement, though it is willing to train Vietnamese disposal units and help with archival research.[1]

CHRONOLOGY OF VIETNAM-U.S. RELATIONS

1976—United States vetoes Vietnam's application for United Nations membership. Unofficial contacts in Paris and United Nations on missing United States servicemen.

1977—Presidential envoy Leonard Woodcock visits Hanoi on POW/MIA mission. Normalization talks in Paris break down as Hanoi demands billions of dollars in postwar reconstruction aid.

1978—Normalization talks resume, come close to fruition, but fail as United States opts for closer ties with Vietnam's rival China.

1979—Relations deteriorate badly as United States pushes for international isolation of Vietnam over its invasion of Cambodia.

1982-1986—United States delegations visit Hanoi several times for talks on POW/MIA issue.

(continued on next page)

---

[1] The above issues are adapted from an article by Dr. Allan E. Goodman, Professor of International Affairs at Georgetown University, Washington DC, which appeared in "Will U.S.–Vietnam Ties Ever Be Normal?" *Business Times,* January 28, 1995, Special Section; pg. 3.

1987—Presidential envoy Gen. John Vessey holds talks in Hanoi on POW/MIA issue and humanitarian concerns of Vietnam.

1988—United States and Vietnam begin joint field investigations aimed at resolving fate of American servicemen missing from the Vietnam War.

July 1990—Bush administration announces readiness for direct dialogue with Hanoi to reach Cambodia peace settlement.

September—Secretary of State James Baker meets Vietnamese Foreign Minister Nguyen Co Thach in New York—highest level contact between United States and Vietnam since end of Vietnam War.

April 1991—Washington presents Hanoi with "roadmap" plan for phased normalization of relations. Vessey visits Hanoi, wins agreement to set up POW/MIA investigation office in Hanoi. United States announces $1 million dollars in humanitarian aid to Vietnam.

July—United States MIA investigation office opens in Hanoi with staff of five.

October—A peace agreement on Cambodia is signed in Paris, setting in motion a four-stage United States "road map" for normalization with Vietnam.

November—The first round of U.S.-Vietnam talks on normalizing relations is held in New York.

March 1992—United States Assistant Secretary of State Richard Solomon holds high-level talks in Hanoi, announces Washington will provide a minimum of $3 million dollars in humanitarian aid to Vietnam in response to increased cooperation on POW/MIA issue.

April—Washington eases embargo to allow commercial sales to Vietnam that meet basic human needs, lifts restrictions on projects by United States nongovernmental organizations, and allows restoration of direct telecommunication links with Vietnam.

July 1993—United States drops opposition to loans to Vietnam from international financial institutions. United States Assistant Secretary of State Winston Lord visits Hanoi.

August—Three State Department personnel take up posts in Hanoi.

September—United States further eases embargo by allowing American firms to participate in development projects in Vietnam funded by international financial institutions.

January 1994—Admiral Charles Larson, commander-in-chief of the United States Pacific Command, visits Hanoi.

February—President Bill Clinton lifts United States embargo against Vietnam. United States and Vietnam begin talks on frozen Vietnamese assets, diplomatic property claims, and private United States claims.

May—United States and Vietnam agree to exchange liaison offices.

July 1995—President Clinton announces that diplomatic relations between Vietnam and the United States have been normalized.

Source: adapted from *Kyodo News Service, Japan Economic Newswire,* January 28, 1995.

THE BUSINESS

SCENE

*P*erhaps the best thing going for Vietnam is the glowing "Next Asia Tiger" reportage in the world press, which hypes the country's huge, hard-working, highly educated populace and immense cache of natural resources. The government's vigorous propagandizing of the country's priority investment projects, processing zones, and economic reforms makes China's efforts of the late 1980s look downright provincial. Having read the press, investors race in thinking the investment licensing process has been streamlined, the laws are transparent, and export zones offer "one-stop" approval of deals, but once they get in, they meet with one steely impediment after another. To build a factory or a hotel, permit after permit has to be fought for and relationships with ministries and the People's Committee must be cemented over time. Bribes must be paid, or not paid, delicately. It takes forever to get plans reviewed, changed, and approved.

REALITY CHECK:
VIETNAM'S CLIMATE FOR BUSINESS

In May 1994, the SCCI held a conference to listen to foreign complaints. A British citizen working for a French concern was one of the many foreigners who vented complaints at the podium. "When I came here some years ago my hair was still black and now it has turned grey as I've gone through so many complicated procedures regarding your country's investment environment. . . Please help us to be part of your community by abolishing as much as you can red tape and bureaucracy."

Real estate developers complained about getting land use permits and getting their construction permits. As one representative of a foreign construction concern said, "once the investment license is given, nothing is certain as a series of other permits must be procured including the land use permit, the land use grant, the construction permit and others. If there is *karaoke* in your hotel, you seek permission from the culture and information office; if there is a massage parlor, you should ask the public health agency; if besides hotel business you want to arrange some tourist activities, you should contact the Tourism Authority—it just goes on."

VIETNAM'S REAL POTENTIAL

While it is true that Vietnam offers a highly-educated, hard-working labor force and is rich in natural resources, there is much fallacy in this as well. There *are* natural resources in Vietnam but not enough to support a population growing at 2 percent annually, which will exhaust the natural resources before they can efficiently be exploited. Even so, the growth in the oil industry shows little sign of slowing and new findings are often in the news. As far as human resources, Vietnam obviously has quite a labor pool from which to draw. In fact, it could be argued that even with the increase of foreign investment and the growth of the private sector, there will still not be enough jobs created to absorb all the labor. Unemployment and underemployment remain at astonishingly high levels. However, as has been well published, the labor force that does exist can generally be characterized as hard-working, flexible, and fairly well educated, perhaps more in the South than in the North. But it takes a lot of expensive training to get Vietnamese workers to do what you want them to do, and even then, it's difficult because, say foreign managers, "they are adaptable, but only when they want to be." Rather than lead you down the garden path, I will address the following sober-minded question.

What are the problems with Vietnam's investment climate?

Despite all the hype surrounding Vietnam, it should not be surprising to find a long list of impediments to doing business in the country. Some of the most frequent complaints are the bureaucratic hoop-jumping; exorbitant phone, fax, and housing expenses; ever-changing laws; and crumbling infrastructure. Fortunately for the U.S. investor, the embargo prevented U.S. businesses from bearing many of the early costs of Vietnam's opening. That is not to say, however, that substantial costs can be avoided by entering the market now. Vietnam is still in its infancy as it develops and industrializes, and foreign investors will naturally have to share the burdens that come with economic transformation.

Perhaps foremost, investors complain of the country's weak and vast changing legal framework. This is combined with frustration over the investment project approval process, which tends to include the participation of too many government players at both the central and local levels. Investors also complain that they have to hire labor through government labor offices at wage levels above what local companies pay. For foreign ventures involved in import substitution projects, one does not hear complaints of trade barriers or pernicious policies on the part of the government; however, all joint ventures complained of the import licensing protocol, which allows a venture to import a select number of items but requires additional paperwork and licensing should other items be needed in the course of production. Other problems due to lacking infrastructure include constant power shortages and insufficient or unclean supply of water. Rounding out the list of complaints are problems with financing and banking. Foreign ventures find that the local banking sector is undeveloped and in most cases unable to provide working capital, forcing the foreign partner to finance its Vietnam venture from overseas sources solely.

BYZANTINE BUREAUCRACY. Perhaps the most frustrating aspects of investing in Vietnam are the different layers of government. While the SCCI claims to be a "one-stop" center for the foreign investment licensing process and promises to rule on most licenses within 30 days, in reality, investors are often stalled by other ministries, departments, and local administrations. In short, regulations have become regionalized. In many cases, the provincial authorities can wield more power and exert more pressure on the foreign investor than the central government. As a result, getting approvals can take as long as one to three years. In order to combat this problem, new legislation to streamline procedures was introduced in mid-1994, that allows local officials to grant land use permits for smaller projects, while the central government can grant permits for larger projects. In spite of the government's seemingly open foreign investment policies, the bureaucracy's actions speak a lot louder and much more slowly than their words. In 1994, the head of the SCCI admitted to the National Assembly that some foreign investors have had to apply for as many as eleven other permits after obtaining their foreign investment license.

NASCENT LEGAL FRAMEWORK. Ironically, investments in Vietnam require a myriad of permits, but are not safeguarded by a comprehensive system of commercial regulations and law. That is not to say that the government isn't trying to put a legal system in place. One of the most difficult tasks that a foreign investor faces is keeping up with the deluge of new laws that are announced on a daily basis. Unfortunately, government proclamations, laws, decrees, even utterances by officials are made purposefully vague, stripped of the specifics a Westerner needs to understand the rules. Also, legal interpretation differs between North and South. The South puts a premium on local laws rather than those promulgated in Hanoi. The People's Committee at the provincial level typically has more power than the People's Committee at the central level. For example, if you import an item through Ho Chi Minh City and you are paying taxes to the central government, the local committee will ask you to pay additional taxes at the local level. You will scream and yell that you've already paid taxes to the central level, but the provincial officials will say they don't care and demand to be paid as well. The clout is with the province, especially when you are dealing in Ho Chi Minh City.

This will not be the case, however, in all fifty-three provinces of the country.

HIGH COSTS. Probably the most shocking thing awaiting the foreign investor who is accustomed to hearing how poor Vietnam is, or is used to doing business in Southeast Asia, is the cost of operating a business in Vietnam. Even if rental fees don't appear to be too overwhelming, telecommunication expenses will definitely take up a big chunk of an investor's budget. A one-page fax from the Hanoi General Post Office to the United States costs about seven dollars, with additional pages running around five dollars. If someone is unlucky enough to be faxing from a hotel, he or she can expect to pay an average of $10.75 for a one-page fax. Some hotels have even found that guests are willing to pay up to eighteen dollars per page to the United States. In fact, it isn't uncommon for the phone and fax bill at a hotel to be more than twice the room bill.

CORRUPTION. No discussion of Vietnam is complete without the mention of corruption. One would be hard-pressed to find a country in which no government officials took advantage of their position for monetary gain. In Vietnam, the problem is perhaps more understandable given the extremely low salaries of government officials. Billions of U.S. dollars are being promised to Vietnam and the bulk is entering through joint ventures with governmental entities. Certainly, a large percentage of foreign investors have encountered no instances of corruption in their dealings, but for many there is a gray area that they are wary to discuss. Though some would counter this assumption, the Foreign Corrupt Practices Act inhibits the U.S. investor from engaging in payoffs and other corrupt activities, but that doesn't necessarily put U.S. investors at a disadvantage.

Bribery has a rich recent history in Vietnam. After 1975 the Communists set about purging business people, mainly Chinese and later intellectuals, and sending them off to "re-education" camps and so-called New Economic Areas, where they were basically left to eke out a life in the jungle on their own. Thousands of Vietnamese and Chinese-Vietnamese either bribed officials and guards to let them leave the country as refugees and boat people, while others simply disappeared into Cholon where they paid a monthly bribe of a few thousand *dong* to police to keep their cover. Lower-level officials took bribes from private businesses whose owners wanted to stay in business, which they passed along to their superiors. By the time the economy was almost without hope of resuscitation in the late 1980s, the accepting of bribes was virtually the only game in town, as an official's monthly salary equalled roughly the cost of a bowl of soup.

Elements within the government have been trying to eradicate corruption since the late 1980s. Communist Party General Secretary, Do Muoi, calls corrupt officials and cadres "revolutionary mandarins" and he says he wants them purged from the Party. In January 1995, it was reported that registered corruption cases had risen 47 percent over the previous year and involved eighty-eight company executives and seventy government officials. The report stated also that 22 percent of district level Hanoi officials had been disciplined in order to control rampant corruption. In 1994, the former Energy Minister, Vu Ngoc Hai, was sentenced to three years in prison for abusing his power. Ho Viet, Chairman of Da Nang's People's Committee, was axed too, as well as Tran Dinh Dam, the Chairman of the Provincial People's Committee. With the change of the power structure in Da Nang, bureaucratic turf battles, payoffs, and delays vanished almost immediately, to the pleasant surprise of foreigners trying to initiate projects there. With all the effort, however, Party people and high-level ministers somehow keep ending up living in million-dollar French villas and being chauffeured about town in Land Cruisers.

Will Vietam's business climate improve, and how fast?

The climate for business in Vietnam will improve as fast as its economy develops, which it must do by itself. International lending institutions have agreed to inject about $2 billion annually into Vietnam in foreign aid, grants, and loans for the next 6 years.\Foreign investment withstanding this is the key injection of foreign capital—$8.2 billion over the next 12 years. The primary focus of the money will be to rebuild the human resource infrastructure and the physical infrastructure—highways, ports, power plants, administrative processing systems for central government, and so on. Ultimately, the speed with which these projects are defined and implemented will be the primary influencing factor for how fast Vietnam develops. The pace of the spending of these appropriated funds determine the growth of the economy, and thus the rate at which the business climate is improved.

A second factor will be the perception of the value and scope of Vietnam's natural resources by the outside world. This perception will determine the level of foreign investment in the development and exploitation of the country's natural resources. The major portions of foreign investment into the country will come from resource exploitation deals. Oil and gas is the most obvious resource, and has garnered 25 percent of total foreign investment.

A third factor will be how smart Vietnam is in implementing policies that facilitate economic growth and maintain its international comparative advantage. This is an area of deep concern. The country's competitive advantages at present boil down to its cheap labor and hard-working people. The percentage of the population that is highly educated is admirable for a country of Vietnam's economic status, but there remains a major shortfall in highly trained human resources. Does the government implement policies that facilitate or hurt the development of the country? Right now, there are some major policies that are running counter to the best long-term interests of the country in regard to foreign investment. One is the absence of copyright law. Another is a new tax law whereby a foreigner staying in the country more than 182 days per year is taxed 50 percent of worldwide income. China tried this too, as did India, but the fact is, by doing so an emerging country substantially increases the costs incurred by foreign firms to maintain resources in the country. Today, it is cheaper to keep a foreign expat in Singapore than it is in Hanoi or Ho Chi Minh City. Thus, companies station expats offshore and keep them from staying in Vietnam more than 182 days. As a result, Vietnam loses the benefit of having those foreign experts in the country for one-half of the year. It's a policy that is completely counter to the country's long-term best interests.

What will govern how effective that $2 billion annual authorization is will be: (1) the human resource capacity of the people of Vietnam to define and implement projects; and (2) the human resource capability of the International Financial Institutions (IFIs) and the Offshore Development Agencies (ODAs) to define and implement good projects. If Vietnam does everything right, the country will need 10–15 years before it can be perceived as a comparable emerging marketplace.

Should a firm get involved now, and grow with Vietnam, or wait until the country surmounts these obstacles?

Most of the companies going into the Vietnamese market are concentrating on infrastructure, construction, heavy equipment, oil, consumer products, light industrial goods, and services. Exceptionally large investments have been made since 1989 in real estate, telecommunications, oil, and tourism. Even so, there is still plenty of room for more foreign investors in such industries as construction materials and infrastructure, chemicals, fertiliser, cement, motorcycles, and some services. While smaller investors may have a much more difficult time obtaining licenses and surviving in a relatively expensive business environment, they nevertheless do have some opportunities, especially if they can cultivate good relationships and convince authorities of the project's importance.

Whether your company should enter Vietnam or not depends on the type of business. If you are in the hotel business you should be involved now. The same goes if you are involved in the oil and gas business. If you are a provider of consumer products, especially high-end products, you will want to think twice. A consumer market in Vietnam exists, but to enter it you're going to be forced to use Vietnam as a manufacturing platform. In this case, you will have to decide whether, given your company's global strategy, the effort to sell to what is a limited consumer market is worth the expense of producing in Vietnam. Say you are in the business of selling 35 mm cameras. There's not much of a market in Vietnam. Say you're Pizza Hut. Again, there's not much of a market. The expat community alone isn't large enough to support sales of these products. But if you're a beverage company like Coca-Cola, Pepsi, or Schwepp's, it's a good time to get involved. If you are an automobile company, it's already too late because there are only one or two automobile assembly plants with which to manufacture for the local market. And both already have joint venture partners. So it depends on the industry. What should you do? Go to Vietnam and look at your market. In areas where local industry is completely lacking, straight sales without producing onshore are possible.

What is the Vietnamese attitude toward American business, and vice versa?

Even before the lifting of the U.S. embargo, over forty U.S. firms had opened offices in Vietnam, with another fifteen pending. These companies had signed 260 contracts that would be acted upon as soon as the embargo was lifted. Some of these companies included Mobil, IBM, American Express, Boeing, and AT&T. Before the embargo was lifted, a U.S. firm could negotiate a contract down to the signing page, though withhold from signing it. There were a few cases in which the parties involved wanted to engage with U.S. firms and deals were put on hold to wait for the lifting of the embargo. Sometimes it was a case of wanting American technology. In other cases it was a priority not to have the Japanese dominate in a certain industry. Yet other times, it was political, as in the case of wanting Mobil involved in the South China Sea, because having American interests in the region's oil fields would make it less likely for China to start throwing its muscle around in the area. It was rumored in 1993 that PetroVietnam was saving some choice blocks for Mobil, but says Red River's Mel Jackson, "if you ever said that to a Vietnamese, they would flatly deny it and get very angry."

Contrary to many predictions, the lifting of the embargo did not necessarily open the floodgates for U.S. investment in Vietnam. Instead, those U.S. companies that had already been observing the market from their representative offices prior to February 3, 1994, were in a good position to begin formal business activities. However, only a handful of U.S. companies were actually in Vietnam surveying the economic landscape before President Clinton's announcement. Because establishing business ties in Vietnam generally requires a great deal of on-site market research and time-consuming relationship-building, the end of the embargo only marked the beginning of a long process for many U.S. companies without previous experience in the Vietnamese market. As a result, the immediate effects of the embargo lifting for U.S. investment in Vietnam have not been that substantial.

Much of the talk surrounding the controversy over the embargo stressed that U.S. business was somehow "missing out" on a golden opportunity, while the Japanese, Koreans, Taiwanese, Australians, French, Germans, and so on were taking advantage of the U.S. absence in the Vietnamese market. Of course, this translates into a disadvantage for the U.S. latecomers who were previously restricted by an obsolete political tool. However, few foreign business people in Vietnam today would subscribe to this view. Instead, several will tell you that the only thing U.S. business missed out on was a lot of administrative headaches. Other foreign investors have spent considerable amounts of time and money working their way through bureaucratic vagaries and surprises, while also coping with the challenges of an immature market. In fact, the United States may have chosen to enter the elusive Vietnamese market at an optimal time: it's late enough that investment procedures are much more streamlined, the Vietnamese themselves have grown more accustomed to dealing with Western businessmen, basic concepts are now more widely understood, and the Vietnamese have had 4–5 years to witness the benefits of a market economy. At the same time, it's early enough that the market isn't saturated for any one product, enormous potential exists for nearly every industry, and most importantly, the Vietnamese have not committed themselves to working only with the early birds.

On the Vietnamese side of the equation, not much has changed. While Vietnamese companies can certainly engage in business with U.S. companies and try to export their products, without MFN status, the tariff rates preclude the possibility of a sensible business person choosing to attempt this. Now that liaison offices have been established in Hanoi and Washington, D.C., the next step is to actualize diplomatic relations through embassies, and then MFN will likely follow. Not only do the Vietnamese like and want to work with U.S. businessmen, but they also have a very favorable view of U.S. products and business practices. This view is particularly strong in the South, due to the U.S. presence before 1975. While some might assume that the war left a bad taste in the mouths of Southern Vietnamese, that is not the case. Rather, most people in the South who lived through the war period recall the large number of jobs that the United States provided, as well as the quality infrastructure and products. For the most part, the Vietnamese are pragmatic people who do not feel the need to dwell on the past, and prefer to focus on the betterment of their economic and social condition for the future. You will not face recrimination or outward ill-feeling because you are

American. The Vietnamese perceive "the American war" as only one of many of their triumphs over foreign invaders and they have no axe to grind with us. All they ever wanted was for their country to be free of occupying forces and united. Most of the streets in Hanoi are named after famous warriors of independence who fought the Chinese, the French, and the Japanese—not the Americans. They want to be our equal partner, and are continually perplexed by our seeming fixation on a war that ended two decades ago. They've moved beyond the war and want to develop. Of course, it's much easier to be a good sport when you've won a war rather than lost it.

With the exception of Americans under 25, the war in Vietnam elicits many memories, most of which are emotional. Be warned that in getting your company involved in Vietnam you may run into a boardmember who resists such moves based on his war experience or attitudes about a previous victor over American forces in a war. Anthony Foster has told the *Financial Times*: "every American company is run by lawyers in a way. Lawyers in most companies can and will kill a deal if they don't think it's safe. The bottom line is that with these deals you have to get board approval. If you are a line manager pushing a project you're sticking your neck out against something that can be very emotional."

The flag of the Socialist Republic of Vietnam, or *Cong Hoa Xa Hoi Chu Nghia Viet Nam*.

Helmsman in bronze, "Uncle" Ho Chi Minh in front of the old Hotel de Ville, completed in 1908 and now Saigon's City Hall.

Erected in 1880, the Hotel Continental was visited by dukes and princes, and later became the haunt of journalists and a setting for Graham Greene's 1954 novel, *The Quiet American*.

A cyclone of dealmaking at the bar in the Metropole Hotel in Hanoi.

Present and past blend along Dong Khoi Street in downtown Saigon.

A woman's traditional outfit for work is still the graceful *ao dai,* comprised of a long-sleeved silk blouse over loose-fitting pants.

Retail shops make up the dragon's share of the private economy.

At the Ben Thanh market in Saigon, sellers rent stalls for $100 per month, from which they sell locally made, imported, and smuggled goods.

Town markets—rather than supermarkets—are still where the Vietnamese find any food or household product available.

Schoolchildren enjoy the Ho Chi Minh Museum in Hanoi. Because of recent wars, Vietnam's population is abnormally young, with 39 percent of citizens under the age of 14.

Budget tourists head to Saigon's Central Post Office (Buu Dien Truong Tam) to call home because telecom prices are half what they are in the hotels.

A tenacious sales pitch alongside a foreign tourist's *cyclo*.

Old neighborhoods are razed to make room for high-rent corporate offices in Saigon.

The neo-Gothic towers of St. Joseph's Cathedral have loomed above Hanoi's French quarter since 1887; after the Philippines, Vietnam has the largest population of Catholics in all of Asia.

English Tudor architecture in Saigon? Urban planning leaves much to be desired as state firms and citizens sell their land rights to neglectful developers.

With office rents higher than in Hong Kong or Paris, some foreign firms set up in so-called business centers sprouting in Hanoi and Saigon.

Catering to Hanoi's fast-paced business elite, streetside office service shops provide typing, translation, copying, and even word processing.

Will Vietnam's national bird become the crane—that is, the construction crane? A boom is on to supply office space and five-star accommodations.

Visitors must make the pilgrimage to VietcomBank to cash traveler's checks or make cash draws on credit cards.

PART TWO

Selling to Vietnam

People say [the Vietnamese] have no distribution system. But what about the Ho Chi Minh Trail? What about all the goods that get smuggled in from China? It may look a little different, but it's working. Nothing gets lost. Nothing gets wasted.

EUGENE MATTHEWS,
QUOTED IN *THE NEW YORK TIMES MAGAZINE*

CHAPTER 5

WHAT VIETNAM
WANTS TO BUY

*V*ietnam's trade patterns experienced a jolt of tectonic proportions in 1992, with the collapse of the Comecon trade bloc of former Soviet satellite countries. Since then, Vietnam has had to find new suppliers as well as new buyers of its exports. With great speed and alacrity, Vietnam has done both, finding new export markets in the West and tripling its $700 million total export trade in 1988 to $2.5 billion in 1992.

Where CMEA trade partners once made up 50 percent of the country's imports as of 1988, they now only provide 5 percent of imports. By all accounts, Vietnam has come of age as an emerging market trading partner.

What is the composition of Vietnam's trade?

Part of the country's remarkable success is due to its crude oil exports, which grew from zero in 1988 to nearly $1 billion in

1995; and to rice exports, which increased from zero in 1988 to over 2 million tons in 1995, and made Vietnam the third largest rice exporter in the world, behind only Thailand and the United States. About half of the country's merchandise exports are made up of oil and rice, though seafood and light manufactured goods, such as textiles and handicrafts, are helping to diversify the country's export package.

While Vietnam's exports increased over 20 percent over the year of 1994 to $3.6 billion, imports rose even faster, rising 15 percent to $4.5 billion—good news for foreign suppliers, indeed. However, this has resulted in a $900 million trade deficit in 1994, which is a $10 million increase from the year before. Vietnam's leading export is crude oil, followed by textiles and clothing and marine products.

Do Vietnamese consumers have an appetite for, and the disposable income to purchase, imported goods?

Although Vietnam is one of the poorest countries in the world, with the World Bank citing a GNP per capita of only U.S.$200, national figures do not paint a very accurate picture of disposable income. First, the disparity between urban and rural dwellers is immense. Those in Hanoi and Ho Chi Minh City enjoy a much higher standard of living than those in the countryside. Some estimate that the GNP per capita in Ho Chi Minh City is closer to U.S.$1,000, while that in Hanoi is in the neighborhood of U.S.$800

But that is not to say that Vietnam is not poor. The 72 percent of the population still working in agriculture does not enjoy a standard of living anywhere near that in the cities. Sadly, many cannot even afford a bicycle and earn barely U.S.$50 per year.

One need not be a genius to realize that urban Vietnamese are richer than official figures indicate. Roughly 40 percent of urban households have at least one motorcycle, many of them new Hondas with a price tag of about U.S.$1,700. Given the lack of consumer credit, motorcycles are being purchased primarily with cash up front. According to the World Bank's figures, this purchase would require nearly 9 years worth of income and absolutely no other expenditures. Obviously, the hidden economy in Vietnam is enormous.

Growth of Vietnam's Foreign Trade

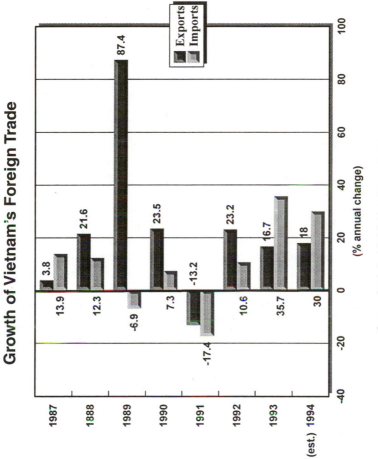

Exports
Imports

(% annual change)

Year	Exports	Imports
1987	3.8	13.9
1888	21.6	12.3
1989	87.4	-6.9
1990	23.5	7.3
1991	-13.2	-17.4
1992	23.2	10.6
1993	16.7	35.7
(est.) 1994	18	30

Source: Statistical Publishing House, Hanoi.

Where is all the money coming from? Are all those years of stuffing gold and U.S. dollars under the mattress at 0 percent interest finally paying off? Part of the money in circulation can be attributed to personal savings during the bleak economic periods of Vietnam's recent history. However, no accurate measures of nonbank savings exist, and the more important sources of wealth seem to be remittances and "unreported" income. (Official reports of annual remittances from overseas Vietnamese put the figure at about U.S.$600–700 million. However, many speculate that the real total has been closer to $1 billion, which is what the government predicted for 1994. While these remittances have a considerable impact on the Vietnamese economy, the majority of the money goes to the South of Vietnam.)

Another important point is that Vietnamese families do not live as nuclear units; instead, extended families live together with as many as three generations in one house. As a result, income is pooled, which increases buying power on a collective level. The foreign investor should keep this point in mind when conducting market research. It is difficult to draw conclusions from the activities of individual Vietnamese consumers; the market must be gauged in terms of families.

Additional income, separate from and far exceeding salaries, plays a big role in the Vietnamese economy. For instance, Vietnamese are rushing to put up buildings for guest houses and business offices. Many of these buildings are erected with cheap materials and labor, and are finished quickly to avoid permit fees. Once these buildings are completed, the landlords can earn high rents from foreign travelers and business people. Consider a guest house with five guests paying an average of U.S.$300 per month. The landlord could receive approximately U.S.$1,500 each month. Of course, only a fraction of that amount will be reported for tax purposes, especially because the tax rate is considerably higher for those housing foreigners. Even after taxes, one family could easily retain U.S.$1,000 without one household member having another job on the side, which is rarely the case.

Consider also that almost half of the households in Hanoi and Saigon contain three or more generations of people. Thus, family income is more important in analyzing the Vietnamese market for durable consumer goods than individual income. In an estimated 30 percent of households in these cities, four or more income earners reside. Add to this the fact that extended families often own businesses together and pool their income. Therefore, when we look at the countries' per capita income of $200 and conclude that Vietnam lacks purchasing power, we are missing the point.

The typical Vietnamese consumer is extraordinarilyy provincial, however. In a recent survey conducted for *VietNam Today,* only 34 urbanites out of a total of 3,184 interviewed had been overseas, only 10 of whom were male, while a mere 106 had traveled domestically at all. The surveyors concluded that "most consumers are thus not aware of the fact that a number of products exist outside their neighborhood, which can provide an answer to their—as yet undiscovered—desires or needs." The surveyors concluded thus, that "a good brand name, and innovative packaging should [allow a company] to become a clear cut brand leader in a short time, and get consumer loyalty for years to come."

Popular purchases include motorcycles, and home appliances such as televisions, stereos, and kitchen goods. Women are becoming more concerned with fashion; that is, hygiene and beauty products. Almost any such product is available at local markets, but the prices reflect transportation costs—and then some. For example, a tube of Colgate toothpaste will cost U.S.$3.00 and a bottle of Pantene Shampoo may cost as much as U.S.$9.00. Even so, it is surprising to see the brands that consumers have access to if they have the money and are willing to pay the price. Of course, a great deal of these goods are smuggled in from China, where trade and distribution systems have about a 10-year lead on Vietnam.

While there is definitely demand for upscale Western goods in Saigon, and to a lesser extent in Hanoi, it is unlikely that many people will be able to afford them for a while. However, those with access to remittances may comprise a submarket for such goods. In Saigon, 75 to 80 percent of households have televisions, while the figure for Hanoi is a bit lower. The government broadcasts programs on four channels. StarTV, BBC, and CNN are available at first-class hotels and in the homes of expats with satellite dishes. A satellite dish was the hot ticket item until the government cracked down on their proliferation. They cost about $800 and a citizen is supposed to obtain a license to buy one, but just like buying a license to build a house or operate a motorcycle, most overlook the formality.

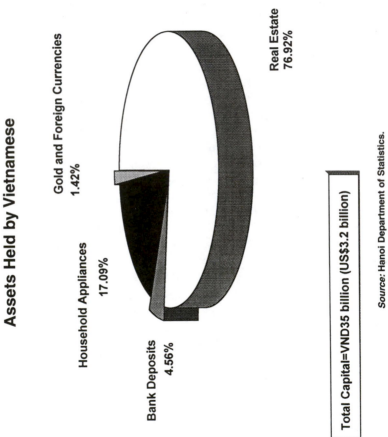

Assets Held by Vietnamese

Gold and Foreign Currencies
1.42%

Real Estate
76.92%

Household Appliances
17.09%

Bank Deposits
4.56%

Total Capital=VND35 billion (US$3.2 billion)

Source: **Hanoi Department of Statistics.**

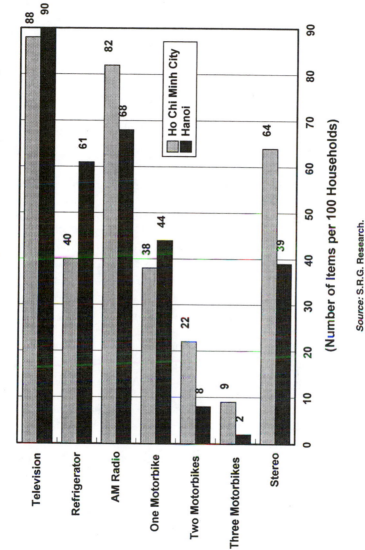

Consumer Product Ownership in Hanoi and HCM City

Ho Chi Minh City
Hanoi

(Number of Items per 100 Households)

Source: S.R.G. Research.

What are the selling opportunities in Vietnam?

At this early stage of economic development in Vietnam, some sectors are obviously more profitable than others. The Vietnamese government is very active in identifying those areas where investment is desired. For the most part, "desired" foreign investment projects overlap with profitable selling opportunities for foreign suppliers. In December 1994, the SCCI released a list of 150 desired projects that favored agricultural and food-processing industries as well as the northern provinces around Hanoi. The SCCI has even named those industries that are among the most promising for U.S. investors, including oil, natural gas, and electronics. The following section will provide a look at different sectors of the economy and the growth prospects for each.

TEXTILES. History has shown that the textile industry is usually the first to take off at the beginning of a country's economic development. Vietnam does not appear to be an exception to the rule. According to forecasts, the textile industry is supposed to grow at a rate of 14 percent annually, with exports increasing from U.S.$200 million in 1993 to U.S.$2 billion in 2005. To reach this target, the government predicts that investment capital of U.S.$2.1 billion will be required. Current activity in the industry supports the forecasts. Textile firms have been busy importing new equipment. One result of the surge in machinery imports is that textile production was up from 1,200 tons for all of 1993 to around 3,000 tons for the first half of 1994. While most of Vietnam's textile and garment export used to go to the former Soviet Union and Eastern European markets, new markets are opening in Western Europe and other Asian countries. Once MFN is granted, the United States will undoubtedly serve as a large export market for "Made in Vietnam" garments.

Closely related to the textile industry is the cotton industry. Each year, Vietnam's textile and garment industry consumes about 70,000 tons of cotton, creating ample opportunity for vertical linkages. As of now, Vietnam is importing the majority of its cotton, but has designated areas for cotton cultivation in Long An, Dac Lak, Dong Nai, Khanh Hoa, Binh Thuan and Ninh Thuan. With the introduction of high-yield cross varieties of cotton and advanced cultivation techniques, cotton could make an attractive import-substituting foreign investment.

CIVIL AVIATION. With the flood of curious tourists and business people that have already begun to visit Vietnam, the state of the civil aviation industry must be upgraded as soon as possible. This has implications for two different areas of the existing aviation infrastructure. First, older aircraft will be phased out as fleet sizes are increased. Vietnam Airlines is presently undertaking this task. Older Russian planes are gradually being grounded and should be completely out of use by 1997. In addition, the state airline says it will be purchasing thirty to forty new aircraft between now and the year 2000. Passenger traffic on the carrier has increased by an average of 30 percent annually since 1987, and the airline expects to be carrying 4 million passengers by the turn of the century. The growth in this industry bodes well not only for Boeing (which plans to sell Vietnam eighty passenger jets over the next decade worth up to a total of $5 billion) and Airbus, but also all related industries.

Second, airports all over the country need to be rehauled, if not completely redesigned and rebuilt. Several groups have been vying to upgrade Hanoi's international airport, Noi Boi, one of the smallest and most poorly equipped airports in any of the region's capitals. Over the next three years, passenger volume is expected to double and the two run-down terminals that comprise Noi Boi Airport have already reached capacity. At this point, it appears that a Japanese group has the advantage due to substantial amounts of Japanese aid offered for improvement of the airport, but like most things in Vietnam, only time will tell. Tan Son Nhat Airport in Ho Chi Minh City was recently refurbished and is in much better condition than Noi Boi, but it still doesn't meet the standards of most airports in Asia. A host of smaller airports throughout the country is in great need of modern equipment, new facilities, and expanded runways. The Vietnam Civil Aviation Department has already begun to undertake this project, but foreign assistance will be integral to its completion.

COMPUTER TECHNOLOGY. Although Vietnam has come a long way from the Soviet Minsk 22 computer of the late 1960s, the country nevertheless has a lot of catching up to do. One example of Vietnam's lag is that there are 3 computers for every 10,000 people as compared to Indonesia where there are 3 computers for every 1,000. With a view to upgrading the country's computer technology, the Technology Promotion Department of the Ministry of Science, Technology and Environment (MOSTE) adopted IT2000 (Information Technology to the year 2000) in August of 1993. Under this plan, the government will spend U.S.$300–500 million over the next 6 years to create a national data communications network and establish a domestic industry in component manufacturing and software development. Priority will go to the financial sector, education, and all government agencies, where 80 percent of the country's computing allegedly takes place. At this point, it looks like only big-name computer firms will be given preference for government contracts, but that doesn't include the immense computer market that will open up in the private sector.

Current government estimates say that there are about 40,000 computers in use in Vietnam, but the market is growing at a rapid pace. In 1993, the computer market amounted to around U.S.$20 million, and according to computer experts already in Vietnam, the PC market is doubling every year. However, with annual household incomes being as low as they are in Vietnam, it is unlikely that individual consumers will be able to afford computers for a while. Certainly, some urban consumers with more disposable income will begin to consider computer purchases soon, but it's hard to say how large that market will be. Companies such as IBM and Unisys saw the country's potential early on, and are busy gaining a foothold in a market where nearly all computing equipment is imported and import duties are quite low: 5 percent or less for microcomputers and peripherals.

The success of foreign firms in plugging into the country's science and technology opportunities became apparent in a report produced by UNIDO/UNDP, which conducted a study of the electronics and information technology sector.

> Apple has provided the Ministry of Education with equipment for a small training unit. Compaq has offered to equip a similar unit elsewhere and to run seminars on microcomputer applications for government staff in Hanoi. Hewlett-Packard will create its own 'open systems center' in Hanoi. IBM, which came back to Vietnam somewhat earlier, in September 1993, has not only signed a dealer-contract with its former South Vietnamese company which survived the embargo years as a service firm under a different name but

with some of the same IBM 360 computers from pre-1975—but also with two local distributors in Hanoi. Like Hewlett-Packard, IBM will create its own Institute of Science System (for education and applied research) in Production in Vietnam. Digital Equipment (DEC) exposed its technological capabilities and know-how in a highly-esteemed series of seminars on open systems, but is now building its organization for its products and services. Oracle has visited the country, but has not started commercial operations.

Another related opportunity is computer-training centers. Information technology is lacking in Vietnam, where there are no graduate CS, MIS, or computer engineering programs at any of the universities or polytechnics. While Vietnam's education system struggles to keep up with the fast pace of change in the country, private schools are filling the demand for English, computer, and business training. Some companies have already begun to set up joint ventures for this purpose.

CONSUMER ELECTRONICS. One need not walk the streets of Hanoi or Ho Chi Minh City long before realizing the potential of the consumer electronics market in Vietnam. Shops are set up everywhere with stacks of televisions, stereos, recorders, video cameras, and CDs. Moreover, Vietnamese consumers are not just looking for a bargain; quality is in demand and it's associated with price. Those that can come close to affording it, prefer upper-end models. Such brands as Sony, JVC, and Samsung have found success in Vietnam thus far, and others are quickly entering the market.

While the demand for electronic equipment and appliances is growing rapidly, domestic manufacturers have yet to supply products that are competitive with imports in price and quality. Most of the products seen on the street are imports, or are smuggled in from China and Thailand. Even basic items such as electric bulbs, switches, plugs, and wire still come from China and Thailand. Electric fans provide a good example of the inefficiency afflicting this sector. About 5 million fans are sold annually in

---

[1] Jan Annerstedt and Tim Sturgeon. "Information Technology in Vietnam." April, 1994. UNIDO/UNDP project DP/VIE/89/002, pg. 26.

Vietnam, and while there are dozens of domestic manufacturers, the majority that are purchased are imports due to price and quality. Similar stories can be told about electric cooking stoves and irons. When it comes to appliances such as refrigerators, washing machines, and vacuum cleaners, only imports are serving the market. As a result, there is ample opportunity in this industry for foreign investment, and domestic manufacturers are actively seeking foreign partners to produce high-grade electrical appliances. The Vietnamese government is also encouraging joint ventures and technology transfer in this sector.

The outlook for television sales in Vietnam is particularly bright. Currently 21 out of every 100 families nationwide have a television, and most are older sets that will be replaced in the near future. Between 1991 and 1992, the number of television sets in Vietnam increased from 2.2 million to 3 million, and forecasters say that the amount will continue to rise by one million annually up to the turn of the century. About 80 percent of the market is supplied by imports or imported kits assembled by domestic manufacturers. Of the twenty-five domestic television manufacturers, the largest and most successful is Hanel, which covers about 20 percent of the market. Hanel recently entered into a joint venture with Daewoo to manufacture television tubes, which marks the largest investment in electrical appliances thus far in Vietnam. According to reports, smugglers used to corner one-third of the market, but it is now much more difficult to track how many kits are coming into the country. To encourage more domestic production, the government passed an increase of the import tariff on SKD color-television kits to 15 percent from 10 percent that became effective January 1, 1995.

FOOD PROCESSING. Predictably, food processing is one of the best light industries to enter in Vietnam. Although Vietnam has a wealth of natural resources for this industry, it desperately needs modern equipment and advanced technology. There is a huge market not only for processing equipment, but also for agricultural equipment used in all stages of production. A survey conducted by the Ministry of Agriculture and Food Industry (MAFI) in early 1994 came to a fairly obvious conclusion: Vietnam has a very low level of agricultural mechanization. To fill the void, tractors, tillers, engines, and water pumps are among those machines in the greatest demand. Since the state ended subsidies for the purchase of agricultural equipment, farmers are demanding reasonable prices for high-quality models with good guarantees, but they're buying about 30,000 engines and 12,000 other pieces of equipment annually. Joint venture link-ups to produce food products for the domestic market portend a great deal of promise. One prime example is ASHTA International's $18 million joint venture to produce dairy products, which will involve the establishment of two modern dairy farms, one in Ha Tay Province in the north and the other outside of Saigon. ASHTA is contributing $12 million, and the partner is Vietnam's National Dairy Company (VINAMILK).

AQUAPRODUCTS. Anyone even glancing at the amount of water bordering Vietnam's long coastline should be able to guess that a substantial amount of Vietnam's food comes from the sea. In fact, unofficial data shows that 3 million tons of marine products can be caught annually, including 2 million tons of fish. About 50 percent of Vietnam's provinces and cities are coastal, as are 110 of the country's districts. Around 1 million tons of fish and shrimp are caught in these districts every year, of which about 50,000 tons are exported. The export earnings from aquatic products account for about 10 percent of total export earnings and are continually increasing, especially in key markets like Singapore, Hong Kong, France, Australia, Taiwan, and Britain. In the nine months of 1994 alone, Vietnam's seafood industry earned U.S.$367 million in exports, more than all of 1993.

Some of the disadvantages facing the aquaproducts industry can be overcome with foreign investment. For instance, over 70 percent of the fishing ships are very small-scale and at least 15 years old, with less than 22 horsepower. As a result, most shipping can only be done near the coastline at a depth of less than 100 meters. A fleet of larger, more powerful ships would not only improve the annual yield of seafood, but would also prevent many of the destructive activities that are taking place along the coastline by local fishermen. Competition has been growing in the industry, but there is certainly room for more efficient technology. Presently, there are sixty-five fish-processing plants, of which twelve are run by Seaprodex, Vietnam's largest state-run aquaproducts enterprise. Additonally, there are sixty aquaproduct freezing plants, including five that specialize in dried products.

The government manages collection points along the coast, which purchase fresh products from local populations and bring them to processors.

COFFEE AND TEA. Despite the use of antiquated processing equipment, Vietnam's production of coffee in the 1993/1994 season was 11 percent higher than in the 1992/1993 season and exports were 9 percent higher than the previous year. Moreover, Vietnam produces high-quality coffee that is gaining more world recognition. Coffee is in high demand worldwide, and while Brazil has cut back on coffee investments, Vietnam has invested in high-yield coffee. Right now, Vietnam is among the world's top ten robusta coffee exporters and expects to capture fifth place by the year 2000. Roughly 70 percent of the country's coffee, mainly robusta, comes from Daklak in southern Vietnam. Foreign investors are starting to take a look at this sector because with advanced processing facilities, it has the potential to be a major revenue earner by selling directly to the world market, rather than to traders.

Vietnam has 70 different tea factories, which employ 189,000 workers and produce about 40,000 tons of dry tea annually. Like the coffee industry, tea producers are operating with outdated equipment. Even so, tea exports were projected to double between 1993 and 1994. If the Union of Tea Agro-Industrial Enterprises' masterplan for the tea industry comes to fruition, the production of tea will increase 50 percent in 1995 and nearly 300 percent by the year 2000. To realize this goal, the government is calling for U.S.$70 million in investment. All factories are looking to foreign investment to upgrade processing equipment and seven northern provinces are hosting projects specifically asking for foreign investment. The most capital-intensive project is in Vinh Phu province, calling for U.S.$19 million to renew three factories and replant or newly cultivate 5,000 hectares. Other projects are sited in Son La, Ha Tay, Tuyen Quang, Yen Bai, and Thanh Hoa provinces.

MEDICAL EQUIPMENT. The question is not whether Vietnam needs medical equipment, but whether it can afford any. Vietnamese hospitals and medical clinics are all ill-equipped, and many have to adopt unsafe practices such as reusing gloves and needles because of limited resources. In the public sector, there simply isn't enough money to purchase needed equipment, and most hospitals are almost exclusively relying on donations. However, it seems that private clinics are acquiring supplies and pharmaceuticals. Some private physicians are even reselling pharmaceuticals directly to patients out of the office, even though it's illegal. The pharmaceutical market is expanding, but consumers cannot yet afford to buy medication in large packages. For this reason, pharmaceutical companies are selling their products in individual packages.

A limited number of facilities have ample resources to buy medical equipment because they're catering to foreign expatriates. These types of hospitals and clinics will multiply now that the government has thrown open the health care industry to foreign investment. Foreign companies can now operate wholly owned medical services, though the government obviously favors joint ventures with existing hospitals. At least three U.S. companies have already applied to operate joint venture hospitals in Ho Chi Minh City and Hanoi. First Choice Realty and Investment, Inc. and Real Estate Medical Investment Trading, Inc. have proposed a joint venture with Hanoi's main military hospital worth $10 million.

Auto Industry. With such a low GNP per capita, there certainly isn't much of a domestic market for automobiles, but the government would like to see the industry develop for other obvious reasons, such as hard currency earnings. Companies like Toyota, Mitsubishi, General Motors, and Chrysler have already begun to lay the groundwork for their entrance and others are sure to follow. In order to boost local production and domestic purchases, the government increased import tariffs in July of 1994 to 200 percent from 150 percent for passenger vehicles with less than five seats. The Vietnamese government has also been encouraging foreign carmakers to enter into deals with Mekong Corporation or Vietnam Motors Corporation (VMC), the two local auto manufacturers. Both of these companies are joint ventures and are assembling such vehicles as Mazda 323s and 626s, and Renault's new 1800cc model. In May of 1994, Mitsubishi formed a JV, known as Vina Star Motors, which will assemble the Delica minibus. Daimler-Benz is also planning to start producing commercial and passenger vehicles by the end of 1995. With all of these players entering the market, there will be a great need for components, which are now all imported. All of the plants in Vietnam are assembling imported kits, but there are plans for domestic manufacturing of parts in the future. Vietnam has set a local content goal of 30 percent for joint venture manufacturing in the automotive industry, set to be attained within the next ten years.

MOTORBIKES. Motorbikes seem to be replacing the bicycle as the mode of transportation in the urban areas of Vietnam. Honda has enjoyed the booming market and now other motorbike companies have begun to compete. One such company, Vietnam Manufacturing and Export Processing Company (VMEP), a Taiwanese company, is offering their 125cc Bonus motorcycle on credit to Vietnamese consumers. Since hitting the market in July of 1993, they claim to have averaged monthly sales of 2,000. To discourage imports of whole motorbikes and knockdown kits, the Finance Ministry recently raised tariffs on motorbikes from 50 to 60 percent, on semiknockdown (SKD) kits from 45 to 58 percent, and on complete knockdown kits from 35 to 52 percent. The government hopes that this move will promote domestic production and raise tax revenues. Given the rising level of disposable income in Vietnam, the motorbike industry should continue to be a good bet well into the future.

What is the market for capital goods?

ELECTRIC POWER. Anyone who has spent the summer in Hanoi knows that power outages can be frustrating, to say the least. "We sat here in the office last week," says William Howell, who represents IBM Hanoi, "on Wednesday, Thursday, and Friday, and we were without electricity three-quarters of all three days." Computer users also have plenty of horror stories to tell about spontaneous outages. Realizing the precarious state of the national electricity grid, the Vietnamese have made energy production a priority in their development plans. For many years, the case was that the South was starved for power, while the North had more hydroelectric power than it could use. To overcome this situation, the 500 kV trans-Vietnam transmission line, carrying power from a hydroelectric station north of Hanoi to southern Vietnam, was switched on in May of 1994. However, many problems remain and a substantial amount of investment

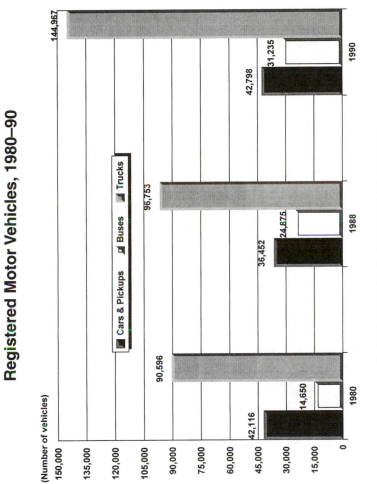

Registered Motor Vehicles, 1980–90

(Number of vehicles)

Source: Police and Traffic Department, February, 1993.

is still needed. For one thing, rural areas are lacking sufficient electric power. In fact, rural people are still relying on firewood and straw for 75 percent of their energy, and on charcoal, kerosene, and electricity for only 10 percent. In mid-1994, the Vietnamese government set a target of expanding the national power network to every district in the country. Another problem has to do with the different levels of potential on Vietnam's electric grid, which necessitates many kinds of transformers, insulators, and other accompanying equipment for operation and maintenance. The plan is to replace the archaic 3kV and 6kV potentials with 20kV ones, but 10kV, 15kV, and 35kV potentials are also in use. Foreign assistance and equipment will undoubtedly be needed to unify the system.

On average, power production in the 1990s has increased by 9.3 percent annually, and Vietnam's energy ministry estimates that U.S.$3.5 billion will need to be invested in electricity services by the end of the decade. To supply the amount of power that will be demanded, the Electrical Equipment and Technique Corporation predicts that Vietnam will need 740 neutral transformers, over 16,000 distribution transformers, and over 360,000 tons of high-tension equipment, particularly the 110kV and 220kV transformers. All of this equipment will have to be imported, so the market is wide open.

As for large projects, Vietnam's hydroelectric potential is among the greatest in the world. The Japanese have already begun hydroelectric projects in the North, but there is ample need for such BOT projects in other regions of the country. Vietnam is also looking for foreign investment to build nuclear reactors. In late 1991, high reserves of uranium were found in Quang Nam-Da Nang, and the government is hoping to use this resource to generate electricity. Vietnam already has one nuclear reactor in Dalat, which was built in 1956, shut down during the war, and rehabilitated in 1983 with help from the former Soviet Union. Its major function is to produce and analyze radioactive isotopes for medical use, though it also generates up to 500kW of electricity. Vietnam has three main utilities underneath the Ministry of Energy, Companies 1, 2, and 3, which correspond with the northern, central, and southern regions, respectively. Private sector power projects would most likely have to be done in cooperation with them.

TELECOMMUNICATIONS. After energy production, telecommunications ranks second on the government's list of priority infrastructure development projects. Since opening up to foreign investment, the government has had no shortage of bids from telecommunication companies, and now that the United States has entered the scene, the competition is even stiffer. In a country with only 200,000 telephone lines, 6,800 public phone boxes, 8,000 fax machines, 12,000 mobile phones, 50,000 pagers, and 500 magnetic card phone boxes, the market potential is vast. At present, Vietnam has only 1 telephone for every 350 people, 80 percent of whom reside in rural areas. Some predict that the need for telecommunications in the countryside could amount to U.S.$200 million in possible sales over the next 5 years.

In 1994, Vietnam spent $80 million on improving its post, telecommunications, and phone services; the figure is slated to rise to $400 million in 1995, bringing the number of telephones to one phone per 100 people. The Vietnamese government would like to see 3 to 4 phones per 100 people by the turn of the century. At the current rate of phone connections, they just may realize that goal. In the first half of 1994, an average of 413 phones were connected daily in Vietnam, bringing the total to 346,934 for the whole country by mid-June.

In mid-1994, Prime Minister Kiet scrapped the Vietnam Post and Telecommunications monopoly, triggering the formation of at least two companies that claim to have access to military telecommunications: the Saigon Telecommunication Post Corporation (STPS) and the Military Telecommunications Company (MTC). Both firms are relying on foreign technology and equipment and at least five North American and Australian companies have already made offers. This is somewhat indicative of what has been happening at the central level. Rather than creating one national system and contracting with a few big companies, the government has offered contracts to several companies to develop different areas. Unfortunately, Vietnam already has twelve different switching systems, where most developed and developing countries have no more than three. On the bright side, Vietnam can look forward to high-speed data transmission and video conferencing in the near future through its connection with the TVHK optical fiber cable that joins Thailand, Vietnam and Hong Kong. The good news for the foreign investor is that telecommunications will no

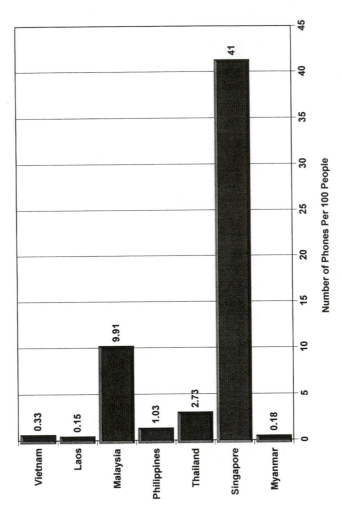

Asian Telecommunications Compared

Number of Phones Per 100 People

Source: Asia Pacific.

Country	Number of Phones Per 100 People
Vietnam	0.33
Laos	0.15
Malaysia	9.91
Philippines	1.03
Thailand	2.73
Singapore	41
Myanmar	0.18

doubt offer good opportunities in Vietnam for the next 15 to 20 years.

BUILDING MATERIALS/INFRASTRUCTURE/CONSTRUCTION. Infrastructure projects and construction are definitely two of the hottest areas to be involved in right now. In one of the largest foreign deals in Vietnam, Japan's Mitsubishi Materials Corporation and Nihon Cement Company have signed a 50-year joint venture with the State-owned Vietnam Cement Corporation south of Hanoi to build a cement plant to fuel the country's construction boom, in a deal worth $347 million.

Vietnam needs everything from roads and bridges to housing and office buildings. Property developers have wasted no time entering the market, but they're running into problems securing permits and evacuating local populations. As far as infrastructure projects are concerned, many of them have to be BOTs and are riskier because the return on investment is less certain. However, Vietnam is receiving aid from the World Bank and ADB to upgrade roads and bridges. Although Vietnam has 65,000 miles of roads, only 12 percent of these roads are paved, and about half have been rated by the United Nations as poor. Of the country's sixteen airports, only three are international airports: Noi Bai at Hanoi, Tan Son Nhat at Ho Chi Minh City, and Da Nang. Vietnam also plans the construction of ten industrial parks throughout the country where foreign firms in all economic sectors can set up manufacturing, build and operate infrastructure services, and process products for export.

With all of this activity, the most promising sector may be building materials such as cement and steel. Several JV cement plants have already been proposed to take the place of the low-quality cement that is currently produced in Vietnam, but the demand will still exceed the domestic capacity. The steel industry also has a lot of room for growth. Projected demand for 1995 is 70,000 tons and 1.5 million tons for the year 2000. However, the present annual production capacity of all Vietnam's steel mills is only 500,000 tons. In reaction to this gap, eight separate foreign investment projects have been dedicated to the steel industry. According to the government, a lot more are still needed. At this time, all mills are producing steel from scrap metal, but Vietnam is estimated to have 600 million tons of iron ore reserves for the production of high-grade steel.

NATURAL RESOURCE EXPLOITATION. Although Vietnam is renowned for its considerable oil and gas reserves, the country is also endowed with a plentiful supply of other valuable natural resources. Vietnam's Quang Ninh province and Red River Basin, for example, together possess 6.5 billion tons of anthracite coal and several hundred billion tons of brown coal. Vietnam also has a respectable reserve of metal and mineral ores: 1 billion tons of iron ore; 4 billion of aluminum; 1 billion tons of phospate; 21 million of chromitite; and 600,000 tons of copper, to name a few. Vietnam has vast forest resources too, with over 57 percent of the country covered with 9.3 million hectares of forest. At this writing, the exploited timber output is only 4 percent of Vietnam's total exports, far below the potential. The table below provides an exact accounting of the country's key natural resources.

Resource	Reserves	Location(s)
Anthracite Coal	6.5 billion tons	Quang Ninh Province
Brown Coal	Several 100 billion tons	Red River Basin
Hydrogenous Coal	500 million tons	N/A
Fat Coal	40 million tons	N/A
Uranium	N/A	Lao Cai and Hoa Binh Provinces
Iron Ore	1 billion tons total	
	600 million tons	Thach Khe Mine
	100 million tons	Quy Xa Mine
	70 million tons	Right bank of Red River
Manganese Ore	5 million tons	N/A
Chromite	21 million tons	N/A
Copper Ore	600,000 tons	Lao Cai & Son La
Sulphur Ore	200,000 tons	Chieu Hoa, Phu Hoat, along Da River in Da Lat, and Cho Den Mine in Bac Thai Province

(continued on next page)

Resource	Reserves	Location(s)
Oxide Ore	300,000 tons	N/A
Gold Ore	100 tons	Kim Boi, Yen Na, Trung Mang, Dak Pek, Pak Lang, and Bong Mieu Mines
Aluminum Ores	4 billion tons	Southern Plateau and Vietnam-China border
RE_2O_3 Ore	9 million tons +	Phong To and Lai Chau
Quartzite	30 million tons +	N/A
Dolomite	12 million tons	N/A
Graphite	12 million tons	N/A
Fluorite	9 million tons	N/A
Barite	3 million tons	N/A
Phosphate	1 billion tons +	Lao Cai Apatite Mine
Oil	5 million tons/year	Bach Ho
Titanium Oxide	N/A	Nghe An and Thuan Hai Provinces
Precious Stones	N/A	Lao Cai, Yen Bai, and Lam Dong
Bauxite	N/A	Lam Dong
Tin	3000 tons/year	Cao Bang, Nghe An, Bac Thai, Vinh Phu and Tuyen Quang

Sources: Khac Binh, "Foreign Investment in Mineral Exploitation Needed," *Saigon Times,* No. 95, July 29–August 4, 1993, p. 24; and Nguyen Huong, "Vietnam: Rich or Poor in Mineral Resources," *Vietnam Economic News,* Vol. III, No. 30, July 23–30, 1993, p. 6.

ENVIRONMENTAL PROTECTION. Environmental protection has only recently received extensive governmental attention in Vietnam. In fact, Vietnam did not begin serious research of the country's environmental problems until 1982, 7 years after reunification. Before that time, the government had been preoccupied with several years of war, which had exacted a heavy toll, both in terms of the environment and the economy. Although the Vietnamese government has since moved swiftly to produce decrees and set up an institutional framework for handling environmental affairs, it was not until December of 1993 that the National Assembly passed the country's first Law on Environmental Protection, which became effective on January 10, 1994. Before this time, various ministries had drafted ordinances on ministry-specific environmental problems, but none of the ordinances had been accorded the force of law.

In terms of foreign investment projects, the Vietnamese government requires environmental impact assessments as part of the feasibility study, which is submitted in application for a foreign investment license. Eight copies of the feasibility study are circulated to relevant ministries, including MOSTE. Theoretically, any one ministry can block the application based on insufficient information in the feasibility study. However, in practice, MOSTE does not actually wield enough power to demand better environmental provisions in the face of opposition from such ministries as Heavy and Light Industry or Construction. Ho Chi Minh City, with a population density of over 1,961 people per square kilometer, has suffered the most environmentally from population growth, urbanization, and industrialization. Without any water treatment systems, all 100 kilometers of Ho Chi Minh City's canals are heavily polluted with sewage and effluents. Air pollution levels range from two to ten times in excess of international standards. Every day, 3,000 tons of garbage are produced in Ho Chi Minh City, yet the landfills cannot accommodate this level. Moreover, landfills are not lined and runoff seeps into nearby watersheds. In addition, smoke and noise caused by vehicles, old transport trucks in particular, are becoming increasingly critical sources of irritation.

Currently, the government is drafting legislation to set standards, but there are a host of issues that must first be addressed. Which standards to adopt is obviously the most difficult question. Standards could be based on international criteria, but then the government must make realistic adjustments for Vietnam's level of economic development. Developing countries all over the world face the challenge of reconciling the need for economic betterment with the need to protect the environment. In a country as poor as Vietnam, this conflict is particularly glaring. Presently, there are two sources of funding for environmental projects. MOSTE receives money from the central government, but in reality, hardly any projects are fully funded by the Vietnamese state. Most of the support, about 80 percent, comes from UNDP, UNIDO, and bilateral aid primarily from Sweden, France, Japan, Holland, and Australia. At the provincial level, money is allocated by local authorities, but the amount is minuscule relative to need. Vietnam's deficiencies are not only limited to financial resources. Most ministries lack the training and technology that a substantive environmental transformation would demand. For example, although MOSTE is staffed with about fifty engineers and Ph.D.s, virtually none of them have been trained abroad, unless it was in the former Soviet Union or Eastern Europe where the environment was hardly a major concern.

Because Vietnam is essentially at the starting point of environmental protection, there is a great need for more basic research of such factors as water and air quality. Considering that the profits of state enterprises fall well short of the amount needed to invest in cleaner technology, the only realistic option that environmentally conscious enterprises have on their own is proposing tax exemptions and reductions in budget contributions. One of the biggest pollutants in Vietnam, a cement factory outside of Ho Chi Minh City, is currently looking into updating its equipment in coordination with a Swiss company. As of August 1994, the bill had already reached U.S.$6 million, a figure far beyond the reach of any state enterprise in Vietnam.

The ideal solution for these enterprises is to enter into joint ventures and benefit from the technology transfer contribution of the foreign party. One promising note is that over 100 foreign delegations came to the Hanoi Urban Environment Company in 1993 to inquire about investment opportunities. This same company is now building a garbage treatment plant to produce microorganic fertilizer with U.S.$800,000 funding from the UNDP.[2]

---

[2] This section is adapted from an unpublished paper written by Tamera Richardson at the Graduate School of International Relations and Pacific Studies at the University of California at San Diego, and who assisted in the research for this book.

What is the market for services?

Some of the first U.S. business people to enter Vietnam were those in service trades like law, consulting, and accounting. Predictably, this industry is more hassle-free when it comes to getting governmental approval relative to other industries, such as construction or manufacturing. Interestingly, there has been substantial overlap in these professions. To their benefit, they have succeeded in creating some markets for themselves by getting involved in the foreign investment process. Many firms prepare the feasibility studies for foreign investors, thereby standardizing the process and making the SCCI and foreign investors more reliant on their expertise. They also play a crucial role in training Vietnamese counterparts, introducing international business practices, and standardizing reporting. For those approaching the Vietnamese market for this purpose now, it may be much more difficult than before because of market saturation and competition. Ever since the lifting of the embargo, lawyers and accountants have been flooding Vietnam in hopes of bringing the formerly isolated country into the 1990s.

ACCOUNTING. In April of 1994, the government declared that all accounting reports of companies with foreign investment are required to be audited by an accounting company, and ever since, the demand for accounting services has been rapidly increasing. Vietnam has three state-run accounting firms: the Auditing and Informatics Service Company (AISC) owned by the Ho Chi Minh People's Committee, and Vietnamese Auditing Company (VACO) and Auditing and Accounting Service Company (AASC), both owned by the Ministry of Finance. International accounting firms with offices already in Vietnam include Deloitte Touche Tohmatsu, Ernst and Young, Coopers and Lybrand, Price Waterhouse, Arthur Anderson, and KPMG Peat Marwick. Ernst and Young claimed to have a turnover of U.S.$2.7 million in 1993, with 80 percent of that coming from the South and only 17 percent from the North. However, with the growing number of foreign companies that are setting up shop in Hanoi, business is sure to expand in the North.

Note: For information on the Advertising industry, see Chapter 8, page 127; for information about the Banking industry, see Chapter 12, page 190.

INSURANCE. In 1994, new government regulations opened up the insurance and reinsurance industries to a whole range of companies, including JVs, wholly foreign-owned, and branches of overseas insurance agencies. Previously, only the state insurance company, Baoviet, operated in the market. Insurance companies in Vietnam may undertake only certain types of insurance coverage, such as life, assets, losses, vehicles, ships, civil liabilities, cargo transport, aviation, credit, and financial risk insurance. In order to engage in insurance activities, a Certificate of Qualification must be obtained. Vietnam's primary insurance regulation, article nine of the Law on Foreign Investment, 1988, states: "Assets of the joint venture shall be insured by the Vietnam Insurance Company, or by other insurance companies to be agreed upon by both partners." However, the word "assets" is not defined, and therefore it is unclear which type of assets should be insured, against what kind of risk, and based on what value. Because the law doesn't even require that foreign companies insure their assets in Vietnam, many have opted for off-shore insurance. However, with the recent opening of the market and the continued improvement of the legal infrastructure, more foreign companies may start to use insurance companies in Vietnam.

LAW FIRMS. Ironically, foreign law firms in Vietnam are doing anything but practicing law. According to Vietnamese law, foreign law firms aren't even allowed to give advice on Vietnamese law, to participate in any court proceeding as lawyers, or to represent clients before Vietnamese courts. However, foreign law firms can hire Vietnamese in accordance with the current labor regulations of Vietnam, and such persons can give advice on local laws. These restrictions haven't stopped over ten foreign law firms from opening up offices and at least five others from applying for the purpose of consulting. Foreign investors are relying heavily on the advice of lawyers for making investment decisions, obtaining licenses, negotiating contracts, and drafting JV documents. Some foreign law firms are even publishing foreign investment guides for would-be clients. For the most part, the government recognizes the role that foreign law firms play in providing investor confidence, but also justifiably worries that allowing foreign law firms to practice Vietnamese law may make for an overly litigious atmosphere. Of course, this limits the scope of activities that law firms can engage in and makes competition even more fierce.

TOURISM. Where in Hanoi can you order *escalope de porc* for $4 and a glass of good Bordeaux for $2? Try the unbelievably authentic Cafe de Paris in Hanoi, opened by a French engineer named Maurice Lassalle, who can be seen regularly in the streets of the capital on his motorscooter passing out flyers to tourists and newly-arrived expats. Mr. Lassalle has tapped into Vietnam's share of the world's largest industry—tourism.

Nearly four times the number of tourists who visited Vietnam in 1990 visited in 1994—1,018,000 foreign tourists. Tourist authorities expect 3 million visitors to come through the country each year by the end of the century. Tourists come mainly from the United States, Australia, Canada, and France, though overseas Vietnamese only account for 15.6 percent of the total. All of this is good news for the hotel industry; there are only 18,000 hotel rooms of adequate quality for foreign visitors in the entire country, as of this writing.

In a day and age when the world population is traveling much more, Vietnam's lush greenery and untainted beaches couldn't remain a secret much longer. Developers and investors from all over are scurrying to get a piece of the huge tourism market that is predicted to take off in the near future. Over 1 million visitors went to Vietnam in 1994 and the country expects to receive 3 million by the year 2000. Tourism is the fastest growing business in Vietnam right now, with the number of tourists increasing by 50 percent annually. Travel companies see Vietnam as an important link in an expected surge in travel to and within Asia. Tourist receipts in the Asia-Pacific region are estimated to account for 30.6 percent of worldwide revenues by the year 2000, and air travel in the region is expected to grow at 7.5 percent annually. However, tourism hasn't really started booming yet. Many foreign visitors are coming to Vietnam for business purposes. Even when tourism does take off, the projected 3 million by the turn of the century is still a far cry from Hong Kong's 8.9 million annual visitors, or Singapore's 6.4 million, but it would be a huge leap from the 20,000 who visited Vietnam in 1986.

Ever since Vietnam opened its arms to foreign investment, the tourism industry has been getting a lot of attention. In fact, tourism ranks second only to the oil sector in attracting investment dollars.

This is good for Vietnam because it is estimated that the sector needs at least $40 billion in investment to upgrade its infrastructure.

In the 6 years since Vietnam opened up to foreign investment, U.S.$1.5 billion has been slated for ninety-seven hotel and tourist village projects, 20 percent of all foreign capital commitments. Most of these will open in the next 2 to 3 years.

Several investors in Hong Kong, Singapore, and Taiwan are pouring money into new hotels to fill the void. Vietnam has only about 32,000 hotel rooms, but not all of them are up to international standards. The number of international-standard hotel rooms is expected to jump from its current number of 18,000 to about 28,000 by 1997, but that still isn't going to be enough. There is a lot of potential for international-standard hotels in coastal locations like Hai Phong, Hue, Da Nang, Nha Trang, and Da Lat, but even Ho Chi Minh City is predicting a shortage in spite of all the hotels that are going up there. Unfortunately, unless services, transportation, and other tourist-related problems are solved, Vietnam may find itself with too many hotel rooms!

Unlike Thailand, Vietnam wants to pursue a strategy that caters to upper-end tourists to elevate the image of Vietnam. In 1991, specialists of the World Travel Organisation (WTO), who made the Vietnam Tourism Development Master Plan, suggested that Vietnam select visitors by turning to high-level tourism, geared only toward the most wealthy. This strategy would distinguish Vietnam from other countries in the region that have already established low or medium-level tourist networks. This plan has its advantages and disadvantages. First, Vietnam cannot possibly hope to fulfill the needs of higher-class travelers until it has fully developed the concept of "service." Moreover, the transportation system and basic infrastructure needed for high-level tourism is nowhere close to being sufficient. In fact, these basic factors, as they exist now, do not even meet the needs of backpackers.

Given this, the foreign investor may have a window of opportunity by investing not in hotels, but in entire vacations. For example, cruises along the coast of Vietnam are currently doing well because they don't require passengers to spend the whole time experiencing the not-so-pleasant aspects of tourism in Vietnam. Resorts may be another good option, but it's difficult to get approval for enough land from the People's Committee unless you have the right local partner; for instance, the People's Committee itself.

CHAPTER 6

ENTERING
THE MARKET

*G*iven that before the collapse of the Berlin Wall, Vietnam conducted its trade primarily with Eastern Bloc countries using a semibarter system, and was restricted from dealing with Western countries because of the U.S. embargo, no one can belittle Vietnam's adroit shift to Western-style trading and the rapid growth of its export markets. The country had to learn the ways of Western trading and international payments, as well as pay for imports with convertible currency rather than in ruble-denominated currency, and contend with international competition overnight.

How does Vietnam manage its foreign trade?

With *doi moi,* Vietnam replaced an earlier system of import quotas with one of import tariffs to control the volume of foreign goods into the country. With tariffs high, however, smuggling has remained rampant; the use of import licenses to provide additional control over imports is a unique—albeit vexing—aspect of the business environment. The main authority for regulating and registering import and export in Vietnam is the Ministry of Trade and Tourism which hands out the necessary licenses and permits to importers. All companies are required to obtain a Foreign Trade Permit before engaging in the import or export of goods. Private companies, collective enterprises, and state enterprises can apply for permits. State-owned company permit applications increased dramatically to over 1,000 in 1993, up from a mere 300 2 years earlier. Given that the private sector is producing a growing share of exports, a significant recent development is that private firms have been issued trading permits. Private companies still have to conduct their trading business through an authorized foreign trade corporation, which possesses direct trading rights and charges a commission for its services. For a company to obtain direct trading rights it must have a legal capital of $200,000 and an annual turnover of roughly $4–5 million, restrictions that tend to greatly limit the expansion of the foreign trade business sector. Also, a trading permit allows the firm to import only a listed number of goods, rather than import any foreign goods. For a company to import an item not listed on its original trading permit, the company will have to apply for a separate trading permit altogether. Most imports are handled by Vietnamese trading companies who are licensed to handle a range of commodities brought in by importers, which will be discussed in detail in the following chapter.

What are Vietnam's import/export regulations like?

Vietnamese import/export regulations are relatively uncomplicated. The problems encountered by many foreign companies and investors are due mainly to varying interpretation and implementation by local Vietnamese authorities. Inexperience and lack of knowledge of how to implement regulations has resulted in headaches and costly delays.

A wide range of goods are covered by import duties. Rates range from 0 percent to 50 percent of the price. Duties on cigarettes, tobacco, beverages, and alcohol, however can run in the range of 80–150 percent. Quotas still apply to goods exported from Vietnam, subject to existing agreements between Vietnam and her trading partners, though export duties apply only to specific raw material items, including fish, coffee, nuts, seeds, metals, and wood products.

Previously, for each consignment of goods, joint venture companies were required to apply for an import or export license. Recently however, a general license for certain products has been issued, which is valid for 6 months. While the 6-month license greatly reduces delays and paperwork, some of the major problems facing foreign business entities still need to be addressed. Given that support and spare parts industries are scarce in Vietnam, you cannot simply pick up the phone and order, say, a new fan belt for your backhoe. You'll have to import it, and thus obtain a license to do so. The prudent joint venture manager lists every conceivable spare part, belt, filter, nut, and bolt that could be needed on the joint venture's original import/export application. When coupled with Customs delays, the unforeseen need for support products from abroad could bring a venture to a standstill. As an Australian construction executive explained: "Say you need an oil filter. Normally you'd fly it in from Bangkok immediately. But that would arrive before the bill of lading, which must come in first. And it might not be listed on your original import license. You could write a book just about the import licensing process."

Joint ventures, wholly foreign-owned ventures, and business cooperation projects are allowed specific exemptions on import duties with regard to the following items: (1) materials and equipment forming part of the capital contribution of fixed assets; (2) materials imported for use in production of exported goods (duty is paid upon entry into Vietnam, then reimbursement will be made upon the export of the finished goods); (3) the transfer of technology as part of the capital contribution of the foreign party's initial capital expense; and (4) duty on exempt goods, unless they are sold into the Vietnamese domestic market.

VIETNAM'S IMPORT TARIFFS ON SELECTED PRODUCTS

Categories/Items:	Rate (%):
Automobiles	100
Cassette players	40
SKD form	30
CKD form	7
Ceramic products	20–30
Clothing accessories	20
Computers/peripherals	5–8
Electrical machinery	15
Electronic parts/components	5–10
Footwear	40
Furniture	30
Garments	40
Glassware	20
Hand tools	20
Iron and steel	0–10
Jewelry	30
Radios	20
Small household electrical appliances	30–40
Telephones	40
SKD form	30
CKD form	7
Television receivers	40
SKD form	10
CKD form	7
Toys	10
Watches (clock movements)	20
Watches and clocks	30
Woven fabrics of cotton	35
Yarns of cotton	20
Yarns of manmade fibers	20

What's involved in obtaining an import license?

Apply for an import license with the Ministry of Trade and Tourism by providing copies of the bills of lading (listing container contents) and a commercial invoice from your supplier. (See appendix for address.) The Ministry will normally approve your application within 5 days. Experienced shippers say it is wise to apply for your license well in advance of your cargo's arrival. To avoid port penalties and mounting fines and delays, obtain copies of bills of lading and invoices from the shipping line or freight forwarder while your cargo is in transit. Supply a copy of the bills of lading and supplier invoices to Customs along with a copy of your import license. Arrange for inspection with the Customs head office as well as the port authorities. Remember to watch out for sudden changes in import regulations. Several containers of "previously-owned" cars and motorbikes are sitting stranded on the dock at Ho Chi Minh port due to a recently imposed ban on importation of used vehicles.

The information sources listed below will help you stay abreast of changes.

MARKET INFORMATION RESOURCES

The Vietnam Business Journal
(English bi-monthly)
VIAM Communications
381 Park Avenue, Suite 919
New York, N.Y. 10016
Tel. (212) 725-1717

Vietnam Courier
(English weekly)
Contact the Vietnam News Agency in Hanoi

Vietnam Investment Review
(English weekly)
56, Nha Chung Street
Hanoi
Tel: 266740

Vietnam Economic Times
(English monthly)
10, Duong Thanh Street
Hanoi
Tel: 243037/036
Tel: 252875

Vietnam News
(English language daily)
79, Ly Thuong Kiet
Hanoi
Tel: 268211

Vietnam Today
(English monthly)
Hanoi Press Bureau
32, Hai Ba Trung Street
Hanoi
Tel: 260382

You might also contact the following organizations which publish Vietnam business-related information:

U.S. Department of Commerce
The World Bank
United Nations Development Program
Asian Development Bank
Hong Kong Trade Development Council

What goods are prohibited from being imported or exported?

The Ministry of Trade and Tourism has directed that certain items are prohibited for import. These prohibited goods are:

1. Previously-owned consumer goods, particularly, motorbikes or vehicles with less than twelve seats, garments and textiles, and electrical appliances (except those approved by Customs).

2. Explosives, weapons, ammunition, and similar devices and equipment.

3. Narcotic drugs of any kind.

4. Decadent or reactionary literature.

5. Firecrackers and toys morally harmful or detrimental to public order.

6. Left-hand–drive vehicles (unless for special purposes, and by special permission).

Another list was published in mid-1994 in conjunction with the Ministry of Culture and Information that bans the import and export of the following "Cultural Products."

IMPORTS THAT ARE BANNED

1. Products whose content tends to react against the State of Vietnam.

2. Products propagandizing depraved lifestyles or violence or that are contrary to Vietnamese morals or customs.

3. Slanderous materials or products intent on offending the honor of Vietnamese citizens or organizations.

EXPORTS THAT ARE BANNED

1. Handicraft products, works of art, or antiques of Vietnamese origin, or those of foreign origin that have been in Vietnam a long time and have cultural or historical value.

2. Objects owned by historical-cultural monuments or museums.

3. Objects and statues of the Buddha.

4. Publications banned in Vietnam or abroad.

Is it necessary to open a representative office in Vietnam in order to sell there?

The advantages to having a physical presence in the country are self-evident, and setting up a Rep Office is the best way to do this. On the surface the law appears to be straightforward and simple—just make an application, pay the fee, and open the doors. Unfortunately, Vietnam considers Rep Offices purely to represent the company's overseas office, not as existing for investment, marketing, or trading purposes. Rep offices therefore fall under the authority of the Ministry of Trade and Tourism (MOTT), as they are looked upon as existing only to *promote* trade.

What are the steps in setting up a Rep Office?

Contact the MOTT to set up a Rep Office in Vietnam. (See appendix for address.) You should receive a written decision within 60 days after submitting your application to MOTT. There is no Rep Office Division in the ministry, so frustrating and inexplicable delays are common. Hiring a local consultant, accountant, or lawyer to help with the procedure is probably wise.

The application for an office license must be in prescribed form on company letterhead, notarized, and submitted in duplicate in Vietnamese and English. The application should be accompanied by a copy of the Articles of Association and a notarized Certificate of Incorporation, if any, of the applicant; a certificate from a bank or the applicant indicating the applicant's prescribed capital; and a copy of any signed project contract with an authorized Vietnamese legal entity. Also, include your firm's current brochure. Send the application to the MOTT and the People's Committee with jurisdiction over the area where the office is to be located. Within 30 days of receiving the application, the People's Committee is required to advise the MOTT of its position in regards to the application. Within 65 days of receiving the application, the MOTT is required to notify the applicant of its decision. To obtain a license, you will pay a flat fee of $5,000 ($4,000 for nonprofit offices); the license will be valid from 1–3 years. At the end of the period, an additional $5,000 must be paid, and likewise for each additional extension.

Within 60 days of the Rep Office's license being issued, an application for registration of the Rep Office's activities must be submitted to the relevant People's Committee. The application should provide the following information:

- address of the office;
- number of foreign and local staff;
- process date or commencement date of operations; and

- nature of activities in which the Rep Office will be engaged.

  The application must be accompanied by:

- a copy of the Rep Office license;
- a copy of the letter of appointment of the chief representative;
- the resumé of the chief representative, and any other foreign person working in the office;
- a copy of the lease of the proposed office premises; and
- copies of employment contracts for any Vietnamese to be employed immediately.

Four copies of the application must be submitted in Vietnamese and English. Each copy must be signed by the person nominated to be the chief representative. The People's Committee should issue a registration certificate within 15 days of receiving the application. Once you've received a Rep Office license and registration certificates, you will have 60 days to complete the formalities of actually opening the office, or your license will lapse. Fortunately, officials are flexible and will usually grant leeway if a sincere effort to follow procedure is observed. The procedural priorities for opening an office entail four basic steps best undertaken in the following sequence: (1) renting an office, (2) hiring staff, (3) registering with the local People's Committee, and (4) opening a bank account.

RENTING AN OFFICE. Office space is in short supply and thus expensive, even by world standards. There are at present only six modern office buildings able to provide basic services of air conditioning, telephone hook-ups, and lighting. These buildings each accommodate only twenty-five office units. Only 0.5 percent of the 250 foreign companies (each with an average staff of seven) requiring office space can be accommodated at this time. With many more foreign companies applying for licenses daily, offices are temporarily being set up in hotel rooms and hastily converted houses, which are also in short supply.

A survey by the property firm of Richard Ellis found that one square meter of prime office space in Ho Chi Minh City can now rent for as high as U.S.$475 per month, higher than any other capitol city in Southeast Asia. On average, however, office space runs U.S.$35-40 per square meter per month, as the following table indicates:

REGIONAL COMPARISONS OF GROSS MONTHLY RENTS

City	Offices (per meter sq.)	Residential (3 bedrooms)	Industrial (per meter sq.)
Bangkok	$24	$2200–3600	$7
Hanoi	$35	$3000–5000	$4-5
Ho Chi Minh City	$40	$2000–5000	$6-7
Hong Kong	$65	$6000–8000	$14-21
Jakarta	$17	$2000–3000	$4
Kuala Lumpur	$28	$2000–3000	$6
Singapore	$50	$1600–2800	$16
Taipei	$45	$3700–4400	$8

Source: Richard Ellis (Thailand), Vietnam Fund.

Should you encounter difficulties finding space, state-owned "service companies" exist that act as brokers to find and rent office space on a commission basis. They can also help in qualifying landlords (who must be authorized to rent to foreign firms), finding and hiring local staff, and securing a lease. (See page 268 in the appendix for a list of office and labor service companies in Ho Chi Minh City.)

One alternative to renting your own office is to set up shop in one of the new "business centers" going up in Hanoi and Ho Chi Minh City, which are specifically licensed to rent to foreign firms—a generally hassle-free way to go. Rents run $80–$100 per month per square meter inclusive of all services. The dream office site is in a refurbished French villa left from pre-Dien Bien Phu days. With the defeat of the French in 1954, most of these houses were nationalized to house governmental departments. Going this route is not easy and definitely not cheap, but it can be done. In a scheme announced in 1993, the Hanoi Land and Housing Department plans to rent 450 such villas to foreigners. The former occupants are to be relocated.

Restoration can be between U.S.$300,000 and U.S.$1 million depending upon the condition of the villa; rents can soar to between U.S.$6,000 to U.S.$12,000.

Rep Offices are not permitted to conduct business transactions, sign contracts, or receive money, though it's no secret that hundreds of Asian business people have entered the country, rented a hotel room, and started selling goods without any license at all.

HIRING STAFF. At a Rep Office, you are required to go through a state-run labor agency to hire needed staff. If they can't provide you with the people with the skills you need, then you can advertise on your own. But once you've hired someone, the person must register with the government agency. Some offices pay salaries directly to the agency and the agency pays the worker. Of course, most expats don't recommend doing this. If at all possible, pay the worker directly.

The existing hiring protocol goes like this: the Rep Office contracts with the Service Company who receives the employee's salary. The Service Company passes roughly half of the gross salary on to the employee, who, in turn, must then pay out 10 percent to the MOTT. Of the 50 percent that the service company retains, it pays 10 percent to MOTT. When you first receive your Rep Office license, the agency will normally limit you to hiring only four persons. After operating for 6 months, you can apply to hire more staff, by giving proof of the amount of business you are doing to the MOTT. At least in Hanoi, it seems there is no uniformity in salary scale among the four official employee service companies. (For more about worker recruitment, training, and wages, see chapter 10.)

REGISTRATION AND REPORTING. Once you have rented your office and hired a staff, you are required to register with the local People's Committee. The documentation must be in Vietnamese and English (French or Russian are permitted as well), and prepared in four copies. Within 15 days of application, registration should be issued. Twice annually, in January (1st–5th) and in July (1st–5th), you are also required to submit a written report summarizing the office's professional activities to MOTT and the People's Committee.

OPENING A BANK ACCOUNT. Without a People's Committee Registration Certificate, the country manager cannot open a bank account, so you will have to plan on carrying large amounts of cash for start-up expenses. All initial funds must be transferred to a MOTT account at the VietCombank. With notification of their receipt made, a separate license can be issued by the Account Finance Department for the opening of your Rep Office bank account. The flat rate fee charged is $20. An account may then be opened by the authorized foreign representative at any bank preferred. Overseas transfers can be done directly after that.

CHAPTER 7

CHANNELS

OF DISTRIBUTION

*L*ike any socialist economy, Vietnam's is characterized by scarcity of goods and a thriving black market of smuggled goods. Due to the scarcity of essential goods consumers and end-users traditionally *pulled* products into the markets, rather than manufacturers and distributors *pushing* products into the market in response to customers' tastes and preferences. Very little product promotion or advertising was used; there was little brand awareness, and virtually no Western-style marketing was employed as of the advent of *doi moi.*. However, there was a huge black market trading in smuggled goods that came over the border from China or by sea, that rivaled the Ho Chi Minh Trail in moving a variety of goods to consumers who could pay for them both secretly and without interruption. Scarcity and smuggling—these are the dual influences that have molded Vietnam's current distribution system.

What does Vietnam's goods distribution system look like?

One looks for signs of a formal distribution system in Vietnam's cities, but they just aren't there. No eighteen-wheelers unloading at the rear of a supermarket, or containers loaded on the flat-bed cars of a passing freight train. Then a cyclo driver passes by with Sony Trinitrons stacked seven high. Then another, laden with Samsung computer monitors. How do they balance all that stuff, you wonder. It's then you realize that you're looking at Vietnam's distribution system!

The fine selection of sophisticated Western manufactured products in Vietnam reflects the refined art of smuggling in Vietnam. A World Bank report, written in 1992, estimated that about 40 percent of all imports entering the country are smuggled, most entering through Cambodia or China. During the war, with the right connections and enough cash you could buy an American tank in Saigon. The networks are still there working alongside the expanding new system of Western-style retailing. Much of the smuggling has now died down, in part because most of the major Japanese and Korean electronics manufacturers are now producing in the country. The price of a Sony television in a local electronics shop and one that is smuggled is now roughly the same, so the attraction of smuggling televisions has waned.

Most products that enter the country end up in the hands of private wholesalers before they move on to subwholesalers and then to retailers, though a sizable proportion of distribution is handled by State wholesalers and then private or state-owned subwholesalers before arriving at retailers' shops. Either way, once foreign products reach the hands of private traders, the original suppliers lose virtually all control of their products as they move through distribution channels. Product price becomes unstable as margins fluctuate widely between wholesaler, subwholesaler, and final retailer. This makes the notion of sales strategy somewhat problematic because there is little method by which to set prices or govern supply as a product moves along the distribution chain.

What are the characteristics of the country's retail sector?

As for retailers, the majority of them are privately owned, but many are state-owned as well. (Of the 45,000 officially registered retail units in the country, two-thirds are in private hands with some 14,000 owned by the state. Total retail sales of consumer goods rose 26.7 percent between 1993 and 1994, reaching 85.25 trillion *dong*, the equivalent of roughly $8.5 billion. State-owned commercial agencies handled 23.6 percent of the total.) Retailers can buy product from wholesalers or subwholesalers as well, or act as agents for local or foreign suppliers, or simply display signs indicating that they are the agent of a firm when they are not. Their profit margins are razor thin, between 5 and 10 percent of the wholesalers' prices.

The heart and lungs of Vietnam's distribution network—both wholesale and retail—is Ho Chi Minh City. Because Ho Chi Minh City is the country's clearing house for the distribution of goods (even those that come from the North), wholesalers travel to Saigon to buy goods for distribution to the market. The city is home to 32,000 privately owned shops and retail outlets, 3,000 state-owned trading enterprises, and 6,500 such establishments that are collectively owned. Eleven of the city's 150 markets are engaged in wholesale trade, 7 are engaged in both retail and wholesale trade, and the remaining 132 are in retail trade alone. Packed with food stalls, piles of materials, and sleeping and working bodies, the markets are where the retail action is. Ben Tranh Market in Saigon does about U.S. $50 million in annual sales.

Most goods are sold out of tiny streetside retail shops or in huge indoor markets similar to those you find in Mexico, or to a flea market in England. Peculiarly, the same items tend to get sold on the same street. To find a part for a motorcycle, you venture to Motorcycle Street; to buy CDs, you go to the street where every shop sells CDs. On Electronic Components Street you find a surprising degree of variety; many foreign suppliers such as Sony, Thompson, and Samsung have signed up official retail agents. The tradition of single-item street distribution has early roots. In the Old Quarter section of Hanoi, each street was named after the goods produced along it, from hats to horsehair, and each *pho,* or passageway, was partitioned from the next. As villagers migrated to the city, they specialized in one craft, with which they eked out an existence in the city as an exclusive guild. So you have to walk for four blocks to buy four different items. The good news is that the cyclo drivers seem to know where to find just about everything. I needed to buy microcassettes for a dictaphone in Hanoi,

Share and Growth of Retail Sales

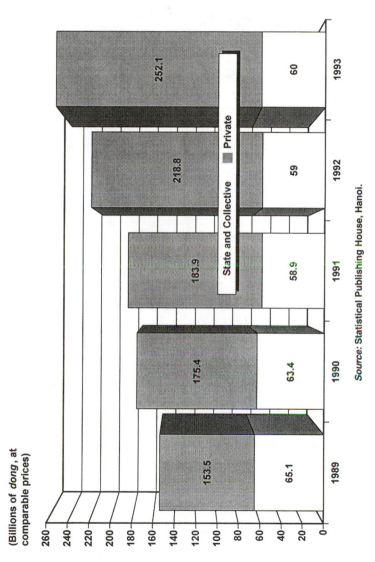

(Billions of *dong*, at comparable prices)

State and Collective ■ Private

	1989	1990	1991	1992	1993
State and Collective	153.5	175.4	183.9	218.8	252.1
Private	65.1	63.4	58.9	59	60

Source: Statistical Publishing House, Hanoi.

which seemed about as possible as finding Ho Chi Minh statues in a Wal-Mart. I asked a cyclo driver. He found out from a television repair shop where to find the tapes and took me there. Was this "Microcassette Street"? Figuratively, it was.

Vietnam's streetside distribution speaks volumes about the unformed notion of competition at this stage in the country's transition. On these product-specific streets, no shop owner or vendor tries to undercut the others. "They band together as a proletariat mass," a Canadian shopper told me as she searched in vain for a bargain in a Saigon market.

Can foreign firms operate a distribution network in Vietnam?

The Vietnamese government prohibits foreign companies from participating in the distribution of products within the country. Even if you have a general trading license, you will need to deal through a so-called foreign trade corporation in order to bring products into the country. Joint ventures are not allowed to import as foreign trade corporations either; they can import only those goods listed on their license. "[Importing] is not allowed because we want to attract foreign direct investment in production," says Nguyen Huy Phi, Deputy General Director of the Trade Ministry's Foreign Investment Department.

In fact, foreign companies *can* distribute their own products in Vietnam, but with certain restrictions. To quote Mr. Nguyen: "Foreign companies can market in Vietnam through Vietnamese agencies or through joint ventures, through 100 percent foreign invested enterprises, or through Business Co-operation Contracts to sell their products. In cases where they have set up factories to market their products, they can set up their own system of distribution, but only for products made here. Another method is by making contracts with Vietnamese companies to sell their products."[1]

Pepsi and Castrol are among the handful of foreign companies that have successfully set up and controlled an independent distribution system—and at a high cost. Pepsi can't run all the routes that it wants, and with Hanoi having to be supplied from Ho Chi Minh City, and with trucks leaving only every three days,

---

[1] (Quotes are from: "Distribution: An Official View," *Vietnam Economic Times,* July 1994, pp. 24–25).

its challenge of going it alone is daunting. "Our distribution is good," says Castrol Vietnam's General Director George Webster to the *Vietnam Economic Times,* "we are perhaps the only product in Vietnam that is in every province." Castrol's fleet of twelve trucks is bolstered by others contracted out in the provinces.

Through what channels does a product move into the market?

A product to be distributed in Vietnam may orginate from one of three sources: a locally produced product, an imported product, or a smuggled product. The smuggled product will normally enter the country and end up in the hands of a private wholesaler, where it will be distributed to local retailers.

A product produced locally will find its way to retailers in one of three ways. First, it may be delivered directly to a private wholesaler who will move it to subwholesalers and then on to the retailers. Second, it could be sold to a state-wholesaler, and then moved to subwholesalers and then on to retailers. Third, it might be moved directly through the retail agent for the company producing the product, directly to local retailers and into the market.

An imported product goes throught a number of additional steps on its way to the final retailer. First of all it must pass through a Vietnamese port, say the port at Ho Chi Minh City. There it must pass through Customs and duty is paid. Next, a foreign trading company will likely have taken title to the imported goods as the primary buyer in the transaction. Because the foreign trading corporation cannot legally import from outside Vietnam, the next step in the chain is a licensed importer, which will likely be a state-owned government trading company, which will take an added commission on the sale. At this point, the foreign product can move either to a state-wholesaler or to a private wholesaler, or to both. From there the state-wholesaler and/or private wholesaler can move the goods to subwholesalers, and then on to the retailer. Additionally, the state-wholesaler may move the product into state stores, which are located in most of the major cities.

Once goods are purchased by wholesalers in Saigon, they are moved by truck to outlying provinces and up Highway One to the cities in the North. This explains why prices tend to be higher in the North than in the South. Once goods reach local areas, they are warehoused. Next, subwholesalers and retailers come to the warehouse to see the merchandise and to buy (rather than wholesalers going to the retailers and actively pushing product into the market). There simply does not exist a Vietnamese distribution company that can move product nationally. Few of them can move product across an entire province. The subwholesalers are extremely local in orientation.

How should foreign suppliers approach the task of distributing product in Vietnam?

Your best strategy is to avoid beginning with a grand plan to distribute to the entire country, but rather to focus on the South, generally, because most goods distributed to all parts of the country pass through Saigon. Most consumer product suppliers acknowledge that the "market of 70 million" is unreachable at present—to reach 5–7 million consumers is a more realistic goal at the outset. Your distribution team will thus want to headquarter itself in the South. Later, Da Nang, Hanoi, and Hai Phong can be added, where local distribution links are currently in place.

Second, you need to realize that between the licensed importer, which is usually State-owned, and the ultimate retailer, the price of your product will be highly unstable and perhaps uncontrollable. Thus: "Brand selling is tough because you can't control price and image," says consultant Mark Gillon. "Eli Lilly sells drugs which are 60 percent image and packaging. But here, it's hard to get retailers and wholesalers to maintain image and price integrity. People want shampoo, not Breck, and they want it at a good price." Experienced foreign suppliers have learned over time what the exact margins are in each link of the distribution chain as their product moves from wholesaler to subwholesaler to retailer. They can thereby set their export price accordingly. Heavy promotion of high-profile products such as Coca-Cola, Pepsi, and Kodak film, eventually stabilizes the price because retailers come to agree on an appropriate price expected by the consumer. If the local retailer marks up the price on a product because you tell him to, the product will just sit. Retailers don't undercut each other. Prices are thus fixed though adjustable; the point is that *they* fix them and the foreign firm can't.

What is the process by which a foreign company sells through a
foreign trade corporation to an end-user?

Unless you have successfully obtained a trading license in
Vietnam, which few foreign companies have, you will have to
work with one of the two types of Vietnamese trading companies in order to import your product. The so-called foreign trading corporation is a traditional fixture in socialist economies,
which acts as a membrane between enterprises and the outside
world. In China, the countries of Eastern Europe, and Vietnam,
the foreign trade corporation was the link, as well as the buffer,
between the state-owned enterprise and both its foreign suppliers and its foreign buyers. On the one hand, they have provided
a method by which the central government can control the
spending of precious foreign exchange on imports. On the other
hand, they insured that the state enterprises remained ignorant of
their customers' tastes and preferences, needs and demands. As
in China, Vietnam employs foreign trade corporations to act as
intermediaries in the country's import-export trade. Only a select
number of powerful state-owned enterprises, foreign joint ventures, wholly foreign-owned ventures, and licensed trading companies may independently import and export from within
Vietnam.

The two types of trading companies are Government Trading
Companies (GTCs) and Foreign Trade Companies (FTCs). A foreign supplier can work with either type of company to export
goods to Vietnam, as both types are experienced and equipped to
offer distribution services for a negotiated fee—a 2.5 percent commission on CIF is common. Government Trading Companies are
usually subsidized and state-owned firms weaned on the socialist
command-style economics. They're accustomed to doing what the
government tells them to do: when to buy, when to sell, and so
on. They are not marketing-oriented as a typical Western trading
house. They do not pursue new markets and often lack the foreign exchange to select and target foreign products for specific
markets. They are, however, mandated to act as an importing service and Customs broker. They are to be found in every business
sector and are well-known to distributors as well as end-users. If
a commissioned-based agreement is not to your liking, they may
be willing to consider a profit-sharing arrangement wherein they

distribute your product in exchange for a cut of the margin between your selling price and the price they charge the end-user. A 30-percent cut is common, but start out by offering 20 percent. Don't be surprised if a GTC requests a sum of start-up capital to get things started.

Foreign Trading Companies are an entirely new breed in Vietnam and much more Western in orientation than GTCs, though they cannot yet legally offer import services to the foreign supplier. They do maintain representative office presence in Vietnam, conduct market research in a Western manner, hire and train sales teams to sell specific product lines, and are in the process of forging important contacts in their chosen business sector. In short, they are becoming specialized market developers and distributors. FTCs enjoy greater autonomy than GTCs because they are not controlled by an overseeing ministry. They can also reduce the risk for the foreign supplier, because they can take title of goods *ex factory* (outside Vietnam), which frees the supplier from liabilities associated with shipping and warehousing. Unlike GTCs, Foreign Trading Companies aggressively push products into new markets and might even be willing to share some of their office space for use by your representatives to facilitate the training of their staff, customers, and to orchestrate the sales effort. Perhaps the best strategy is to hook up with an FTC to begin the effort to market your product, while also linking up with a government trading company (GTC) to handle the actual importation.

How does the foreigner locate an appropriate wholesaler?

"Wholesalers in Vietnam are," as a French consultant told me, "basically people with a lot of money in dark corners." The big wholesalers in Saigon are typically Chinese shadow tycoons, but there exists a number of state-owned ones as well. The number of private wholesalers is expanding rapidly and is quickly coming to overshadow the state-owned distributors. In part because they have built their empires on smuggling, wholesalers tend to be secretive and difficult to locate. Sometimes they are simply one person at an office in a market in Saigon. For this reason personal ground-level contact-making is in order. You may find a wholesaler by attending trade fairs, talking to other foreign companies, and interviewing retailers of similar products. If you can't find an entity large enough to generate an order, then you have to talk to your competitors (it's a young enough market so people are willing to talk with one another about such things), as well as trading companies, in order to find a suitable wholesaler. I can also advise roaming the large Saigon markets and talking to vendors of goods similar to yours. (See the list of trade contacts in the appendix.)

What is the situation regarding the shipping of goods and materials into Vietnam?

Vietnam's two major ports, at Hai Phong and Ho Chi Minh City, both lie several miles upriver from the sea and are shallow. Thus, most shipments headed for Vietnam must first go to Singapore, Hong Kong, or Kaohsiung, Taiwan, where they can be offloaded to smaller feeder ships of up to only 10,000 deadweight tons. Obviously this pushes up shipping rates into the medium-to-high range—as much as $5,000 per container from U.S. West coast ports to Vietnam. Feeder service to Ho Chi Minh City runs several times a week, but service to Hai Phong is less frequent. From West coast U.S. ports, expect up to 30 days to get a container to Vietnam, about twice as long as to nearby Thailand. A local go-between may be useful in obtaining accurate shipping information, which is often in vexingly short supply. Also, the handling capacity of Vietnam's ports is limited. Due to a lack of cranes at Ho Chi Minh City harbor, ships arriving there need to be self-geared. Hai Phong harbor has only a few cranes capable of handling up to 50 tons.

Vietnam's ports are currently jammed with container ships bringing goods, materials, and machinery to fuel the expanding economy. In a report produced by the Danish shipper, Vaersk, Ho Chi Minh City handled 190,000 containers in 1993, and probably more than 300,000 in 1994. Hai Phong harbor is expected to jump from 54,000 containers in 1993 to 75,000 in 1994. The massive increase in port activity, combined with Byzantine regulations requiring import licenses for each shipment, is causing costly delays for importers at dock side.

Can goods and machinery be transported by air into Vietnam?

The two major airports in Hanoi and Ho Chi Minh City are in not much better shape than the ports. Heavy bombing during the war damaged Hanoi's Noi Bai airport, such that it can handle only small cargo loads brought in by passenger jets. Ho Chi Minh's Tan Son Nhat Airport currently lacks the equipment to handle the huge payloads of commercial airfreighters. Moreover, warehousing facilities amount to open-ended sheds that spill out onto a parking lot at peak season, which is also the peak rainy season.

Veteran shippers recommend seafreighting cargo to Singapore and then airfreighting it from there, at least until the airports are brought up to standard. You will, of course, need to allow more time for this—figure 3 to 4 days seafreight and 1 day turnaround time to airfreight. This costs more but may be more efficient.

Once materials arrive in port, can they be transported easily within the country?

Freight forwarding is a young concept in Vietnam; the idea of internodal transfer, (moving containers between ships, trucks, and trains) is still unfamiliar. Historically, when a shipment arrived at port it was unloaded piece-by-piece and reloaded onto whatever was to transport it elsewhere. Suddenly, containerization has come to Vietnam. Most imported goods now come by container and are moved by truck, not train. Rail transport, in fact, is down 10 percent since 1988, and still fading. Partly because rail transport averages about 20 miles per hour, it takes two days for a train to make the 1,000 mile run from Hanoi to Ho Chi Minh City, and products frequently arrive damaged. By its own estimate, the Vietnamese government calculates it would need $547 million between now and the year 2000 to rehabilitate the lines connecting Hanoi and Ho Chi Minh City, and the one to Lao Cai on the Chinese border.

Local truckers are about as unreliable as the roads are poor. Indigenous trucks are largely owner-operated and few are regularly available. Major roads often have stretches that lack paving, and one must cross weight-restricted bridges or give way to ferry crossings and bicycle traffic, as well as passing livestock and rice spread out to dry on the road. It can take up to 8 days to reach Hanoi from Ho Chi Minh City on Highway 1, the only road linking the country's Northern and Southern regions.

Burmah Castro, a 3-year-old joint venture, sought to distribute the lubricants turned out by its plant near Ho Chi Minh City to the rest of the country. The company purchased a fleet of trucks, which are kept in a warehouse at the plant in Ho Chi Minh City, and in Da Nang. Hanoi shipments go by sea because the time to ship there by truck would be one week each way. Things are changing, however. Projects involving the upgrading of Highway 1, Hanoi's airport expansion, and developing Vung Tau as a deepwater port to serve Ho Chi Minh City, will improve the situation.

Are there problems with Vietnam's Customs?

Customs in Vietnam is a disaster. The government has done nothing (as of this writing) to clean up the Customs system, and as a result, it is impossible to move goods in and out of the country efficiently. Customs officials are typically unfamiliar with many of the Western products imported; not having even seen the products before, they are understandably cautious, and thus slow. When they encounter unfamiliar cargo they may draw out the process for days. Different Customs agents interpret the tariff regulations differently. One month the rate is 20 percent, the next it's 80 percent. Often the product you want to import is simply not listed in the regulations, which causes delays. You have to renegotiate every time you import the item.

IBM recently tried to bring in 500 copies of the OS/2 operating program to give away to various government agencies so that they could try out new or more advanced software. Each set includes 18 disks. Customs looked at the shipment and realized it was comprised of 9,000 diskettes. Too many, they said, for a free giveaway. They refused to allow IBM to send them back, too, and confiscated them. "Maybe they realized each of the 9,000 diskettes was worth a buck on the open market," muses William Howell, who represents IBM in Hanoi.

Keep in mind that it is not uncommon for importers to "grease the wheels" with incentive money to get your application to the top of the stack. Mark Gillon says: "You pay $200–300 to the Customs guy when you go to the dock or he comes to your factory."

Just one more Customs war story: "We had a pretty unpleasant experience with Customs in Hai Phong when we were trying to bring in equipment from Singapore," remembers Mel Jackson of Red River Oil Company. The company was trying to import office equipment and a car. The problem was in setting an official exchange rate for the tariff payment. Customs tried to set the rate at 9,900 *dong* per dollar when the actual official rate had moved to around 10,600. Customs claimed that the rate used was set at the time Red River ordered the car, which Jackson called ridiculous. The discrepancy doesn't sound like much until you calculate what Red River was expected to pay in import duties; on the car alone the duty was 100 percent. By law, Customs was to be paid in *dong* rather than dollars, which, at the inflated exchange rate, generated a handsome illicit profit for Customs officials of $5,000. Red River fought, but finally gave in and paid.

WAREHOUSING. The warehousing situation in Vietnam is described by expats as appalling. Machinery might sit 45 days getting wet and rusty. The end-user balks at accepting it when he sees its condition, and insurance companies ask the foreign supplier why it took so long for them to be notified.

CHAPTER 8

ADVERTISING
AND PROMOTION

I strolled into a Vietnam Airlines office in Ho Chi Minh City to buy a ticket to Hanoi. Inside, I found what appeared to be a professional photoshoot in progress with a photographer snapping photos of smiling and bashful ticket sellers. Lighting assistants held strobe lights aloft as mystified tourists and harried business travelers hurried to reserve seats and purchase their tickets. I figured the photographer had been hired by *Time* or *BusinessWeek* to illustrate some article about the meteoric success of Vietnam Airlines, one of the country's few state-owned success stories. But after introducing myself I found that the photographer, Gerald Herman, was actually the managing director for a private foreign-owned company in Saigon called Lotus Communications, specializing in business graphics, print advertising, audio-visual programs, and even Macintosh-based multimedia presentations. In fact, Mr. Herman was *working* for Vietnam Airlines producing the company's new advertising brochure. Once considered a "capitalist tool," Madison Avenue-style advertising now fills every inch of visual space in Saigon, and even looms over tranquil West Lake in the country's capitol in the form of gigantic neon billboards.

To what extent are foreign companies advertising in Vietnam?

The first organized promotion of American manufacturing prowess in Vietnam, after the lifting of the embargo, was not a resounding success. The Vietnam Chamber of Commerce & Industry, in conjunction with its U.S. affiliated office in San Diego (which is owned by Viet Kieu), organized the Vietnamerica Expo held in April, 1994 in Hanoi—the first trade exposition in the country attended solely by U.S. companies exhibiting American products. The show was held in the oven-like Giang Vio Exhibition Centre in Hanoi where fifty-two corporate exhibitors paid $500 a square meter for booth spaces. A VCCI representative in San Diego, with whom we spoke, claimed that the event was a grand success, with unexpectedly high Vietnamese attendance, and that "our flags were flying together." The only problem, she said, was that "there were a few products they couldn't get off the dock, so some firms didn't have their samples to exhibit." In Vietnam, we asked James Rockwell, president of VATICO, how the show had gone. "It was awful," he said. In fact, Chrysler executives had asked Rockwell if the company should attend the show. Rockwell, whose wisdom and experience match his Abraham Lincoln looks, advised Chrysler to skip it, explaining that the exhibition wasn't well organized. And sadly enough, the first showing of American products was, indeed, considered a disaster—a public relations Hiroshima that devastated the image of America and its products in a newly-opened market where our reputation for quality had preceded us. The event was, as reported in the Vietnamese press, poorly attended. But worse, as I found out in Hanoi, the event "was a bad showing for American products," as one U.S. expat put it. "It proved to the Vietnamese that American products weren't really that good compared to Korean or Japanese products." When the foreign press picked up the story, it only reported the large number of Vietnamese who attended and concluded the event was a success. Yes, hordes of Vietnamese people were there because they only had to pay 20 cents at the door.

But Vietnamese who walked out of the show were not impressed. Many of the participating U.S. companies were not able to get their products to the site in time for the show because they were hung up in Customs. Boxes of brand name foods sat rotting out on the tarmac at the Hanoi airport. And many firms pitched food product lines without free samples. (The Doritos booth had only seventeen samples of their product, which they had tried to sell rather than give away.) The hall was extremely hot and not well ventilated; the displays looked terrible. Pepsi hung on as a sponsor of the event, but Chrysler and Coca-Cola opted wisely to attend a concurrent trade show sponsored by an international organization, which turned out to be a huge success. We'll come back to whether attending a trade show is a good way to launch promotional efforts in the market. For the moment, let's focus on what's happening in the realm of advertising in Vietnam.

Western-style advertising has already eked out a huge presence in the major cities. Foreign and domestic companies alike strive to build brand awareness in a country where few brands are known and the early bird gets the worm. Billboards and point-of-sales displays are the two most worn methods of marketing, though advertising has made its debut as well. At some restaurants, you sit at a table inscribed with the Tiger Beer label, on a chair inscribed with the Pepsi label, under an umbrella flying the Coca-Cola logo. An indigent foreigner could live for weeks on free Snickers Bars given out as a promotion in food stores and bars. One day a domestic beer company issued free tee-shirts to every cyclo driver in Saigon, and instructed them to meet at a central traffic circle en masse in the busiest part of Saigon, where they peddled around and around for an hour. The shirts were the only incentive. Another company hired motorbike riders to carry signs on their bikes advertising condoms, and carry free samples. In a pub, women will suddenly appear at your table wearing Carlsburg or Guiness tee-shirts touting those brands of beers.

And nobody denies that advertising to Vietnam's nascent consumer class works. J&B has spent heavily to promote its whiskey in Vietnam. All across Asia, Johnny Walker is number one and Chivas Regal is number two, but in Vietnam J&B is number two. The promotion has done its job. If you order "whiskey and Coke" in a pub, the bartender will automatically reply, "J&B?" Shell recently ran successful print ads in all major newspapers in Ho Chi Minh City commemorating Vietnam's Independence Day (1945), when it was liberated from Japanese domination. "Government people love this kind of advertisement," an executive for Vietnam Advertising Agency told me. The law firm White & Case recently ran a similar ad "congratulating" Hanoi for its liberation from the French in 1954.

Should a firm begin promotion of its products and services at a trade show in Vietnam?

Trade exhibitions are constantly being held in Vietnam sponsored by an assortment of international organizations. Most are industry-specific, well-choreographed affairs that generate sizable numbers of deals. Attending one is a cost-effective method of introducing your firm and its product line to Vietnamese end-users, distributors, and agents, as well as government officials. Choosing a competent exhibition organizer is critical, however, as pulling off a smooth trade show, especially in Hanoi, is a job for seasoned organizers only.

What is the size and potential of Vietnam's budding advertising industry?

Although Vietnamese still tend to believe that a good product doesn't really need to be promoted, foreigners' love of advertising has successfully penetrated this infant market where advertising of any sort was illegal only 4 years ago. Predictably, Vietnam lags far behind other countries in the region in terms of dollars spent on advertising. In 1993, Vietnam spent U.S.$80 million, while South Korea spent U.S.$ 4 billion, Taiwan $2.8 billion, Hong Kong $1.4 billion, and Indonesia $627 million. Nevertheless, foreign advertising firms see a lot of potential for advertising products to Vietnam's population of 74 million people.

Advertising seems to be more prevalent in Ho Chi Minh City, where nineteen advertising firms are currently in business. Nearly 700 billboards, the largest source of revenue for most local advertisers, can be found all along Saigon River and atop many of the city's buildings. In Hanoi, the most visible form of Western-style hucksterism are billboards that mar the scenery. One touting

Halida beer overlooks the otherwise bucolic view across West Lake and has citizens torn up about whether billboards in scenic places should be allowed. Actually, there is quite a bit of money to be made in the billboard business. The owners of a building in Hanoi on Hai Ba Trung Street, which carries a huge billboard advertising the Nestle product Milo, nets $4,110 a year. In kind, thousands of owners of street-front homes have erected makeshift scaffolding to hold billboards so they can rent advertising space, while they convert their first floor to be rented to a foreign company representitive office.

Can foreign companies handle their own advertising in Vietnam?

For a foreign company to conduct its own advertising in Vietnam would require having an investment license to do so. If you do not have such an investment license but want to advertise in Vietnam you'll have to engage the services of a local Vietnamese advertising firm. The foreign company could, for example, sign a Business Cooperation Contract or Joint Venture contract with a local Vietnamese advertising agency, as a handful of foreign advertising firms already have. These restrictions have greatly benefitted Vietnamese ad agencies, particularly VINEXAD, which now controls 60 percent of the entire advertising market. The firm has signed cooperative ventures with such foreign firms as J. Walter Thompson of Thailand, Optel Media of Australia, and Densu of Japan. Vietnam Advertising Ltd. in Ho Chi Minh City has also been able to form ties with a major international advertising agency.

What are the various modes of advertising in Vietnam?

About 40 percent of the $25 million spent on advertising in Saigon in 1993 was spent on billboard advertising. Ho Chi Minh City is the most important advertising region in the country, and television is the most direct conduit to the city's urbanites, 80 percent of whom have access to a television. Of note, the World Cup captured a gigantic television audience in Vietnam, which also saw a repeating barrage of commercials for Milo, Ovaltine, Coca-Cola, Dunhill, and BP, among others. The Vietnamese had bags under

their eyes for weeks because they had to watch the soccer match-
es live as replays were not shown. And get this: it was perfectly
okay to show up late for work or do a less than adequate job during the day because you had watched the World Cup. Everybody
was talking about it constantly. Most companies, however, are
content to buy billboard space and basically slap up posters and
other displays wherever they can. They hire cyclo drivers to wear
tee-shirts or give them logo stickers, give free samples to stores,
and so on. Electronic billboards have also recently been introduced.

The promotion of Vietnam's investment opportunities is perhaps where most local advertising energy is spent. State companies advertise as much to sell their products as to advertise for foreign joint venture partners. Some stores now keep lists of their
customers, which they sell to foreign advertising agencies for
building databases of high-income urbanites. The first section of
the Vietnam phone book is dedicated to foreign investment,
including a recitation of the most important investment laws,
addresses of government trade and investment agencies, Rep
Offices, and tax information—all in English.

How do the Vietnamese regulate advertising in Vietnam?

The Ministry of Culture is the key watchdog on advertising,
but district entities also get involved, including the local People's
Committee. Restrictions on advertising limit liquor advertising to
posters, and prohibit messages and innuendo that go against
socialist morality. Winning approval of a license application
requires dozens of official stamps of approval, or chops, and the
submitting of innumerable notarized copies of documents to meet
the stipulations for outdoor advertising. For this reason nine out of
ten advertising billboards in Saigon are unlicensed; many companies simply purchase land-use rights, pay off local officials, and
erect their billboards without a license. And even with full government approval, you never know when the government might
intervene. In one case, the Vice Premier was trying to watch a
movie on television, and got so annoyed at all the advertisements
that he single-handedly had advertising on television temporarily
cancelled. The Vietnamese Advertising Agency gingerly had to
inform its clients that their spots went unaired and would be

rescheduled, a representative of the company told me. Due to the bureaucratic morass surrounding the advertising industry, most foreign entrants engage one of over fifteen advertising agencies in Vietnam—two are private companies—to handle their promotion needs.

What are the rates for advertising in Vietnam?

Television and radio commercials can cost anywhere between U.S.$40 to $250 per minute; a typical spot on television runs $200 in Ho Chi Minh City. Billboard space on the road to Hanoi's Noi Bai airport costs about U.S.$ 250 dollars per square meter per year.

Will it be necessary to educate customers (and officials) in order to sell in Vietnam?

Education and training is central to any serious effort to sell sophisticated products and services in Vietnam. Advertising is simply not enough to bring a buyer to the table. You will have to consider four types of customer education, three of which you can't expect to be paid for. The first will be educating government sector entities, including state-run companies, as to the technological capabilities of your product line relative to the standards of your industry. Second, you can expect to have to make a major investment in educating your business partners so that they can effectively sell, install, and support your products. Third, part of the marketing process will be to educate and train potential customers to understand the product line that you offer. Finally, a major investment will also be necessary to train customers to utilize what you sell. Only the last type of training earns you a penny. Thus, alongside a planned advertising campaign aimed at industrial users, consider sponsoring technical seminars for end-users and their overseeing ministry. If your product is high tech, a great deal of reputation building can be achieved by interfacing with Vietnam's various technological institutes, which can provide references to high government people as well as technology importers. (See page 185 for a list of these entities.)

PART THREE

Investing in Vietnam

It's not that the Vietnamese don't trust foreigners; it's that they don't want to be devoured by foreigners and they don't want to be dependent upon them. They know, given their history, that they can go it alone once they're given the proper tools and the financing, both of which they are acquiring with great alacrity and speed.

STEWART STEMPLE,
MANAGING DIRECTOR, VIETNAM
BBI INVESTMENT GROUP, CHARTERED

WHY INVEST
IN VIETNAM—
AND WITH WHOM?

*S*ince Vietnam introduced its Foreign Investment Law in 1987, the country has been the recipient of over $10 billion in foreign investment capital, though the government admits that only about 40 percent of that amount has actually been invested in the country. By any standard, this represents a spectacular performance given the country's small size, the U.S. embargo in place during all but one of those years, and the undeveloped state of commercial law and industrial infrastructure in Vietnam.

Which commercial sectors are targets for foreign investment capital in Vietnam?

Foreign investment in Vietnam rose 45.4 percent in 1994, totalling $4.07 billion in that year, with $1.1 billion actually realized. By the middle of 1993, over $6 billion in foreign investment

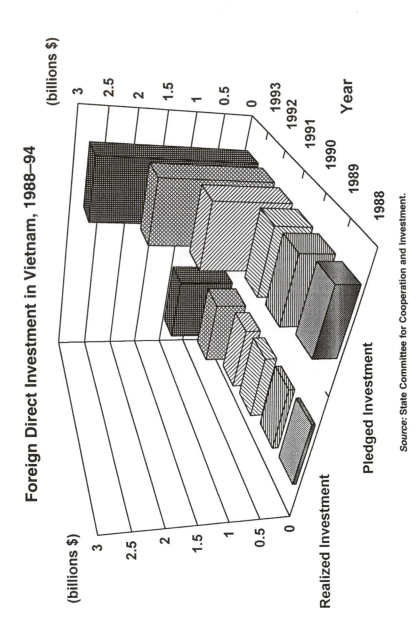

Foreign Direct Investment in Vietnam, 1988–94

Source: **State Committee for Cooperation and Investment.**

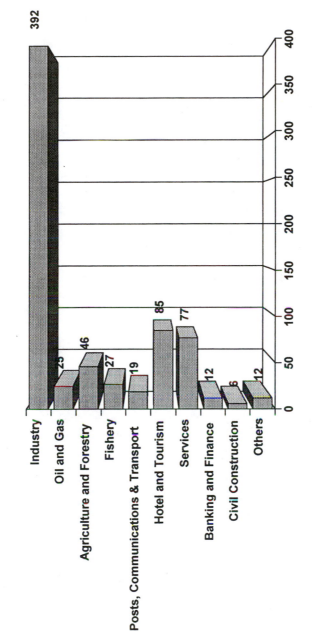

Number of Licensed Foreign Investment Projects in Vietnam, 1988–1993

Industry	392
Oil and Gas	25
Agriculture and Forestry	46
Fishery	27
Posts, Communications & Transport	19
Hotel and Tourism	85
Services	77
Banking and Finance	12
Civil Construction	6
Others	12

Source: **State Committee for Cooperation and Investment.**

had been approved, though only a fraction of that had been allocated. The lion's share of investment has gone into the oil and gas sector, accounting for 37 percent of total investment realized ($1.428 billion) between 1988 and 1992, while most of the light industrial foreign investment has gone to setting up garment and footwear manufacturing. Second to the oil and gas sector is the tourism industry, including the building of hotels.

Which countries are Vietnam's important investment partners?

Taiwan is the largest foreign investor in Vietnam, followed closely by Hong Kong. In the first year of investing after the lifting of the embargo, American companies invested in 28 projects worth $270 million; the United States is ranked 14th among foreign countries investing in Vietnam. Taiwan was the leading investor for 1994, with 180 projects valued at about $2 billion. Most of these projects are fairly small and concentrated in construction, building material and textile industries, food and wood processing, and shoe-making. Hong Kong investors were a close second with 170 projects worth more than $1.7 billion (Hong Kong dollars have flocked to Vietnam partly in search of a haven before Hong Kong reverts to Chinese rule in 1997).

What types of foreign ventures are allowed?

There are five basic forms of investment contracts allowed in Vietnam: joint ventures, wholly foreign-owned companies, business cooperation agreements, processing agreements, and build-operate-transfer (BOT) agreements.

In a *joint venture,* as well as a wholly foreign-owned venture, the Vietnamese side normally contributes land-use rights, some machinery and buildings, and its labor force. Joint venture negotiations tend to pivot on the issue of what percentage of equity will be comprised of the land contribution from the Vietnamese side. The going range of valuation is between 25 and 35 percent. Valuation of the existing building and equipment is often a sticking point. The existing equipment often comes from the former Soviet Union and was purchased in rubles, a currency that has been devalued over the past few years from a rate of 1 ruble to $2 down to 4,170 rubles to $1. Thus, an accurate valuation of a

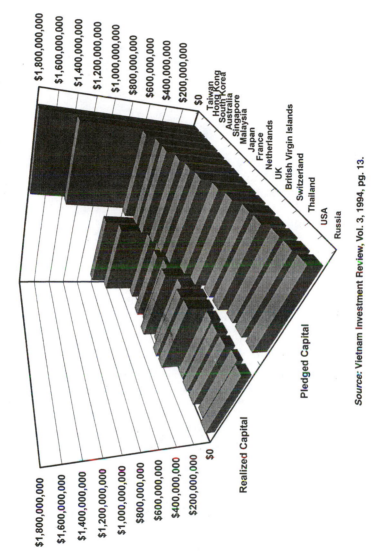

Top 15 Country Investors in Vietnam (through 1994)

Source: **Vietnam Investment Review, Vol. 3, 1994, pg. 13.**

Vietnamese company's assets is virtually impossible. Added to this is the fact the Vietnamese partner will attempt to overvalue the land as much as possible, going so far in one case to "account for every tree and every garden" that exists on the property to be used by the joint venture, says Stewart D. Stemple, a consultant for BBI Investment Group, which is building a resort in Da Nang.

The Vietnamese partner will typically ask that its equity share in a joint venture escalate over the duration of the venture, say, from 30 percent to 50 percent. Duration is limited to 70 years. Be warned that the board members of a joint venture must vote unanimously for an important decision to be made, without regard for the relative equity share in the company. Thus, owning 51 percent of the venture does not garner managerial control in practice, as any decision can be nullified by a single vote cast by anyone. Conflicts have occured because Vietnamese partners often balk at spending money on marketing and advertising (because they tend to be unfamiliar with their cost), while the foreign side pushes to do so.

Of important note, the government will determine whether your joint venture is to be deemed an "important economic establishment," which may, under the law on foreign investment, require the venture to increase the Vietnamese party's capital contribution to the venture, and thus increase its equity share. It remains unclear what criteria are applied in defining important economic establishments, but certainly large projects in telecommunications, oil and gas, and transportation may well be defined as such. These are points for your lawyer in Vietnam to help clarify and make transparent.

In a *wholly foreign-owned* venture, you don't have to negotiate a contract with a Vietnamese party, and you retain total control of the management of the enterprise. Unfortunately, the Vietnamese government frowns on this form of investment unless the foreign side can justify that a joint venture is unworkable; for example, because of the project's size or scope. Permanency is not gained by establishing a wholly foreign-owned venture, as they are granted a maximum 70-year duration like joint ventures. Moreover, the law on foreign investment provides that wholly foreign-owned enterprises may be subject to a "buy-in" stipulation, whereby Vietnamese parties are granted the opportunity to acquire an ever-increasing share of strategic ventures wholly owned by foreigners, though it is not known how, or if, the foreigner will be compensated. If the experience of China and Taiwan are any guide, one can predict that Vietnam will loosen regulations concerning these ventures eventually, especially as Export Processing Zones come online. A strategy worth pursuing right now would be to move 10–20 percent of your production to a low-cost labor operation located in an EPZ in Vietnam, and to ship to captive markets in other countries in Asia. Shoes and textiles would be a good choice.

A *business cooperation contract* is rather like a simple partnership in which the foreign partner and the Vietnamese entity are free to agree on whatever contract terms they wish without all the restrictions and legal headaches involved in forming a joint venture enterprise or other legal venture. *The Vietnam Investment Review* is an example of a venture based on contractual business cooperation between an Australian publisher and a government agency in Vietnam. However, these contracts will still need to be approved by the SCCI, which will require an annual report to be submitted, along with accounting records. Profits earned by the Vietnamese side will be taxed at local rates, while profits earned by the foreign side will be taxed at foreign investor rates. In a business cooperation contract (BCC) make sure that you stipulate in the contract that the assets you bring to the venture will remain yours at the end of the contract and in such case that the agreement is terminated prematurely. With these ventures, the SCCI takes responsibility for determining, through its own calculations, the profits that the BCC earns, taking into account that the Vietnam side will be taxed under Vietnamese tax rates and the foreign party taxed under the tax rates of its country. If at all possible, your lawyer, when negotiating the agreement, should attempt to make the SCCI methods for profit calculation as clearly-defined as possible before approval of the venture is granted.

For companies wishing to produce footwear, clothing, or electronic components, a so-called *processing contract* might be the most appropriate form of doing business. In this arrangement the foreign company provides the equipment and technical know-how, while the Vietnamese company provides the factory space and laborers. The foreign company ships in needed raw materials and the Vietnamese company assembles and processes them for shipment back to the foreign party for eventual distribution.

Vietnam's five processing zones are set up to facilitate this sort of "South China" type of deal.

In a *build-operate-transfer* (BOT) arrangement, the foreigner agrees to build infrastructural property such as a bridge, road, or power station, which it will be allowed to operate and earn a profit from over a given period of time. After the negotiated duration has expired, the infrastructural property is transferred to the Vietnamese without further compensation. A tentative list of BOT projects was released by the government in late 1994, and includes projects such as two coal-fired and two hydro-powered energy projects, two toll roads, three toll bridges, two water supply projects, and five waste treatment facilities. The question for potential investors in BOT projects is a simple one: Is the project economically viable? That is, will there be enough traffic to support the necessary tolls to earn out a toll bridge, for example. Often one can successfully convince lower-level managers of such projects, especially those associated with the SCCI, to comprehend the commercial realities of a BOT project, but convincing high-level government officials, who may be politically motivated to initiate such projects, can be a much greater task.

How is foreign investment regulated in Vietnam?

Foreign ventures are authorized and supervised by the State Committee for Cooperation and Investment (SCCI), which has the discretionary power, in the words of a World Bank report, to "suspend or revoke a foreign investor's business license or even dissolve a joint venture if there is a breach of law or deviation from the investment objectives or incorporation conditions. This wide authority is not tempered by a corresponding right to appeal SCCI decisions."[1] Foreign projects are, however, guaranteed against expropriation or nationalization; their duration can be set for between 50 and 70 years.

The government encourages investment in priority areas by offering tax breaks, including: a 2-year tax holiday with a possible additional 2 years at 50 percent of the normal tax rate, and a low-

---

[1] David Dollar et al., "Vietnam: Transition to the Market," The World Bank, September, 1993. pg. 85.

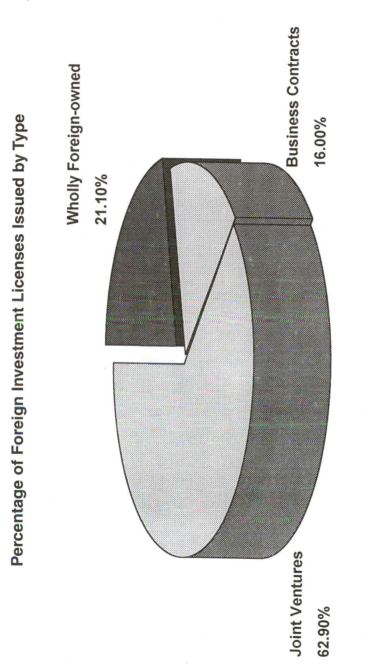

Percentage of Foreign Investment Licenses Issued by Type

Wholly Foreign-owned
21.10%

Business Contracts
16.00%

Joint Ventures
62.90%

Source: State Committee for Cooperation and Investment.

ered corporate income tax rate (10–15 percent) as opposed to
21–25 percent. There are also exemptions on import duty for
machinery, equipment, and raw materials to be used in export
industries.

Does the government require foreign ventures to export production, or are so-called "import substitution" ventures permitted?

High tariffs on consumer goods, and other goods, height-
ens the strategic attractiveness of setting up import substitution
ventures that can sell their output to domestic markets. Though
there are no clear-cut guidelines for such ventures, foreign
invested companies that produce needed materials, such as
cement and steel, may be permitted to sell up to 100 percent of
their production on the local market. For those selling garments,
toys, and electronic consumer products, the percentage of
domestic sales allowed will be much lower, around 20–30 percent of production with the rest being exported. Especially
Japanese and Korean electronics manufacturers of consumer
goods have moved into Vietnam to both produce finished products, but also to set up parts manufacturing. The reason is that
by 1995 over one million televisions will be sold in Vietnam
annually, and duties on imported finished products run around
60 percent, but are only 40 percent on semifinished products for
home appliances. Tariffs on finished products are expected to
rise in the coming months. Thus, for them to be on the inside
producing behind tariff barriers appears to be a wise strategy
indeed.

Will the Vietnamese approve a small- or medium-sized venture?

With so many projects being set up in the country, the
Vietnamese tend to focus on large companies that have large projects in mind. Small ventures are not attractive because they do
not represent large cash infusions from foreign partners. To sell a
small venture, try to lay out the project in clear, simple language
using photographs in your presentation to describe the project.
You may have to sell the concept of "services" as a profitable

form of business, as opposed to manufacturing or resource exploitation.

To what regions of the country is foreign investment going?

The South has attracted about two-thirds of foreign investment, but this proportion is expected to come into balance as the North increases its investment promotional efforts and improves its general business climate. In 1994, Ho Chi Minh City attracted $967 million of the capital in 117 projects; Hanoi attracted $891 million in 68 projects.

After Hanoi and Saigon, other important points for foreign investment included Hai Phong in the North and Dong Nai and Song Be provinces in the South as emerging sites for foreign investment. Dong Nai ranks third in foreign investment after Hanoi and Ho Chi Minh City. Thirteen projects have been licensed in Hai Phong for a total of $292 million, and 20 have been licensed in Song Be Province worth $240 million, all in 1994.

DA NANG. One of the most exciting commercial regions of Vietnam is Quang Nam-Da Nang Province, located on the coast approximately midway between Ho Chi Minh City in the south and Hanoi to the north bounded on the west by 150 kilometers of beautiful white sand beaches, (made familiar to Americans by the television series *China Beach*). It was here that the U.S. Marines landed in 1965 in the first troop invasion of Vietnam. A different sort of invasion is taking place today. In 1992, Da Nang saw only 16,000 foreign visitors; by 1993, the figure doubled to 33,000. The Quang Nam-Da Nang Tourism Department estimates that 1994 will bring 100,000 foreign visitors and by the year 2000 they expect around 500,000 tourists. Not only do foreign tourists favor Da Nang's beaches and points of interest, but the department expects an additional 500,000 domestic tourists by 2000 as well. Companies from all over the globe (mostly from the United States) are scrambling to get a foothold and land prices are soaring. In Non Nuoc, located 10 km from Da Nang City on the beach, one square meter of land sold for $200 in 1993; by May, 1994 the price had risen to $1,000. Richmond Smith of Mbf Indochina Ltd. had plans and government approval for a $1.2 million 60-room hotel upgrade project in 1992 at Bac Mai An, 6 km from Da Nang. Soon after his license was approved, Smith concluded that his plans were shortsighted. Within a year, he cobbled together a partnership that included Furama Hotel Enterprises and Marc Farber to start construction of The Indochina Beach Hotel. The $24 million hotel will be open at the end of 1995. The BBI Investment Group, chartered, of Los Angeles has signed a $258 million memorandum of understanding to expand and remodel the Non Nuue Hotel. The project stretches along 5 km of beach and includes an 18-hole golf course.

What are the advantages of locating a venture in an Export Processing Zone (EPZ)?

Five EPZs are either under construction or already functioning in Vietnam today. In 1993, investment in EPZs was up 40 percent over 1992 to U.S.$ 2.7 billion, with 836 licenses granted. That brought total pledged capital in EPZs to an impressive U.S.$ 7.5 billion. Incentives for potential investors include million-dollar commitments to improve local infrastructure, tax holidays of 4 years, and a low 10 percent profit tax, a big incentive over the 2-year holiday and 15–25 percent profit tax offered to non-EPZ investments.

Unlike the export processing zones in the rest of the world, Vietnam's EPZs seem to have most of the right ingredients for success. According to the World Export Processing Zone Association (WEPZA), of the 200 EPZs worldwide, only about 10 percent of them succeed, and these are in Asia and Mexico. WEPZA has established ten criteria that an EPZ must meet in order to succeed, and EPZs in Vietnam lack only a few. The most pronounced shortfall, as you would expect, is in the area of support industries. Investors are hopeful that local entrepreneurs will soon come online to fill the gap by manufacturing semifinished goods and spare parts, creating a flow of domestically produced goods into EPZs and stimulating the local economy. At present, however, the government dictates that EPZ companies can only sell to domestic Vietnamese buyers possessing import licenses; thus, the sold goods are taxed as imported goods.

The Export Processing Zones in Vietnam are listed in the table below.

VIETNAM'S EXPORT PROCESSING ZONES

Zone Name	Location	Date Established	Size of Zone in Hectares	Infrastructure Investment Capital
Can Tho	Can Tho	November 2, 1993	57	U.S.$8.1 million
Da Nang	Quang Nam	October 21,1993	120	U.S.$24.0 million
Hai Phong	Hai Phong	January 1,1993	300	U.S.$150.0 million
Linh Trung	HCM City	August 8, 1992	60	U.S.$14.0 million
Tan Thuan	HCM City	September 24, 1991	300	U.S.$89.0 million

Source: Vietnam Economic News, Vol. 9, March 8, 1994, pg. 13.

TAN THUAN. Located near Ho Chi Minh City, Tan Thuan had made itself known through extensive marketing. The biggest attraction is its streamlined licensing procedure. The simple 14-page license application is submitted to the Ho Chi Minh City Export Processing Zone Administration (HEPZA), not to the SCCI, for processing. The HEPZA processes the application in 3 months from submittal. A foreign entity must provide evidence of financial background and investment plan details, including production expenses and profitability projections for the first 3 years of operation.

LINH TRUNG. Also located near Ho Chi Minh City, hundreds of foreign business missions have applied for licenses to set up in Linh Trung EPZ. Of the thirteen foreign companies actually licensed in Linh Trung, Japanese firms are by far the largest investors, comprising over 30 percent of land leased for export production. Manufacturing activities involve electronics (14 percent), textiles (13.5 percent), sporting goods (9 percent), and plastic/toys (3 percent). All of the projects are 100 percent foreign-invested projects; as of the summer of 1993 no joint venture projects have been submitted.

HAI PHONG. Established in early 1993, construction of the Hai Phong EPZ is still underway. The master plan and design has been approved and the Hai Phong EPZ administration is processing some thirty-five applications from various countries wishing to invest.

DA NANG. Established in January 1994, the Da Nang EPZ is being built by Massda, a joint venture company between a Malaysian company called Masacorp, and Danepzone (the Da Nang EPZ development company). Already, it has been flooded with applications from Japan, the United States, Thailand, Singapore, Malaysia, Korea, and Europe. At present, the EPZ is trying to modernize its administration and construct infrastructure.

CAN THO. In November 1993, Can Tho EPZ set out in a different direction than other EPZs, funded and constructed by its locality without help from foreign parties. The administration and staff are working out details and preparing to process investor applications from Indonesia, Thailand, Singapore, and the United States.

Can manufactured products be easily sourced from Vietnam?

Most suppliers provide ample quality in terms of workmanship; however, they lack international exposure to business practices familiar to Westerners. They have years of experience trading with the former Soviet Union, trade that was conducted largely via barter arrangements. Thus, they have little knowledge of their competitors in the rest of Asia, nor do they fully understand that they must price their goods in accordance with what those competitors are offering. Their quotations often come in extremely high—"totally unrealistically high," as one foreign buyer put it.

If you don't know which factory might be in a position to supply the product, you can choose to approach the relevant ministry to recommend a factory to you. If you know of a factory that produces what you want, you should go straight to them. Talk directly to the managing directors of producing state-owned enterprises first. There are quota allocations given each state company for exporting its goods to the Western countries. (Quotas don't yet exist vis-a-vis the United States because of the absense of MFN.) The first thing to check is whether they possess the necessary export quota. The ministry will have awarded the factory a certain allocation. The manager will provide you with a list of the factory's allocations for each country of the world, and how much of the allocation remains to be filled. Ministries that control enterprises often withhold quota allocations from them for unknown reasons; in short, the enterprise you may want to deal with might have to negotiate long and hard with its overseeing ministry before winning the necessary quota you need. Moreover, once you present your order, the enterprise may have to go to the ministry to request an additional quota, which can take 3–6 months to obtain. This still unresolved problem can make it tough to plan for a buying season.

What kind of license do you have to obtain to source goods from Vietnam?

With a Representative Office license, you can carry out the functions of an export buying house and source produced goods from Vietnam. The exchange of monies will still be between the offshore buyer and the State enterprise producing the goods. The

Rep Office or export buying house is restricted to coordinating production, ordering, checking quality control, and facilitating shipping.

FINDING A LOCAL INVESTMENT PARTNER

Foreign executives working in Vietnam make no mystery about their, as consultant Mark Gillon told me, "almost total dependency on the local partner." Given the number of participating official parties in a venture and the necessary approvals that have to be obtained, matrimony with a local partner who is both familiar with the bureaucratic apparatus and adept at finessing it is—at least at this early stage of the Vietnam investment game—more of a requisite than a choice. That doesn't mean you have to accept a shotgun marriage arrangement with an unattractive local company. Picking your partner is perhaps the most important decision you'll have to make.

What should a foreign partner look for in a Vietnamese partner?

Evaluating partner enterprises in Vietnam cannot be said to be as complicated a process in Vietnam as in other transitioning economies. Normally, all that a state company is going to be able to contribute is its land; the existing machinery in a factory probably won't impress you, nor will it be upgradable in most cases. As Mark Mitchell, Director of VATICO in Saigon told me, "You are starting from scratch in most cases—starting greenfield companies. A piece of land with possibly a few delapidated buildings sitting upon it." Thus, the task of evaluating an enterprise as a potential manufacturing partner begins by asking: what experience and expertise does the partner have, and how good is its land?

"The partner that we met seemed to know what they're talking about," says Al DeMatteis of DeMatteis Vietnam, a land development firm. "They were in the development business already and they are a subsidiary of the Ministry of Defense. They have an office building down in Ho Chi Minh, and they have Saigon Village. They've been in this before."

Through your partner you might also gain access to its contacts, an asset of immense value to outsiders. In fact, one of the De Matteis' partners is a local architect, who, says DeMatteis, "is very good for us because of his relationship with the Chief Architect's Office. He happens to be a very good local architect also." Most foreign joint venture partners seek local partners who wield lobbying power with local (if not central) government officials, but who are willing to take a backseat in the daily management of the operation. While the foreign partner takes care of managing the operation, the local partner can tweak the local bureaucracy and lobby for fast decisions, help the venture acquire scarce local materials, get imported goods through Customs, and basically act as an interface with local government authorities. Does your candidate partner in Vietnam have such clout, and is it willing to watch and listen, rather than meddle in managing the enterprise? (The "sleeping partner" approach should not, however, be allowed to drive a wedge between the foreign partner and government officials, such that they forget one another exists.)

The local partner might also have some kind of a distribution network in place. Before the U.S. embargo was lifted Pepsi had come into Vietnam, built up government connections, and signed numerous memorandums with local beverage companies that had strong distribution capabilities. Coca-Cola, on the other hand, held back, and sold product into the country through a Southeast Asian affiliate. When the embargo was removed, Pepsi won an investment license and entered the market, as did Coca-Cola. But Pepsi's approach proved to be the wiser of the two because it had tied up with partners who could distribute, while Coca-Cola lost time and a major share of the Ho Chi Minh City market.

Lastly, in an industry where Vietnamese exporters must abide by a quota system in order to sell their production overseas, you will want to choose the partner enterprise that wields the most clout amongst the quota-granting government agencies in charge. Let me offer an example. Vietnam controls the exploitation of its forests by placing quotas on exporters, rather than attempting to control the cutters. Thus, as a joint venture partner of a Vietnamese wood products company, Norway's Scansia hooked up with the Vietnam Wood Products Company to form a joint venture called Scanviwood, which is a state company with limited experience in Western-style marketing and finance, but which wielded significant leverage in hard bargaining with the government in increasing its quotas for exporting wood products, which the joint venture sells mainly to the European Union.

How do you locate an appropriate business partner?

To locate an appropriate partner in Vietnam, you will want to pursue two avenues at the outset. First, meet with the relevant ministry that controls your industry, which can introduce you to the various enterprises under its aegis who might be suitable partners. The Ministry of Heavy Industries will keep a running list of companies for which it desires to initiate automobile manufacturing joint ventures, for example. Second, meet directly with enterprise directors who operate companies in your industry. (See the appendix for addresses of ministries and key factories.) An enterprise director may be willing to get behind your proposal and take it to the ministry for review. You have to play it by ear as to which of these two approaches will pan out fastest.

At the same time, try the following approach strategies as well. The key matchmaking service in the country is the Vietnam Chamber of Commerce and Industry. The organization provides contacts, visas, and introductions to suitable Vietnamese partners with surprisingly little tendency to introduce only those partners whom the *government* might deem suitable. Introductions to potential partners can also be facilitated through the local or city Foreign Economic Relations Department, usually established by the local People's Committee. You might also check with the Foreign Trade Development Center (FTDC) in Saigon, which publishes a list of "projects calling for investment." Should you be interested in implementing a small project in Vietnam, check with the Ministry of Agriculture. Agricultural projects have great potential because Vietnam is known to be a breadbasket for the ready markets of Asia. A foreign businessman recently told the *Vietnam Economic Times* that "with markets like Hong Kong and Singapore a few hours away, it makes fresh produce a real possibility."

If none of these tactics work, you can engage one of a plethora of organized local companies, often started by moonlighting State officials, which bill themselves as investment consultants. Many offer "package services" including introductions to venture partners, negotiations, and contracting.

Can foreign firms enter partnerships with privately owned Vietnamese enterprises?

Though private enterprises are permitted to enter into joint ventures with foreigners, the overwhelming majority of joint ventures are between either state-owned enterprises and foreigners or Vietnamese state agencies and foreigners. But partnering with private companies is legal, as long as the person or company has a license to be in business. Individual entrepreneurs in Vietnam who possess a license to do business are relatively rare. "A foreign company coming in to do joint manufacturing is not going to do it with a private company," says Mark Mitchell of VATICO. Most of the private sector is made up of small shops, and major manufacturing accounts for very little.

But the private sector is gaining fast, and soon companies will emerge that will have the funding and the initiative to be effective joint venture partners. With reforms initiated in 1986, the private sector has been encouraged and placed on an equal footing with the state and cooperative sectors. Though the average private enterprise in urban areas employs only fourteen employees and is capitalized with $30,000, many are larger. Moreover, government officials have taken interests in the newly formed private companies and thus, the largest private companies have indirect government backing.

THE EMERGING PRIVATE SECTOR. When private business became legal with *doi moi*, people like Mr. Le Van Kiem literally went into their backyards to dig up their gold. They pulled dollars out of their mattresses, and notified relatives overseas to send money so they could start up businesses. Mr. Kiem founded Huy Hoang, which became involved in everything from garment manufacturing to construction property and development, tourism to banking and investment. Soon, Mr. Kiem became Vice Chairman and one of the main shareholders of V.P. Bank, a joint stock partnership between the state and private sector. The company's turnover in 1995 equalled $32.5 million, just 5 years after being started in 1990 with $1 million.

Private enterprises are typically constrained by a shortage of capital, limited access to long-term capital, lack of land and buildings, uncertainty regarding the legal atmosphere in regard to business, a lack of business skills, and high taxes. "For Vietnamese business people," Mr. Kiem says, "raising capital is the greatest problem. Banks only make short-term loans at rates of more than 30 percent. We had savings to put into a business. Once it was up and running and there was cash flow, problems were easier to deal with."[2] Private enterprises are typically funded by idle savings or remittances, rather than capital loans from banks. However, authorities believe that local Vietnamese have hidden away between $1.83 billion and $2.74 billion, which they remain hesitant to invest in Vietnam for fear of possible nationalization, or changes in the legal framework. While foreign investors have brought in nearly $10 billion to Vietnam, domestic investment remains negligible. Part of this has been due to the fact that foreign investors enjoy preferential advantages that local investors do not, such as a ceiling of 25 percent on corporate profits, as opposed to the 40–50 percent tax rate for domestic manufacturers, and tax-free imports of raw materials, equipment, and vehicles. The Domestic Investment Law (DIL), recently submitted for consideration by the National Assembly, is intended to level the playing field and encourage local Vietnamese to invest in their economy.

---

[2] Kieran Cooke, "Vietnam Slips Uneasily Into Capitalism," *The Financial Times,* Jan. 13, 1995, pg. 25.

CHAPTER 10

PROJECT APPROVAL

AND START-UP

*C*ommercial decision-making in Vietnam is done through a system of clearly defined procedural steps—by the book. The bureaucratic hurdles are many and the job of winning final approval of a complex project, especially one involving the renovation or demolition of inhabited buildings, is nothing short of Sisyphean. To prepare yourself, approach the task accepting that the system, no matter how inefficient and irrational it might appear, won't be bent to make your life easier. If a situation requires that you have to accomplish Step Three before Step Two, you'll find that officials cannot, and will not, accommodate; *they* can't bend the system, and either can you...even if you scream and yell and stomp your feet and get red in the face.

What entities will be involved in the approval of a foreign project?

Whether or not a project will need national as well as local approval will always *depend*, even though there are magic numbers, like "under $30 million" can be approved locally and a "300-room hotel or less" doesn't need to go to Hanoi. The first consideration will be the dollar amount. The second will have to do with the sector in which the venture exists. And the third will be its impact on local residents, natural resources, and the surrounding community. (The requirement that all projects valued over $40 million must pass through the Prime Minister's office is one regulation that you can count on.) Thus, no matter how large the project is, every telecommunications project, for instance, will have to go to Hanoi for approval, as would an electric power plant. Because of its cross-province impact, a highway project will involve local entities as well as central. To renovate and expand an outdated office building, a firm would need to engage with the People's Committee at the provincial level, as it is responsible for handing out building permits, demolition permits, and coordinates the eviction of people from land to be developed. Los Angeles-based BBI Investment Group, Chartered, was granted the rights to develop a large piece of land in Da Nang only after the SCCI approved the project and the proposal was submitted to eleven different ministries for approval.

Projects that ostensibly fall under one ministry, such as a recent water project in Saigon, may ultimately require multilevel approval. Each entity will have varying degrees of authority over your project depending on its nature and industry. The People's Committee won't have the meddlesome authority over a manufacturing project that it would over a construction project, for example. The relevant ministry will have more control over a manufacturing project and less over a land development project.

Hence, the approval process for investment projects varies greatly depending on these criteria. Suffice to say, however, that a typical small-scale investment project would include the following players, if not many more:

- People's Committee of the city or of the province, which will play a role in evaluating the suitability of the project, arrange for land use, and ensure the necessary supply of utilities;

- Ministry of Finance, to which the venture must submit financial records;

- State Committee for Cooperation and Investment, which attends to all aspects of evaluating and licensing foreign projects;

- The Chief Architect's Office of the city, which evaluates building plans; it's not uncommon for it to lop off three or four floors of a planned structure, so start high—literally— and be willing to bargain;

- Any number of other government ministries, agencies, and commissions that wield responsibility and/or authority over the commercial area in which you are involved:

> Ministry of Trade and Tourism
> State Planning Commission
> State Bank of Vietnam
> The Ministry of Tourism
> The Ministry of Posts and Telecommunications

What are the regulatory steps in getting a project approved in Vietnam?

The size and business sector of your project will determine how it moves through the approval process. Projects to be evaluated are lumped into three groups, known as Groups A,B, and C. Group A projects are those of national interest, having a capital investment of $20 million or greater. The Vietnamese define areas of national interest as telecommunications, precious resources, transportation, real estate, pharmaceuticals, banking and finance, import/export trading, and tourism. A heavy industry project with a capital investment of $40 million or greater is automatically considered a Group A project, as is any other project having a capital investment of $30 million or more. Group A projects also include those that will significantly affect the environment or require a large land area. Group A project applications require the approval of the Prime Minister, who will base his decision on the recom-

mendations of the National Project Evaluation Council. This council is chaired by the State Planning Committee, and includes representatives from other ministries, state bodies, and local authorities involved in areas relevant to the project.

Group B includes heavy industry projects having a capital
investment of $30 million or greater, and projects in other sectors
having a capital investment of $20 million or more. Applications
for Group B projects also require approval of the Prime Minister,
who will base his decision on the recommendations of the State
Committee for Cooperation and Investment (SCCI) and the
Chairman of the National Project Evaluation Council. All other projects are in Group C, and are approved directly by the SCCI.

What is the role played by the State Commission for Cooperation and Investment?

The SCCI is required by law to process licenses within 3
months. That sounds well and good, but those 3 months must be
preceded by additional arduous months of obtaining approvals
necessary to compile the dossier of documents necessary to apply
to the SCCI for an investment license. Al DeMatteis, president of
DeMatteis Vietnam, bent my ear on the phone about this in Hanoi:

> Everybody thinks that you form a joint venture—they throw in
> the land, you throw in the financing, you get an SCCI
> license—and the land is yours to use. Well, it's not that way.
> It's a very complicated procedure to get a land-use permit.
> And the only way you're going to get a construction permit is
> when you get approval of the land-use permit. But the land-
> use permit goes to everybody and his mother-in-law to sign!

Both the Vietnamese and the foreign partner in the venture
must engage with four different departments to obtain approvals
before seeking SCCI go-ahead: the Chief Architect's Office, the
Urban Planning Institute, the Land and Housing Department, and
Construction Department. (This applies generally to the entire
country, but to Ho Chi Minh City specifically.)

Once the SCCI receives a properly prepared application for
a license, it must evaluate the project in terms of its necessity, location, the local partner, labor supply, and the assets possessed by

Project Approval Process

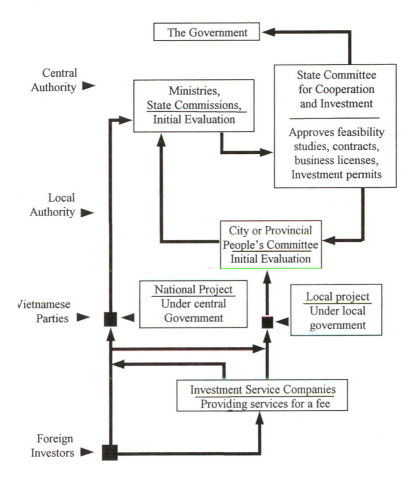

the local partner to succeed with the project. The SCCI then sends eight copies of the application to its main office in Hanoi, and normally two copies to the People's Committee with oversight of the project. With all of these approvals obtained, the foreigner can move on to obtaining a construction permit.

Will it be necessary to visit Hanoi to get a project approved?

"Ho Chi Minh City may have the right people and the right facilities," says a Bangkok-based businessman working in Vietnam. "But Hanoi still has the power and ultimately it's still very much up to them."

Any time that you are dealing with a state company, make sure to visit with its overseeing ministry in Hanoi, and not just its local office in Da Nang or Saigon or elsewhere. The people whom you deal with in Saigon—a manager or a director or an official—will perhaps claim to wield much more autonomy and authority than he or she really does, vis-à-vis people in Hanoi. Don't take their word for it when they say that "you don't need to see anybody in Hanoi." Check for yourself. "Ultimately you will have to deal with the ministry in charge in Hanoi," says Mark Mitchell of VATICO.

Much of dealing with Hanoi officials is a matter of corporate lobbying, relationship-building, and posturing. Anthony Foster, a Vietnam representative of the law firm Freshfields, has admonished incoming insurance companies that they need to lobby the Vietnamese government by buttressing their corporate image and reputation:

> The Finance Ministry is likely to look more favorably on applications from companies with a good reputation, based in countries which have invested heavily in Vietnam....Applicants may be wise to marshal support from whatever source they can, such as influential members of the Vietnamese community, diplomats from home, and customers with major ventures in Vietnam.[1]

---

[1] Anthony Foster. "Vietnam: The Orient Express—Vietnamese Market," Reuters' *Post Magazine,* January 12, 1995.)

Part of this process is meeting with skeptical officials who tend to be suspicious of foreign firms' intentions and, like bureaucrats anywhere, risk-averse. DeMatteis Vietnam has won two SCCI licenses, probably the only U.S. company that has done so, and it did this all in one year. I asked Mr. DeMatteis to explain his success. "You've got to present yourself properly to the government authorities. You have to let people know that you know what you are talking about," he said.

Will residents occupying land to be used need to be relocated and compensated by the venture partners?

The people evicted from land on which you want to build will have to be relocated, and the People's Committee will ask you to pay for their relocation. The fee isn't high per person, but it can add up if scores of people currently live there. "And the People's Committee is notorious," says a Japanese consultant to the hotel industry, "for not getting the people out." Months after Contech began construction on its office tower located next to the Metropole in Hanoi, the people who live there have not been evicted or compensated by the People's Committee, which was supposed to have done so. So the company moved ahead to demolish the existing structure anyway once they had obtained a demolition license. Indeed, Hanoi's own People's Committee recently had to scrap the relocation of 1,000 households at a cost of $20 million so it could renovate and rent 150 French-style villas in Hanoi because of difficulties relocating the current residents; if the People's Committee has such problems, a foreign investor can expect even greater problems in this regard.

The relocation process begins with the People's Committee surveying all affected residents. People are divided into three different groups based on the value of their homes. Residents can accept cash as compensation or demand that the joint venture provide a new house to be built for them. Most people take the cash because they can build their own home for a pittance relative to the cash amount forthcoming. There are 214 homes occupying the land upon which BBI Investment Group of Los Angeles wants to build, in Da Nang. The firm has offered to build additional homes, which are normally very small, at a reasonable cost.

Unfortunately, there is also a graveyard on the land and the People's Committee wants $50 per grave to move all remains to another site. Looking ahead, BBI consultant Stewart Stemple paints a worst-case scenario in which, because they are Confucians, East Asian tourists may not want to stay in the hotel because it will be built on burial grounds. Moreover, the Vietnamese are extremely sensitive about moving the graves of their ancestors, and the People's Committee has made it no secret, says Stemple, that the issue may be the most critical one that the project will encounter.

WORKING WITH VIETNAMESE LABOR

How productive is the Vietnamese worker, and in what sector of the economy do most work?

Of the 33 million Vietnamese workers and farmers (47 percent of the total population), only 10 percent of the country's workforce is employed in the state sector, including Party workers. The rest work in the non-state–owned sector, including agriculture collectives, private enterprise, and foreign ventures. Note that the private sector is made up mainly of *household* enterprises, which account for 84 percent of employment. They employ two to five people and are likely to remain very small and localized.

Though the number of state-sector workers is relatively small, Dr. Carolyn Gates, a fellow at the Institute of Southeast Asian Studies, has written that they "continue to occupy an elite position not only in the workforce, but also within the entire political economy." Add this to the perks of working in a state factory, like free medical care, and Vietnamese labor, as Dr. Gates says, "continues to be drawn towards—or chooses to remain—in the state sector by the value of state position, 'the desire for a pleasant life,' and the attraction of tangible benefits not readily available elsewhere." In fact, when the welfare component of a worker's wage, and nonmerit-based social and bonus funds are added up, nominal wages for state employees of $.50 per hour rise to as high as $10 an hour in many state enterprises. Moreover, as Dr. Gates says, "workers, who are paid for a 48-hour work

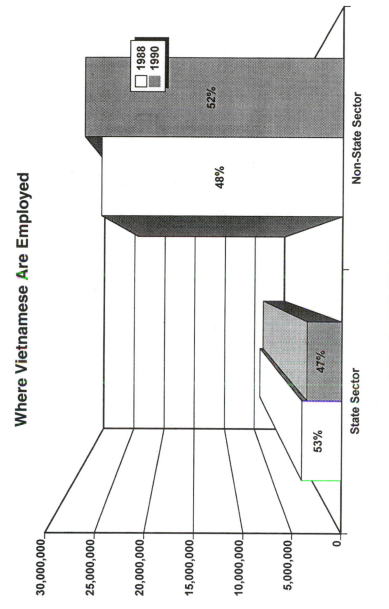

Where Vietnamese Are Employed

1988
1990

52%

48%

Non-State Sector

47%

53%

State Sector

30,000,000

25,000,000

20,000,000

15,000,000

10,000,000

5,000,000

0

Source: General Statistical Office.

week, may be working no more than a few hours a week because
of insufficient work or ineffective management."[2] Thus, in the
State sector, worker productivity and efficiency can be said to be
frightfully low.

State-owned enterprises (SOEs) have been shedding surplus
labor to the tune of 800,000 people over a 3-year period during
the early 1990s. The trend has been for unemployed state workers
to seek new jobs in the private sector, especially in the emerging
foreign sector. Foreign-invested enterprises employ 65,000
Vietnamese working fulltime and have already generated more
than $1 million in construction-related jobs.

Does a free labor market exist in Vietnam?

Basically yes, with the following caveat. Most young people
seek work in foreign-invested enterprises and private companies,
and thus, managers of SOEs have to constantly fight braindrain as
their staff leave for positions where wages are higher. For this reason, says Dr. Gates, "managements of SOEs are using legal and
extra-legal measures to discourage their best workers from seeking employment elsewhere, including transfers from one state job
to another....in general, state organizations use labor regulations to
restrict labor mobility." Thus, for a worker to change companies
can be fraught with official hassles, and considering the risk of loss
of perks, trained labor in the state sector doesn't migrate to growth
opportunities as readily as it should.

Can skilled workers and managers be recruited?

It's not hard to find people to hire, but it's very difficult to
find aggressive young people who possess even limited training,
let alone technical skills. A Canadian company representative
recently phoned his boss back in Canada and informed him that
he couldn't find a qualified Vietnamese manager after two years of
hunting for one. His angered boss replied: "You mean that out of

---

[2] Carolyn Gates. "Vietnam's Growth Constrained By Ineffective Management of
Labour." *The Straits Times* (Singapore) Jan. 5, 1995, pg. 27.)

74 million (highly qualified, highly educated, hard-working people) you haven't been able to find *one* qualified manager?" For this reason, you need to prepare—mentally and financially—to train people from scratch. One American lawyer we spoke to in Hanoi normally expects to get fifteen letters a day out of a secretary. In Vietnam, she says, she is lucky to get four, and her other Vietnamese employees think she's a slave driver. Motivation may also be lacking. The only suggestion this woman's Vietnamese staff has ever made to improve the functioning of the office was to give the employees another break...and they already get a 2-hour lunch!

Joint ventures and wholly foreign-owned firms can utilize the services of a government-run labor agency or advertise for staff. Fortunately, a government labor agency cannot require you to hire a person whom they recommend; in one case, all 700 people referred by a government labor agency to the New World Hotel were rejected. The hotel opted instead to advertise on its own, mainly through English-language schools, to find needed people.

The small corps of skilled people who can speak English are in acute demand by foreign offices, and these people know it. Often, they take a job and two weeks later start demanding more money, and move on if they don't get it. Foreign managers whom we spoke to claim to "know who these people are now" and refuse to hire them. The same has happened in China where firms have decided in many cases it's better to hire someone with no experience at all, and train them, rather than to hire an experienced job hopper.

One last point: take care that the people you hire aren't "being watched" by the government, or for that matter, are not politically active people. This may not sound very liberal-minded, but one company hired its own people and three days after they had signed them up with the local labor agency, the police showed up and informed them that they could not hire them because they "had criminal records" and "were political problems." The foreign firm dispatched its local partner to convince the local authorities that "there would be no political activities allowed at the joint venture," and the firm was allowed to keep the employees. This is not an isolated case.

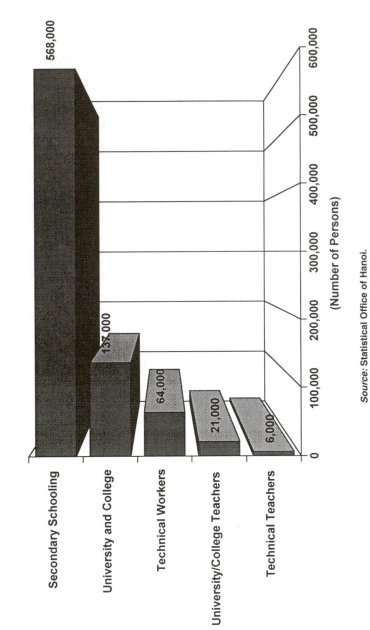

Number of Trained Vietnamese (1992)

(Number of Persons)

Secondary Schooling — 568,000
University and College — 137,000
Technical Workers — 64,000
University/College Teachers — 21,000
Technical Teachers — 6,000

Source: Statistical Office of Hanoi.

What worker rights—including minimum wage—are
guaranteed by Vietnam's labor laws?

Vietnam's Labor Law provides workers 1 day of rest per
work week, 12 holidays a year, the right to strike in extreme cases
after negotiations have broken down, and a 30-minute lunch period. Vietnam's minimum working age is 15 years and 13 for
apprentices. The minimum wage was recently lowered from $50
per month (6 days of work per week) to $35 per month in Saigon
and Hanoi, and $30 per month elsewhere, though one hears com-
plaints about some foreign ventures that pay less than these
amounts, taking advantage of the government's lax enforcement of
labor laws. However, expect to pay an office staff person between
$60 and $70 per month in salary; $100 a month is necessary to
keep someone who is competent.

Are Vietnamese workers unionized, and are they strike-prone?

One potential liability for foreign companies in the country
is the Vietnamese labor force, which has historically prided itself
on its solidarity and revolutionary strength. A certain degree of
unrest is permitted, where in other socialist regimes it might not
be. Institutionalized worker unions aren't obstreperous, but the
workers themselves can be very demanding of their rights, over
issues of wages, hours worked per week, disability compensation,
and control over the enterprise. When worker strikes in foreign
enterprises occur they are usually warranted. In one venture,
workers struck for 1.5 hours on Christmas Day and demanded a
year-end bonus of the equivalent of $9.50, a daily food allowance
of under $.10, $5.00 in monthly travel allowance, and two sets of
workclothes. In another case at a Saigon toy company, workers
demanded a reduction of their 16-hour working day, safety measures, and that their salaries be paid on time, citing that they had
been paid as late as 2 months in the past.

Large-scale strikes in foreign companies or state-owned
enterprises are presumed to be rare. In a foreign enterprise, workers have the right to form a labor union (and many have been
formed in joint ventures), though they are not known to be dis-
ruptive. In fact they are more of a social group than a collective
bargaining entity.

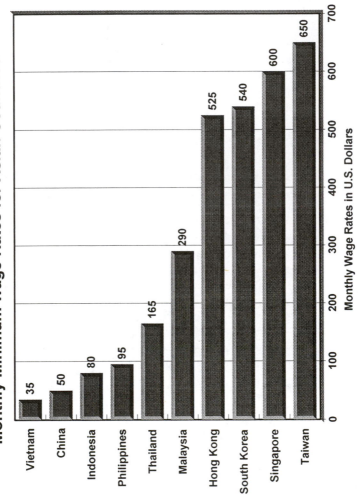

Monthly Minimum Wage Rates for Asian Countries

Vietnam — 35
China — 50
Indonesia — 80
Philippines — 95
Thailand — 165
Malaysia — 290
Hong Kong — 525
South Korea — 540
Singapore — 600
Taiwan — 650

Monthly Wage Rates in U.S. Dollars

Source: World Bank, Trends in Developing Countries.

Should Viet Kieu managers be hired to run a factory in Vietnam?

The Viet Kieu issue is a major one for a company starting up in Vietnam. American companies often choose Viet Kieu to head their organizations in the country, taking advantage of the fact that they speak the language and fit in culturally. But in many cases, the Viet Kieu cause problems because the Vietnamese don't necessarily like them. In the minds of many, they are traitors. An Australian management consulting company with an office in Hanoi conducts staff training and goes into companies to study what's going wrong in U.S.–Vietnam joint ventures. It claims that "nine times out of ten," the problem is that the American company has put Viet Kieus in to run the organization. While, on the one hand, the Vietnamese government wants the Viet Kieu to come back with their money and training, on the other, Vietnamese workers resent them and balk at their attemps to manage them.

Overseas Vietnamese often arrive in Vietnam sporting gaudy hairdos, flashy clothes, and gold watches. They visit their home towns, which they left after the war, to build a house and receive press adulation. Some are considered genuine, others are thought to be greedy. "I never met a Viet Kieu who considers himself Vietnamese," an Australian journalist who lives in Saigon told me. "I was meeting with a Viet Kieu who heads up an American company here and when I said I was Australian, he said 'Awh, you're from the same country I am.' That's the problem—especially among the French Viet Kieus—when they do come back, they look down on the Vietnamese, and are very arrogant sometimes, and they try to dissociate themselves from Vietnamese culture and the Vietnamese people."

TRANSFERRING

TECHNOLOGY

*V*ietnam desperately wants to "catch up" with the rest of Asia, which means acquiring the latest foreign technology and receiving intensive training. Accordingly, the government is trying to provide incentives for technology transfer. For foreign vendors of technology and training, Vietnam should be viewed as a potentially rich vein in one's overall Asia technology strategy. Why? First, there is a ravenous market for consumer electronics based on a population of over 74 million. Vietnam is strategically located in the center of Southeast Asia, where it can easily eke out an important niche in the division of labor among countries exporting electronics. Its work force is well trained relative to other developing countries in the region. And perhaps most importantly, the government has put in place a policy for improving its science and technology sector and pragmatically finding applications for existing information technologies. Moreover, the government seems far more open-minded and less threatened than China in opening up communication links that will allow Vietnamese intellectuals in scientific institutions, as well as ministries and industrial firms, to communicate directly with their foreign counterparts through e-mail and actively participate in international technology sharing over the Internet.

What is Vietnam's attitude toward Western technology?

Along with acquiring foreign exchange, technology and training are considered the most important contributions by foreigners to ventures in Vietnam. But Vietnam's approach to technology acquisition is fraught with contradiction and has underpinnings in its historical experience with foreign powers and their innovations. We will get to more of this later, but for now suffice it to say that Vietnam undervalues intellectual know-how, and this is reflected in its technology transfer regulations, which restrict its overall value in an investment contract. In short, they want state-of-the-art technology, but they don't want to pay for it. There is a great deal of emphasis on software development, yet the country's international copyright law does not yet sufficiently protect foreign software developers from having their software copied in Vietnam. During the U.S. Embargo of Vietnam, software programs could not legally be purchased from overseas and therefore they were pirated on a wide-scale basis. There are currently 45,000 computers running in Vietnam, most of which are operating on DOS-based or Windows software; virtually none of this software was legally purchased.

Vietnam's attitudes about Western technology are founded in its historical relationship with the technologically advanced West. Like China, Vietnamese culture is an agricultural one in which technological innovations traditionally took place in the open and were immediately made communal property. To imitate another's innovation was the highest compliment, while the selling of proprietary know-how was unknown. When the first American, Captain White, came ashore in Saigon in 1820 trying to sell the Vietnamese firearms, books, uniforms, and other merchandise, the young emperor, Ming Mang, offered only to sign a contract to purchase copies of uniforms, firearms, artillery, and books. Captain White turned his ship around and came home, having rejected any contract. The Vietnamese purchased a Western steamship in the 1830s, realizing that it was superior to their own sailing vessels, but did so for the purpose of later dismantling the steamship in a factory built for that purpose in an attempt to copy it; the blueprints for the steamship were, however, not acquired. Vietnamese architecture was traditionally influenced by China, but architects also imitated European characteristics such that you can see buildings in Hue with Western windows and other European elaborations. Early in the 1800s, the Vietnamese sent emissaries overseas to observe Western innovations, and many of these people were quick to note the technological superiority of Western countries. One of these emissaries, Phan Thanh Gian, was sent to Europe, Hong Kong, and Indonesia in 1863. He came back and wrote about the foreigners he had seen in one of his poems:

"Under heaven, everything is feasible for them
save only the matter of life and death."

Although Western countries were superior technologically, Vietnam never opened its borders to rampant borrowing or purchased their technology. And this is one of the contradictions in attitude that we continue to see today in Vietnam. On the one hand, Vietnam attempted to acquire key technologies for military purposes in order to protect its borders and secure its independence; on the other hand, the government of the country was also extremely sensitive to the incursion of Western culture and science entering the country through the acquisition of technology and ideas, because of its potential ill effects on traditional Confucian values and priorities. This was combined with an equally felt threat of foreign Christianity, which seemed to be part of the same package.

In short, Vietnam valued its independence more than modernization. Technology acquisition occurred strictly within the confines of court culture, rather than among the common people. As late as 1835, Vietnam had sent virtually no students abroad to learn about foreign industry or technology. The court had set up a so-called translation office to teach languages to its emissaries for the purpose of diplomatic missions. But the court sponsored no scientific investigations or experimentation, nor innovators or inventors, viewing the spread of Western knowledge into the country as more of a threat than a benefit. Even the trading of European goods was kept to a minimum and tightly managed by the court, restricted to elite luxury goods, which again remained in the confines of the court itself.

Nowadays, the government of Vietnam realizes that it is playing technological catch-up not only with Western countries but also with the newly industrialized economies of its own region. It will drive a hard bargain to acquire advanced technology at bargain prices, attempting to leverage access to its 74-million–person market to compel foreign countries to transfer their technology, much as China has done. Unfortunately for Vietnam, the market that they are leveraging is quite small, and by placing caps on the technological contribution contracts, they may find it hard to convince foreigners to release state-of-the-art technology at all.

What has been the evolution of science and technology activities in Vietnam?

Subsequent to the liberation of the North in 1954, Vietnam adapted the Soviet model for science and technology organization and research and development (R&D) institution building. R&D institutions and colleges were put under centralized administrative control of the government and placed under a fixed budget to conduct mainly theoretical research as opposed to technological innovation. A linkage between R&D institutes and enterprises producing goods never emerged. Many of the institutions conducting fundamental research enjoyed direct material support from both China and the Soviet Union. Like the R&D apparatus in these other countries, the organization of scientific endeavor in Vietnam was administrative in both a vertical and redundant manner.

At the central level, R&D was controlled by three different entities: the State Committee for Planning, the State Committee for Science, and the Ministry of Finance. Under these entities were ministries, national research centers, and ministries of education. Below these three entities was conducted the actual R&D. Under the ministries, R&D units might conduct specialized research for a state-owned enterprise under a certain ministry; R&D units under the control of national research centers and additional units within and under the large universities were controlled by the Ministry of Education. All of this R&D took place under the control of the central government, at that time under the ultimate rhetoric of the Council of Ministers. A similar system was mirrored at the city or provincial level. Thus, the city provincial committee for science and technology, the city or provincial committee for planning, or the city or provincial department of finance would have under its control a number of R&D units existing at the local level. Obviously, these units would fall under local as well as central control, and each R&D unit, whether at the central or local level, was prohibited, generally, from forging direct contacts with one another in a horizontal manner.

As in the Former Soviet Union, the Vietnam science and technology sector has gone through massive changes since the early 1980s. R&D institutions have been granted greater autonomy to pursue the research that they wish, their research has been expanded, and since 1986 the funding for these institutions has increasingly come from service contracts signed with ministries, enterprises, and educational institutions. Few R&D institutes are totally dependent on state funding. No longer are they dependent on ministries above them, nor as administratively separate from industry. Many have been amalgamated into larger entities along the lines of state-owned conglomerates of enterprises and even private firms. Individual scientists have formed private scientific consultancies, some institutes have privatized, and some laboratories have become bottom-line oriented service organizations.

Who conducts R&D in Vietnam?

Presently, there's still little R&D performed by business units in Vietnam. Obviously, this will change as R&D units privatize, but as of this writing most modern technology is purchased rather than developed indigenously There is still little attempt on the part of the government to implement a policy whereby enterprises themselves are asked to organize or fund technological innovation. The source of the technology in the mind of the Vietnamese government continues to be the foreign joint venture partner. Although there has been much debate in Vietnam about transferring R&D institutes to manufacturing enterprises, there are really three places where true R&D is happening. The first is R&D tech-

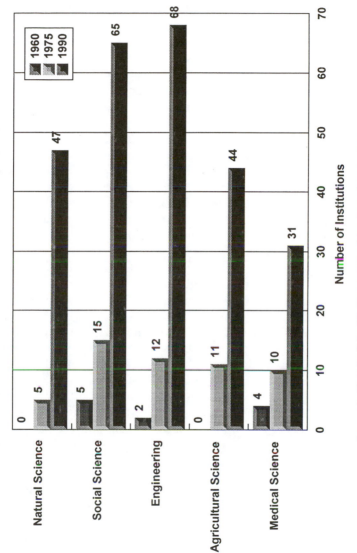

Number of Scientific Institutions in Vietnam

Number of Institutions

Source: Institute for Scientific Management, State Committee for Science.

nical units or laboratories under the aegis of a ministry or government agency; thus, an institute conducting research on textiles would be controlled by an associated ministry controlling textile manufacturers.

Second, a number of universities and higher education departments have the personnel, equipment, and resources to conduct specialized research. Most of these are located in Hanoi and Ho Chi Minh City. Third, there are a number of national R&D institutions with large-scale facilities that do not come under the aegis of any ministry and which conduct research on a contractual basis with enterprises and ministries. An example would be the National Center for Scientific Research (NCSR). Foreign companies will also want to engage with some of the new R&D entities that are taking form in Vietnam, including consultancy firms, technology "service centers," and other privatized R&D centers. Currently, Vietnam allocates 11.67 percent of its state budget for education (1990). About 35 percent of this figure is devoted to higher education and technical and vocational training.

A feasibility study is being conducted for a plan to build the country's first high-technology industrial zone (HTIZ) about ten miles outside Ho Chi Minh City, a 300-hectare project to be built at a cost of $90–100 million patterned on Taiwan's Hsin Chu technological park. Zone planners intend on attracting foreign manufacturing, R&D projects, and education and training projects to generate the development of new technologies emphasizing information software products, electronics, engineering design and graphic designs such as animated cartoons, tropical agriculture products, environment technologies, and advanced materials. The sight is adjacent to the Linh Trung Export Processing Zone, as well as the proposed location for a new national university.

What is IT 2000?

In 1993, the Ministry for Science, Technology and Environment, with the help of UNISYS and Matsui, conducted a strategic review of Vietnam's information technology development and produced a report called "IT 2000 Program," also known as "A Strategic Review of National Information Technology Development." UNISYS conducted and paid for the study in hopes of gaining access to information to further its own business plans

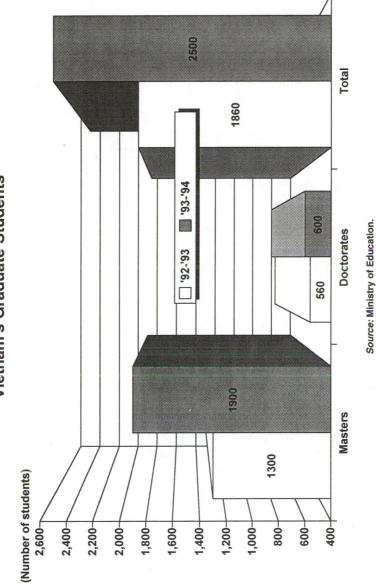

Vietnam's Graduate Students

(Number of students)

■ '92-'93   ■ '93-'94

Masters: 1900, 1300
Doctorates: 560, 600
Total: 2500, 1860

Source: Ministry of Education.

in Vietnam, though the ministry involved has side-stepped making any commitments to UNISYS to purchase the company's product or services, at least thus far.

Six months prior, Prime Minister Vo Van Kiet had issued a decree outlining Vietnam's national IT program, which aimed at generating "better diffusion and application of an existing advanced technology," as a UNIDO/UNDP report put it. The program emphasized developing information technology in each of its business sectors rather than limiting the development of such technologies to central ministries and public agencies. That is, information technology should be assimilated to enhance manufacturing and government administration, and generally support the country's modernization as a whole. The IT 2000 Program outlined specifics for a number of areas. It emphasized implementing faster data communication networks that could integrate the various ministries across the various sectors and locales of the country. It put the priority on computerization to collect and manage data to be used by management of enterprises in the energy sector, the transportation sector, and for making the postal and telecommunication services more efficient. It aimed to increase information technology education in secondary schools on up, as well as increasing training for the country's workforce. It emphasized self-reliance in developing an indigenous information technology industry based on the development of software, both for local and international markets. It emphasized information technology research in experimentation amongst key R&D institutions and universities, as well as the linking of Vietnamese information users to regional and international networks through "open systems" of information exchange, made possible by an active attempt to standardize computer hardware and software systems. The government even formed a national information technology board to span different government sectors. This board is chaired by the Minister for Science, Technology and Environment, and is served by a council that can be called the first national agency for Vietnam's IT development—the agency for the national program for information technology.

How does Vietnam define technology transfer?

The transfer of technological materials into Vietnam is covered and regulated by the Ministry of Science, Technology and the

Environment (MOSTE). In January of 1994 MOSTE issued a circular supplementing, but not precluding, existing regulations on technology transfers. The circular defines technology transfer as (1) the transfer of ownership or the right to use all types of industrial property, including inventions, industrial designs, and trademarks; (2) the transfer through the purchase, sale, or supply (with or without equipment) of technological know-how, technological projects and processes, preliminary designs and technical designs, formulae, drawings, graphs, diagrams, and charts, and other technological knowledge and expertise; and (3) the provision of a wide range of consultant or technical support services. Conventional machinery and materials is not considered technology, and therefore is not affected by the circular. So too, the direct selling and buying of trademark ownership and use rights is not considered technology transfer and is permitted without license or transfer of the associated industrial property.

Are there import restrictions on certain types of technology?

Foreign technology must meet certain standards before approval will be given to import. The technology must enhance production or efficiency, raise the quality of products or improve technological standards, or have the capability to develop new products. It cannot cause harm to the environment or be unsafe. It must make rational and appropriate use of energy, national resources, and manpower.

What government agency approves technology transfer arrangements?

MOSTE must approve all technology transfers contracts and subsequent amendments. MOSTE retains authority over all contracts exceeding U.S.$1 million in value (the source of funding notwithstanding), contracts financed by the Vietnam State Treasury and exceeding U.S.$500,000, contracts impacting national security or defence, and contracts having other exceptional ramifications. MOSTE has delegated approval authority in certain categories, but it still retains approval process control. Contracts valued at less than the above monetary limits and requirements may be dealt with by other ministries or even local governments.

The State Committee for Cooperation and Investment (SCCI) plays an important role in the overseeing and designation of investment-related technology transfer contracts. When applying to the SCCI for an investment license, a copy of the technology transfer contract must be included. The SCCI then determines the value of each technology to establish each party's contribution to legal capital. Thus, the SCCI has a hand in setting the amount of profit earned by each party in a joint venture.

In the event that the technology does not live up to the promises in the contract, adjustments can be made to the royalty rate retroactively. In some cases, revaluation of the legal capital contributions of the joint venture parties will be made.

What are the contractual requirements in a typical technology transfer deal?

Under the terms and conditions specified by the technology transfer circular, you must supply the following information in a technology transfer contract:

1. The identities of all parties and representatives involved.

2. A section defining terms.

3. A statement giving the purpose of the technology transfer.

4. The technology and or services to be transferred, with information on the training program offered and the value of the technology transferred.

5. Provisions outlining the descriptions of the industrial property and the rights to be legally protected.

6. The scheduled time and place for delivery of the technology provided.

7. Outline of the steps taken for efficiency and results, including indemnities, warranties, and specific representations from the technology transferer, in regard to third party and product liability issues.

8. Payment and price terms.

9. Term of the contract.

10. Applicable law provisions and dispute resolution stipulations.

The circular leaves it up to the parties involved to agree upon price and payment terms, on the basis of mutual benefit, but stipulates that the final price should be based upon prices of similar technology in international markets.

What stipulations cannot be written in a technology contract?

There are certain provisions not allowed to be written into a technology transfer contract, and they are as follows:

1. So-called *tie-in* provisions, whereby the transferee is compelled to buy items like raw materials and labor from the transferer, except where proof can be provided that the quality of the finished product requires this and proof that they cannot be purchased elsewhere at lower cost.

2. Restrictions on sales area, price, or quantity of production for products produced with the technology transferred. No restrictions to be made in particular on the export markets or sublicenses for such products.

3. Provisions restricting the transferee from R&D of the technology transferred or to receive similar technology from other sources.

4. Provisions requiring use of suppliers' sales agents except where the transferee can do this more efficiently.

5. Provisions restricting the use, by the transferee, of technology after the expiration of the contract (contracts are limited to a maximum of 7 years) or after the industrial property rights contained in the contract have expired.

6. Provisions requiring royalty payments from the transferee based upon product sales even before the transferee has sold any products.

Note, however, that the relevant authority may, in special circumstances, allow any of these prohibited provisions to be included in a technology transfer contract.

What restrictions are placed on royalties paid to suppliers of technology?

Royalty rates and types of payments will vary depending on several factors. In a direct technology license where royalties are based upon the net selling price, the royalty charged by the licensee agreement can be *no greater than 5 percent* of the net selling price. This is only if the technology is deemed to be "of considerable significance to economic development or the products are of high quality and result in high profitability and a high percentage of the products are exported," states the circular.

Normally though, royalty rates would be limited to 3 percent for patents, know-how, and other proprietary technology. The rate for licensed trademarks has a maximum of 2 percent. Net selling price, as stipulated in the circular, is calculated after the deduction of the cost of packaging, transportation, and indirect taxes, as well as the CIF portion and import taxes on all parts used in the finished product from foreign sources or supplied by a joint venture party. If training, services, and consulting are included with the technology transfer, special considerations may be applied to pricing and payments. These services must be documented by a breakdown of total cost and hours of each consultant and trainer involved.

If the technology transfer is included in the capital investment, or is under a business cooperation contract, then profits may only be disbursed in relation to the portion that the technology contributes to the objectives stated in the technology contract. Importantly, in this scenario the value attributed to the technology transferred cannot be greater than 3–8 percent of *the total invested capital,* exceeding the capitalized land rights and compensation for moving inhabitants. These percentages may be adjusted (with specific approval) in cases where the technology is very sophisticated or the project has small endowment capital.

The circular tries to protect minority Vietnamese interest holders in joint ventures by giving them veto power over technology contract contents and valuation where they hold less than 50 percent interest in the venture.

Subject to negotiation, foreign investors are "encouraged" by the circular to base their royalty calculation upon post-tax net profit (thereby reducing the royalty). Although not required, technology transferers are additionally encouraged to defer royalty payments until after the joint venture technology transferee achieves a positive cash flow.

How do you plug into Vietnam's science and technology/information technology institutions?

I've already mentioned the three key players in Vietnam's R&D apparatus: ministry-controlled R&D units, universities, and national R&D institutions. The largest scientific institution in Vietnam is the National Science Center, with the dragon's share of its resources in Hanoi, but with a branch office in Ho Chi Minh City. It survives by fulfilling contracts from state-owned enterprises and other customers as well as receiving some government funding to cover salaries. As with other Vietnamese R&D institutions, government funding has decreased to the point where the survival of the institute has come into question. The country's flagship high-tech research center, created in 1987, is the National Institute of Technology, which enjoys the status of having the best-equipped laboratories in the country in the areas of electronics and telecommunications as well as a large annual budget. For those of you interested in computing, I suggest visiting the computer center of the Informatics Faculty of Hanoi Polytechnic University and the Department of Computer Science at the Ho Chi Minh City Polytechnic University. Second, the Institute of Information Technology, which is part of the National Center for Scientific Research, is home to 150 microcomputers, two mini-computers, and relatively state-of-the-art data communications equipment. They conduct scientific and technological activities in both the North and the South. One of the software programs developed by the Institute is used in over forty countries, and through its links with the Australian National University it is a server to the worldwide Internet.

Entities in each of these categories would be stops for foreign technology hunters or vendors of technology. Some of the key organizations are listed below. In the field of information technology, the major player is the Union of Electronics Industries under the Ministry of Heavy Industry, which is a conglomeration of the major industrial interests involved in the sector and wields great influence in the formulation of IT policy by the ministry that oversees it—the Ministry of Heavy Industry. Contact with any of these entities is relatively easy to make and should be done so directly rather than through the SCCI or other government investment agency.

GOVERNMENT INSTITUTIONS INVOLVED IN SCIENCE AND TECHNOLOGY

Department of Technology Promotion, Ministry of Science, Technology, and Environment

Institute of Science Management, Ministry of Science, Technology, and Environment

Central Data Processing Center, General Statistical Office

Science, Technology, and International Cooperation Department of the Vietnam Post and Telecom Services

Vietnam Data Communications Company (VDC) of the Vietnam Post and Telecom Services (DGPT)

Industrial Department of the Vietnam Post and Telecom Services (DGPT)

Ministry of Finance

Center for Informatics, State Bank of Vietnam

Center for Scientific and Technological Information (CESTI), Committee for Science and Technology of Ho Chi Minh City

Vietnam Trade Information Center, Ministry of Commerce

Committee for Science and Technology of Ho Chi Minh City

Industrial Firms Involved with Information Technology

Union of Electronics Industries (the VEIC Companies):

   Vietnam Electronics and Informatics Corporation, Hanoi

GenPacific (Ho Chi Minh City)

Veittronics Tan Binh (Ho Chi Minh City)

Viettronics Thu Duc (Ho Chi Minh City)

Viettronics Bien Hoa (Ho Chi Minh City)

Computer, Communication, Control, Inc., Hanoi

Hanel (Hanoi Electronics Corporation)

The Company for Financing and Promoting Technology, Hanoi

CMT (Vietnam Computer Company 2), Ho Chi Minh City

Seatic, Ho Chi Minh City

Lotus Communications, Ho Chi Minh City

Scitec (The Scientific and Technological Cooperation Company), Ho Chi Minh City

R&D and Educational Institutions

Institute of Information Technology

Center for Applied Mathematics and Informatics, Ho Chi Minh City Branch of the National Center for Scientific Research

Hanoi University

Hanoi Polytechnic University

The Ho Chi Minh City Polytechnic University

Lotus College of Information Technology and Management

Institute for Economic Research (IER) of Ho Chi Minh City

Center for Natural Resources Management and Environmental Studies, Hanoi University

Institute for Southeast Asian Studies

Is Vietnam on the Internet?

Vietnamese can communicate with the Internet through three different modes. The Institute of Information Technology functions as the national nexus for linking via modem to the Internet. Through this mode Vietnamese e-mail messages are stored at the Institute and then transferred to the Internet on a weekly or biweekly basis via the Australian National University. Thus, one cannot say that Vietnamese enjoy on-line service to the Internet as of this writing. The other two modes include call-up connection through a modem to a server in Hong Kong, Singapore, or elsewhere and a subscription service that permits interactive communication on the Internet called VIETPAC (Vietnam's Packet Switch Data Network), a joint venture between Vietnam's GDPT (the general directorate of post telecommunications) and the Australian Telstra. Observers predict a great expansion of the numbers of Vietnamese using the Internet because computers can be purchased for $600–700 with only a 2–3 percent import duty.

What is the status of copyright protection in Vietnam?

Foreign publications must be copyrighted in Vietnam within 30 days of being published outside the country for copyright law to apply. Although foreign books and movies formally published and shown in Vietnam are few, the photocopying of books and documents is rampant. Sally Higgins, a partner with BDT & Associates in Hanoi instructed me to visit Trang Tien Street in central Hanoi to pick up copies of recent U.N. reports and legal briefs regarding Vietnam's investment laws and development policies. As I stopped at one of the book stalls set up on the corner and made my desires known, the bookseller dispatched an assistant to run across the street and into a building from where he emerged 5 minutes later with a bundle of nicely copied and bound reports produced by international organizations and law firms from around the world. These reports were commissioned by the Vietnamese government as recently as 2 weeks before they appeared on the street for sale at a price of $5 to $10. Photocopied translations of computer manuals are easily obtainable as well.

Software piracy is rampant. In 1995, there are roughly 50,000 PCs in the country. All of them are running on DOS, Windows, WordPerfect, FoxPro, and Novell Netware. As already mentioned, not one of these packages is paid for. In fact, it was illegal to pay for any of them under the embargo. Up until February 1994, when the embargo was lifted, the Vietnamese had to steal software . . . so why stop now? Given Vietnam's national priority to develop its information technology industry this is one area where the government needs to act swiftly. "How do you develop an information technology industry," asks IBM's William Howell, "if you don't protect the product of that investment?"

Has Vietnam made provisions for trademark protection?

Vietnam provides for trademark registration. Many conditions apply, though they are much the same in the United States and Australia. If your product is registered there, it's likely it can be registered in Vietnam as well. One interesting difference in Vietnam is that brand names must not be offensive to socialist morality.

Registration starts with submitting an application to the National Office for Inventions, which is attached to the State Committee for Science and Technology, or through the Madrid Agreement, of which Vietnam is a member, and which can register trademarks internationally. To avoid lengthy delays the application has to be prepared in the proper form. It may be prudent to hire a lawyer to do this correctly. If the form is prepared properly, the Office of Inventions should approve or deny your application within 6 months. Your trademark will be protected for 10 years, extendable for 10 more at the end of each period. If, within 5 years, you have not used your trademark, it may be forfeited and you will lose your protection, unless you can give good cause for not doing so. If your business ceases to exist or continue its activities, you may lose your trademark protection if there is no legal successor to the trademark.

FINANCING, TAXES, AND DISPUTES

With all the investment that's taking place in Vietnam, one would expect the banking business to be booming. Although about thirty foreign banks have representative offices in Vietnam, nine have branches, and twenty more have applications pending with the State Bank, foreign banks aren't really doing much. Actually, some say that Vietnam is beginning to look "over-banked." The absence of banking and mortgage laws makes medium- and long-term loans too risky to undertake at this point. Other complaints include a minimum capitalization requirement of U.S.$15 million, a turnover tax of 25 percent, and a tax on loans provided by foreign banks of 30 percent, all of which are higher than you'll find in most countries. As a result of all these impediments, banks have stayed away from investment projects and are concentrating their efforts on trade financing, though it doesn't look nearly as good on the books. In fact, margins are very small in this competitive market right now, and a few banks claim to have lost money in the first year or so.

What is Vietnam's banking sector like?

Vietnam's banking sector has expanded greatly in the early 1990s. The key players are four state-owned banks, a slew of foreign-owned bank branches, some joint venture banks, and a large number of share-holding banks with a number of varying ownership structures. The four state-controlled banks include the Industrial and Commercial Bank, the Vietnam Bank for Agriculture, the Foreign Trade Bank (also known as VietcomBank), and the Bank for Investment and Development. Commercial banks tend to operate under very thin profit margins. They are heavily taxed by the government. They're in a difficult position to collateralize loans, given the control of land and assets by the State. And finally, because of a general lack of noncash transactions made in the economy, revenue earned for performing bank services has traditionally been low.

Vietnam's centralized banking system has not yet shed its socialist role of serving as a clearinghouse of funds for financing the State sector. Even credit for financing imports is hard for Vietnamese enterprises to come by, especially private enterprises. With credit scarce and costly, combined with the propensity of new businesses outside the State sector to want to hide their income from authorities, many proprietors avoid Vietnam's banks altogether, depriving the economy of much-needed revenue. In a 1994 survey of small- and medium-sized enterprises in Vietnam, the Central Institute for Economic Development Research found that half of the 120 businesses interviewed in Dong Hai, the business center near Saigon, did not deposit money in the bank, and did not use bank transaction services. Only 25 percent said that they did. Most companies indicated that bank credit is short-term (from 3–6 months in duration), and nearly 40 percent of them indicated that interest rates charged by banks for short-term credit was exorbitant. The government is only now working on a banking law, and the State Bank issued a regulation in the first quarter of 1994 that permits Vietnamese banks to guarantee foreign loan capital. By putting this guarantee in the place of a collateral or mortgage system, the government hopes to win the confidence of foreign banks, which have been very reluctant to lend money. State bank figures show that combined loans among foreign banks amount to only about U.S.$1 million and most of them are short-term loans. Bankers say they are hesitant to lend to state-run or even private Vietnamese companies whose accounts are anything but clear, and where recourse to collateral has not yet been tested. However, some banks are lending against nonproperty assets such as company equipment, and using notarized loan documents against property to get around the lack of a collateral system. Only time will tell whether these schemes are workable, but most bankers appropriately have a long-term view to business in Vietnam. But even under a better banking environment in the future, Vietnam will still be a tough market for foreign bankers due to competition from other foreign banks and from an improving local banking sector.

Four state-owned Vietnamese banks hold full foreign exchange licenses. They are:

Vietnam Bank for Agriculture

VietcomBank

Vietnam Bank for Investment and Development (VID)

Industrial and Commercial Bank of Vietnam

In addition, seven joint-stock banks with foreign exchange holdings have been licensed; their capital is in the form of shares and they appear to be active in offering lending services.

The following Vietnamese banks lend to Vietnamese enterprises:

The Asia Commercial Bank (Asiabank)

The Eastern Asia Bank

The Maritime Commercial Stock Bank (Maritimebank)

The Saigon Bank for Industry and Trade (Saigonbank)

The Viet Hoa Commercial Joint-Stock Bank (Viet Hoa Bank)

The Vietnam Export-Import Bank (Eximbank)

The Vietnam Joint-Stock Commercial Bank for Private Enterprises (VP Bank)

What is the status of Vietnam's capital markets?

Vietnam's capital markets are in a formative stage. Plans to issue international bonds are in the works with a $200 million, 5-year issue currently seeking an international underwriter. Vietnam has only won a single syndicated loan, a $100 million issue for the State Bank of Vietnam put together by the Thai Exim Bank and Thai Military Bank in June 1994. Vietnam's government plans to open a stock exchange in 1995, but that's doubtful. Given the paucity of state firms that operate in the black and the troubles arising from initial privatization attempts, many predict that such an exchange will not be a reality until the turn of the century. At this time, foreigners cannot buy stock in Vietnamese companies, though locals can buy shares in the very few joint stock companies that have been taken public (as of this writing, there are only two). The average dividend yields of these stocks have been remarkable, however, at over 200 percent.

Joint-stock companies are owned by the state, the firm's employees, and local investors, with numerous Vietnam investment funds having been set up for the purpose of raising capital for investment in promising projects. The problem has not been raising money, but finding the promising projects. Unlike in China, the country features a tiny and underdeveloped industrial economy; whereas in China, one can locate 250 automobile factories to consider investing in, you would find only two in Vietnam, and both have already linked up with foreign joint venture partners to raise capital. Currently, so-called Vietnam funds have raised $70–100 million but haven't been able to invest a fraction of that in the country. One of the most promising funds—the Frontier Fund— is managed by a *doi moi* architect, Nguyen Xuan Oahn, whose office is in a gleaming white refurbished French villa on a tree-lined street in the middle of Saigon. I went by to see him one morning just after he had returned from the United States, where he had been promoting investment opportunities to American business executives. The Frontier Fund started with only $7 million, but it invested it in projects and developed a track record with which it was able to attract another $50 million in the United States; Oahn thinks it can attract another $50 million after that. He criticized many of the other funds because they don't take any risks; they don't bite the bullet and invest because few firms meet their stringent criteria. Up until the time of this writing, the Vietnam Fund, one of the first funds, had only invested about $500,000 of the 50-odd million dollars that had been collected. "The funds are having a hard time investing because the criteria is too strict," says Andrew Homan of *Vietnam Investment Review*. "They want 30-percent returns. And they've got to be out in 5 years."

TAXATION IN VIETNAM

What is the corporate tax rate in Vietnam?

Business operations are subject to numerous complex Vietnamese tax laws and levies. Many of these taxes will be negotiated by foreign investors in a business venture and government entities. Petition the SCCI for approval of the tax treatment you want your project to receive. If the SCCI approves a petition for priority status, the terms will be set forth in the project's investment license.

The following taxes will likely apply to your project and its operation.

THE PROFITS TAX. All foreign parties to business cooperation contracts, joint ventures, BOT companies, and foreign investment companies are subject to profit taxes. The profit tax rates for these entities are generally between 10 and 25 percent, but the standard is 25 percent. A 20-percent tax rate can be requested if the project embodies at least two of the following characteristics:

- employs more than 500 people;
- utilizes advanced technology; and
- has at least U.S.$10 million invested.

You can apply for a 15 percent profit tax if your project is:

- an infrastructure project;
- exploits natural resources (except oil, gas, or rare and precious natural resources);

- is involved in "heavy industry" (i.e., cement, mechanical engineering, metallurgy, or important chemical substances); or
- is a joint venture agreeing to transfer its equity to the Vietnamese party.

You can apply for a 10 percent profit tax if your project is:

- a project of "special importance";
- is involved in afforestation; or
- deals with infrastructure projects in areas of difficult socioeconomic or natural conditions.

The new ordinance limits the sundry concessionary rates to 5–7 years for the 20 percent and 15 percent reduction rates, and 3–10 years for the 10 percent rate.

Does Vietnam offer "tax holidays"?

Should your project fall into one or more of the above tax rate categories, it may be eligible for the following tax holidays.

Tax Rate	Holiday Duration	Secondary Rate	Duration
25 percent	1 year	50 percent reduction	up to 2 years
20 percent	2 years	50 percent reduction	up to 3 years
15 percent	2 years	50 percent reduction	up to 4 years
10 percent	4 years	50 percent reduction	up to 4 years

Profit reinvestment can also help reduce tax liability for a project. Should the foreign partner or project reinvest its profits for at least 3 years, that portion of the profit tax may be refunded, under the condition that the foreign party has paid in full its original legal capital contribution. At the end of the project, these reinvested profits may ultimately be repatriated without being subject to any withholding tax.

THE TURNOVER TAX. This tax is assessed upon the gross turnover of all businesses in Vietnam and applies to the sale of goods and services within Vietnam. Goods sold overseas are exempt. The turnover tax rate is generally between 1 and 10 percent, and there are few exemptions, reductions, or holidays. Though easy to overlook, the turnover tax could become a significant part of your tax considerations. In the case of "special services" (turnover of clubs, agencies, or lotteries) the tax rate is between 15 percent and 40 percent.

SPECIAL TAX. Special taxes are levied on certain luxury items such as cigarettes and alcohol. This tax rate ranges from 52–70 percent on cigarettes and 75–90 percent on alcohol. As in the case of cigarettes and alcohol, when the tax is levied on particular products, the turnover tax is not applicable.

WITHHOLDING TAX. When a foreign investor's contributing capital is in excess of U.S.$10 million, the withholding tax is 5 percent. The less the amount of invested capital, the higher the tax, up to 10 percent.

NATURAL RESOURCES TAX. A tax rate of 1–15 percent is levied on the exploitation of Vietnam's natural resources. The definition "natural resources" is extended to oil, gas, minerals, precious stones, forestry products, and fish. The rate will be set according to the type of natural resource and the tax treatment of the venture.

What is the tax rate on income earned by foreigners working in Vietnam?

Personal income tax laws are not yet well defined in Vietnam. Expats living in the country as American citizens are being asked to pay a ridiculous tax rate of 50 percent if their income is over $700 per month. And the tax is on world income! An expat working in Vietnam for more than 183 days over a 12-month period is taxed according to the schedule below:

If your monthly salary is . . .	Your income tax rate is . . .
Under 5 million (*dong*)	0 percent
5 million to 11,999,999 (*dong*)	10 percent less 500 (*dong*)
12 million to 29,999,999 (*dong*)	20 percent less 1,700 (*dong*)
30 million to 39,999,999 (*dong*)	30 percent less 4,700 (*dong*)
40 million to 69,999,999 (*dong*)	40 percent less 9,700 (*dong*)
Greater than 70 million (*dong*)	50 percent less 16,700 (*dong*)

Note: 70 million dong equals roughly $65.

Expats residing in Vietnam for more than 30 days but less than 183 days per year are subject to a flat 10 percent tax rate on earned income. Income must be reported and taxes paid monthly. Expats must present all of their previous income tax receipts before leaving Vietnam, though it is unclear whether this means *permanently* leaving Vietnam, or for any business trip. As with all of these regulations, what really happens will be governed by how they are interpreted and applied.

WHY SOME INVESTMENT PROJECTS FAIL

A disturbing headline appeared at the end of 1993. Out of the first 720 foreign-invested projects contracted in Vietnam, over 100 of them (worth $567 million) were found to have dissolved or revoked by the end of that year. And fifty others were in jeopardy. According to the SCCI, 60 percent of the Vietnam-foreign projects that fail do so because of financial shortfalls, which normally occur between the time that the project is licensed and the time that the license expires. In short, the foreign broker of the deal is unable to sell the investment back home. As an SCCI official recently told reporter Andy Soloman of the *Vietnam Economic Times,* "These people are mostly opportunists and brokers, and these problems occur mostly in the field of hotels, services, and smaller projects."

In other cases, the SCCI has revoked a venture's investment license because the venture was not performing its stated purpose, a right it reserves under Vietnam's regulations. In the most famous case, the so-called International Club, a joint venture between Hanoi Tourist and Hong Kong's Cristal Centre (Asia) Ltd, was licensed to open a hotel in Hanoi, but stopped short by operating only a social club. The club featured a swimming pool, restaurant, and bar, but, as one expat recalled, "It was just a total meat market, filled with foreign dignitaries." It happens that the proprietors were operating a brothel, and the government stepped in to dissolve it after 1 year of operation. Another joint venture hotel set up with Asian money in Saigon was closed down for the same reason. At the time, these closures were seen as examples of the government reneging on foreign investment licenses. But these investors were operating in total violation of their licenses. In yet other instances, project failure has been due to the inability of the local People's Committee to successfully evict and relocate residents occupying land to be used by the venture.

How are commercial disputes settled between Vietnamese and foreign companies?

Business disputes can be resolved in one of two ways in Vietnam. The first is through litigation in so-called economic courts, which are part of the Supreme People's Court at the central level, and the People's Courts at the local level. The second method is through arbitration by the Vietnam International Arbitration Center (VIAC), which functions under the rubric of the Vietnamese Chamber of Commerce and Industry. Another method to arbitrate a case is through the Economic Arbitration Body, which is controlled by the Ministry of Justice, the People's Committees, and Justice Departments in both provinces and cities.

The challenge will not be getting your case heard, but in collecting awards after successfully winning an arbitration. Foreign companies often desire to add a clause into their contracts providing for foreign arbitration should a commercial dispute arise, even though Vietnam has not become a signatory to the 1958 convention for the recognition of foreign arbitration awards. Moreover, chances are low that an award rendered in a foreign arbitration would be honored.

Will these Saigon women ever own the consumer goods that
Western companies want to sell them?

Point-of-sale promotion of foreign brands, including placards, free
giveaways, and hired touts, greets Vietnamese shoppers everywhere.

A photoshoot for Vietnam Airlines' new brochure, produced by Gerald Herman, an American who set up Lotus Communications in Saigon in 1992.

Earlybirds snatched up the French villas dotting Saigon and Hanoi, which they transform into luxurious offices.

An ostensibly authorized Xerox agent open for business in Hanoi.

One of the most successful foreign ventures in Vietnam, the Tiger Beer brewery is located next to a Shell station in downtown Saigon.

A row of decaying *cyclos* (short for the French *cyclo-pousse*) sit outside a new Toyota dealership in Saigon, seeming to comprehend their uncertain future.

"If you leave Hanoi for a week and return," says an expat, "something new will have gone up on the highway to the airport," which is a choked artery at most times of the day.

With 3 phones per 1,000 citizens, Vietnam's telecommunication system is an obstacle to growth. Due to the U.S. embargo, European suppliers lead in bringing the country online.

Many urban poor hail from the countryside, coming to the city to make a better life by selling lottery tickets, cutting hair, or running curbside cafes.

Homeless, often hungry...but happy to have their picture taken and shout "Hello!" to an inquisitive
Westerner.

The Apocalypse Now nightclub in Saigon was one of the first to cater to the foreign business and diplomatic crowd.

Expats complain there's nothing to do in Hanoi for recreation, but this local athletic club sponsors the Hanoi Tennis Open and provides inexpensive training in martial arts.

For Americans over 35, the 1975 helicopter evacuation from the rooftop of the U.S. embassy in Saigon is a deeply etched memory. The building was returned to the U.S. in 1994.

Standing guard at Ho Chi Minh's Mausoleum, where Vietnam's embalmed forefather lies in a glass sarcophagus, though he explicitly requested to be cremated.

Housed in the former U.S. Information Service building, the War Crimes Museum in Saigon features U.S. artillery and armored vehicles as well as horrific photographs (mostly from Western sources).

Riding in a *cyclo*, the author experiences the local adage: "If it has wheels, it's on the road in Hanoi and Saigon."

The infamous "Hanoi Hilton" where American POWs—
mostly captured pilots—were imprisoned, is soon to be
razed to make room for a five-star foreign hotel.

PART FOUR

Working with the Vietnamese

Relationships are everything in Vietnam.

MARK GILLIN,
CHIEF REPRESENTATIVE, MBF INDOCHINA, LTD.

It's a cutthroat and often unscrupulous atmosphere. It's a carpetbagger country out there with a cowboy economy.

AN EXASPERATED AUSTRALIAN BUSINESSMAN

VIETNAM'S

BUSINESS CULTURE

A more subtle obstacle to doing business with the Vietnamese is that of bridging the cultural differences which, if not understood and managed, can work to separate us from them. It's no secret in Vietnam that the commercial mentality of the Americans is perhaps not suited to that of the Vietnamese. The Vietnamese potential partner will want to sit down with you and have tea, and serve you shrimp. Then they might want to take you out for dinner and dancing. Meanwhile, the American wants to talk business immediately because his or her flight leaves in 14 hours. During discussions the Vietnamese want to talk about a number of areas of mutual interest whereas the American mentality is "let's do a deal." American lawyers in the employ of large U.S. firms want to get everything checked and agreements drawn up as fast as possible, while the Vietnamese side is never quite sure if what they agree to today will be something they can agree to tomorrow, given how fast regulations change. As in any Asian country, you're doing deals through relationships, and Americans often lack the patience to build those relationships, over months, to forge the deal that they want to ink today. Meanwhile, the Vietnamese are dilatory and extremely cautious, in part because they are not well acquainted with the concepts and expectations of Western-style business intercourse.

How do the Vietnamese differ culturally from other Asian groups?

The Vietnamese aren't like the Japanese or the Chinese in prizing harmony and protecting face and personal honor. They don't operate with all of the cultural limitations that the Japanese do. They don't have to bow. They don't have to exchange business cards with two hands. At the dinner table, manners aren't formal. They're individualistic where most Asians are group-oriented; they're openly aggressive where other Asians might be more passively aggressive; they can be forthright and rancorous while most Asians are implicit in expression and afraid of giving offense.

But the Vietnamese *are* formal people in that they do expect you to behave in an appropriate manner. Though they are quite flexible and forgiving when it comes to relations with non-Vietnamese, you are expected to be polite and elegant and command respect. That's the ticket—*command respect*, without being domineering or patronizing. If you don't show them respect, they will certainly not want to do business with you. They will accept Western training and accept the fact that you want to run the show, especially within the areas of your expertise. But outside of those areas, watch that you do not talk down to them because you will not be respected in return. Unlike the Japanese, who will bow to you and think to themselves what a jerk you are, the Vietnamese will tell you directly: "You're a jerk," and they won't do business with you anymore. So you have to be on your best behavior, and understand the important aspects of the culture before entering into relations with the Vietnamese, such as the importance of the family and personal relationships.

What are some of the most important aspects of Vietnamese culture and how will these affect business relations with foreigners?

Undoubtedly, the most salient feature of Vietnamese society is the emphasis placed on the family and village. With few exceptions, Vietnamese people value strong family ties. A person's sense of identity is derived from his or her position in the family, which is reflected in the language by the myriad of titles used to address different relatives. As a country, Vietnam is actually a conglomeration of villages that were once associated with clans. In spite of the urbanization that has taken place, the village-oriented psychology of the Vietnamese people remains. Family values take precedence over all other priorities. When you do business with people in Vietnam make sure that you talk about their family, as well as yours. Ask them about their family members and tell them about yours. Bring pictures of your family if you can. When you give gifts, give them to their children and to their spouses. In the South, you will meet with people who have family living in the United States. Take the opportunity to make conversation about where they live and what they do in the States. As relations progress and become closer, gifts for children or other members of the family are not uncommon. (Gift giving will be covered in Chapter 15.)

Another characteristic that is evident among the Vietnamese is a strong sense of national pride. After centuries of successfully driving out foreign invaders, Vietnamese are understandably proud of their accomplishments. To add to the nationalism that already existed, socialist education and ideology concentrated on the nationalist struggle and the triumphs of the Vietnamese people. One-sided accounts of the country's well-being also fueled this type of thinking. Even though Vietnam has admitted the failings of the system it adopted (though it blames a lot of mistakes on the former Soviet Union), the people are nonetheless proud of their abilities, and rightly so. Given the level of poverty that the country has been operating under for so long, the amount of education that individuals enjoy is clearly impressive. In negotiations, this proud attitude may not be perceptible, but foreign business people should be advised to play the power/authority card carefully. Mutual respect is essential; the Vietnamese will not take kindly to condescending behavior from foreign counterparts. "Not being falsely proud is important in Vietnam as it is in China," says Fred Burke of Baker & McKenzie. "Foreigners tend to underestimate Vietnam because they look on the surface of things here, and think it's a poor country, and they just assume that they don't know anything. The Vietnamese don't like to be treated that way."

Even after decades of war and suffering, the Vietnamese are gentle, friendly, and hospitable; but they are also strong, determined, and shrewd negotiators. In fact, they are often quite frank and tenacious.

Finally, the Vietnamese place a lot of emphasis on Confucian ethics, discipline, and harmony, and will try to avoid confrontation if possible. Consequently, politeness is paramount in all business relations. However, politeness should not be taken at face value. Rather than openly disagreeing (at least in the initial stages of negotiation), the Vietnamese will often say "yes" or "maybe" when they really mean "probably not." Little white lies are usually preferable to being offensive.

Is it possible for foreigners to build trust-based relationships with Vietnamese counterparts?

As in most of Asia, business transactions in Vietnam are based on personal relationships. Anyone working in Vietnam will tell you that these bonds mean more to business success there than anything. Because there are so many more foreigners seeking high-level introductions, it is no longer the case that if you are an American in Vietnam you will be able to meet any minister you please. It is through relationships that you get introduced. In Vietnam, relationships are often based on family relations, a shared past, as well as friendships built up over time. Your enduring business relationships with Vietnamese will likely rest on a tripod of trust, mutuality, and respect and will require some time to build. You can't expect to arrive in Vietnam with a prepared contract in hand. While the Vietnamese do tend to like MOUs and documenting drawn-out discussions, contractual agreements come far later in the relationship. Investors are best served by establishing friendships and family connections with potential partners. Furthermore, relationships can be cemented by being as accountable as possible, by acting according to your words.

Trust is hard to win and hard to maintain. In light of Vietnamese history, it is not difficult to imagine how the Vietnamese may have developed a lack of trust for foreigners. Sadly, the divisive nature of modern conflicts has also fostered mistrust among fellow Vietnamese. The informant society that swept down from the North over the whole country after 1975 only served to solidify this mistrust. Sitting in the Binh Soup Shop in Saigon, made famous for being the secret headquarters of the Vietcong during the war, a representative of Mbf Indonesia, Ltd. confided:

> Trust is the most important thing for doing business here because the Vietnamese are automatically suspicious of foreigners—they're suspicious of their *neighbors*. Take this soup shop for instance. What if you were the neighbor of the guy who ran this place who was a major cover for the Vietcong and who wouldn't think twice about slitting your son's throat if he had to? Gaining trust with people who don't trust easily is the key. You have to show that you are willing to sacrifice something and that you're trustworthy, and this takes a while.

So, if you want to go into a joint venture, you need to invest *time* as well as money.

The Vietnamese are prone to suspicion in business not because of historical resentment toward Americans or animosity toward foreigners, but due to their recent experience and lack of commercial knowledge. The trust issue has not been helped by foreign companies that have signed joint venture agreements and then brought in outdated technology, nor by the big-talking foreigners who generate enthusiasm for large projects and then can't come up with the financing to launch them. The trend lately is for the foreign briefcase company to acquire a license to start a project and then to sell the license to a bonafide company that can implement it. This doesn't help the trust-of-foreigners issue either. In fact, the government has recently attempted to crack down on the practice.

Among ministers and officials you will find little knowledge of companies outside Vietnam. An official in charge of hotel construction may not know, for instance, the difference between Hilton, Sheraton, and Holiday Inn. Even if you represent one of these major chains, they may not know who you are. It's difficult for them to know whether or not you're a rip-off artist like the broker who recently squeezed through Vietnam's just-opened doors with a briefcase full of contracts loaded with fine print that worked to the detriment of naive Vietnamese partners. Scores of foreign brokers obtained licenses to build hotels and then sold them to latecomer hotel developers. Many of these projects died on the vine because they weren't practical or financially feasible from the start. Thus, they will want to spend the time to gauge your credibility and find out whether you genuinely have access to capital. They will be concerned, if not paranoid, about legalistic clauses in contracts that they fear could work against them. "Because there is no business law yet," says Nguyen Xuan Oahn, "you cannot trust a counterpart who is not a family member. So you have to share and get to know one another to build trust."

How does a foreigner attempt to build bonds of trust with Vietnamese counterparts?

If you are warm, sincere, tolerant, and respectful, the Vietnamese will eventually come to trust you. And they can be trusted in return. It is simply not the case, as some claim, that they "only trust family members." Perhaps the Chinese in Vietnam only trust family, but they represent a monied class that has been persecuted as an ethnic minority in recent history, and such groupism can be expected.

Foreign firms generate trust by socializing and by addressing the often unstated needs of the person with whom they desire to build trust. The Hash House Harriers is a running club for expats. Red River Oil Company sponsored a run in 1994 for the Hanoi chapter of the club, which they held at the headquarters of PetroVietnam, Red River's client ministry in Vietnam. "PetroVietnam is a pretty conservative group of guys," says company man Mel Jackson. "Well-educated, and trained overseas." Unfortunately, all of the one hundred or so Americans—many from other oil companies—were acting like they normally do on a Saturday afternoon "Hash." The PetroVietnam guys declined to actually run, but they were happy to participate in drinking beer and singing songs. "By the end of event," says Mel Jackson, "we had these conservative guys in the middle of this circle, barely standing up, making loud proclamations about how we were great friends. Another guy from PetroVietnam was going on and on about how we hope we can do this every year!"

Through this socializing, Jackson realized trust was deepened between Red River and the PetroVietnam officials. "On a couple of field trips to geological sites, we've visited native villages and drunk beer together—and got them to a point where anything goes with us." Mel knew he had generated bonhomie when the officials "were finally comfortable telling our driver to stop the car when they had to urinate. They would just say, 'Hey, stop the car, I gotta go to the bathroom!'" Jackson says it's worth being up in Hanoi to develop that kind of close relationship. "The oil guys in Saigon definitely have a more important operational role with PetroVietnam, but they probably don't have the more social role that we have up here. I mean I know the families [of these officials]."

In the following case, the foreign firm addressed the personal needs of an official in order to forge what must now certainly be a bond of lifelong trust, if not obligation. The foreign party is a U.S. real estate development company (which demanded anonymity in sharing this story), which focused on developing an airtight relationship at the earliest stage of its involvement in Vietnam with the head of the People's Committee in a lesser-known coastal province of the country. The man suffered serious heart trouble. The San Francisco-based company flew the man to Singapore, paid for, and "held his hand through," a heart surgery operation. The official was so indebted that he granted the firm the right to act as coordinator of all foreign investment projects in the entire province—a deal that will undoubtedly pan out handsomely for the U.S. company.

WHEN HEART SURGERY
(AND OTHER GIFTS) BECOME BRIBES

How does the foreigner deal with business corruption in Vietnam?

Despite the proclamations about how the government is combating and weeding out corruption—which they are to some degree—it continues to exist at all levels of officialdom. Many expats with whom I spoke didn't want to address the issue of corruption while others spoke of it as an innocuous feature of the business landscape. That is, until I met with one of the most qualified "Vietnam hands" in Hanoi—Stewart Stemple of BBI

Investment Group, Chartered, which is building a $258 million hotel center in Da Nang, at that time the largest foreign land development deal in the country.

Strategic gift giving is a sore spot for Stemple, who works for a company that gives no gifts (or bribes) to Vietnamese counterparts, as a policy. This leaves Stemple in an uneasy middle position between the Vietnamese and American partners. Stemple watches as Asian competitors offer trips abroad and cash bribes to Vietnamese officials. To get a project approved, to get a license, to get a permit, to get something through Customs, bribes are paid on a widespread basis, says Stemple. "This is quite simply the biggest issue we face, but BBI has not given one bribe to get its project approved."

The root cause of corruption in the country is that it has yet to institutionalize the charging of administrative fees such as for building permits, licenses, and so forth. (Imagine the fees to be paid in the United States to obtain approval of a $250 million beachfront hotel complex.) Thus, the system becomes highly vulnerable to corruption by officials. The American side doesn't know whether a viable fee is being charged or they are lining the pockets of officials. "If we don't pay," says Stemple, "we face a delay of 6 months, which costs us 1 million dollars." Speed is vital in the hotel business, and BBI wants to be first in Da Nang. Stemple has pleaded with BBI to allow him to "at least give pens or stickers or stationery," but the company is unwilling. When asked for a bribe, BBI asks for a verifiable consulting invoice, and asks that its Vietnamese partner properly account for every billed hour. Stemple admits that this has caused the project to take longer to get approved and that influence has had to be gleaned through other means, through "pressure on friends." As Stemple warns: "If you give a bribe, every ministry will know about it and you will then have to ante up every time you turn around."

To make a complex story short, here's how things play out. A group of foreign investors comes in with money to invest, say, in real estate. They want to develop some property, and the land they want is controlled by the People's Committee. Fourteen other investment groups are bidding on the same piece of land. Naturally, the People's Committee in charge of the land is in the habit of playing off all investors in order to obtain the best deal— the best deal for the country, but also for themselves. In a deal like this, officials often select the investment group offering the most attractive bribe package. Matters only get worse when a deal gets to the SCCI, say many expats I spoke to. The reason is rooted in the people who sit behind the desks of that august body. Most of the people who work for SCCI, which licenses foreign investment deals, are part of well-connected Vietnamese families, the members of which are often high ministry officials. A well-connected family invariably intends to place all of its sons in government positions. One of the sons is very smart, has earned an engineering degree and was also trained as an economist in Czechoslovakia. The family easily finds him a position at the Ministry of Trade. Another son earned straight Cs in high school and doesn't have a clue about what he wants to do. So they put him in the SCCI. Within a few months, he becomes an official on the take. This is why many expats call the SCCI the "state committee for corruption and investment."

The Vietnamese with whom you deal might be quite bold about asking for bribes, fees, and commissions. They may ask you repeatedly, as one consultant told me ("through peons who come and inform you"), that your company needs to "invite a few officials to the United States." If you ask why, they say because "it would be nice, and that then they will support your project." An official or director might say they "really like your ideas" and "how important it would be for a delegation to visit your factory in the States and while there, to visit Epcot Center." Often this standard request is called "training." In one oil production contract, an American company has committed to spend $200,000 a year on "training" Vietnamese. As an oil executive told me: "That's a lot of money to spend on trips to Singapore, [the] United States, and Europe to hear the Vienna Boys Choir and 'by the way,' meet the CEO of the firm's subsidiary in Austria." One of the English business periodicals in Vietnam is a joint venture between a foreign publisher and a government agency. The deal wasn't approved and licensed until the foreign side supplied the Vietnam side with two new cars and three computers, and this request came from their own *partner.* So you can imagine what controlling ministry people outside a venture often request.

Foreign executives go absolutely nuts contending with the quandary of whether to pay or stake out higher moral ground. "One Taiwanese guy," says Fred Burke of Baker & McKenzie in

Saigon, "literally, came in and said he wanted to *sue* Hai Phong Customs for reneging on a bribe." The man complained that his duty bill was exorbitant given how many times he had treated customs officials to expensive dinners! Often a local "consulting" company is hired to facilitate document processing and is paid a percentage of the total deal. (Such "processing fees" paid are legal under the U.S. Foreign Corrupt Practices Act.) In other instances, a company pays its middle man a "bonus," which is then used to make requisite payoffs to appropriate parties.

Americans in Vietnam must decide whether to follow the law and perhaps their ethical instincts, or do as the Romans do. U.S. trade negotiator Mickey Kantor admits that regarding illicit payments, our rigid antibribery law "puts our business people in a difficult position." That's an understatement. The United States has legislated the most restrictive antibribery laws in the world, while many of its competitors enforce no restrictions at all; Italian, West German, Dutch, and Japanese firms are not only permitted to use bribery to influence overseas entities, they can deduct the value of the bribe from their taxes as a necessary business expense. The Foreign Corrupt Practices Act is an attempt to prohibit U.S. corporations and their agents from bribing foreign officials. Violating it can cost your firm up to $2 million in fines, $100,000 for individuals, and imprisonment of perpetrators for up to five years.

WORKING WITH THE PEOPLE

When managing people in Vietnam, what approach should be used?

The Vietnamese have a phrase about the Japanese: one Japanese is like a mouse, but three Japanese is like a lion. The Vietnamese are the absolute reverse. One Vietnamese is like a lion; you can deal with them one-on-one and you can trust them to do a great job. But deal with a group of Vietnamese and you're dealing with socialism; they will sit around and nothing gets done. The rhythm of work moves at its own pace. Work is a group activity. Co-workers talk, they play, they enjoy one another. To wreak havoc on this family atmosphere in the workplace is to destroy morale, yet changes will have to take place and people will have to be trained if productivity and quality are to be enhanced.

Part of Jason Phua's job at CTS International in Hanoi is to train local state managers to make adjustments in how they manufacture apparel to ensure a higher level of quality. As we talked in his office, the energetic Singaporean suddenly got up and went over to a rack of colorful new clothes. He retrieved a silk blouse and showed me how one of its seams was obviously much different than its opposite. "Workers sometimes don't have the common sense to stop production when there are obvious mistakes. Before you sew, you should know [that this is a mistake]." The factory had made 5,000 of the misshapen pieces. Phua suggests that ongoing training of the supervisor of production is the best route, that to try "to educate all of the workers is not workable." But training must be done with a soft touch.

"Because of the war and their historical experience," he says, "if you push too much, the supervisor will rebel." So Phua urged changes made delicately. "You can't just tell them, and expect them to make the changes," he says. "You've got to check on them . . . remind them."

You will find the people in the South more familiar with Western business practices, while in the North, people tend to be more stubborn, though better educated, and set in their ways. They are prone to reject your ideas for change because, as they might say, "We have been doing it this way for 30 years and it's worked fine all this time without any problem . . . why change now?" Because of their pride, the Vietnamese worker can be stubborn when it comes to changing the way they do things. Staff members say to Mr. Phua: "We understand how to do it; you don't have to tell us." "Do they really know what to do?" I asked Phua. "That's the problem," he says.

"We let them tell us that they know what to do and let them do it. I say, 'if you can't do it, I'll come and tell you what to do. If you think you are good, then show me you are good; but if you can't do it, then let's try my way.'"

Don't assume that the Vietnamese know the basics. A Westerner might know what a soft loan is, what a loan guarantee is, what business fax messages look like, how to make a business telephone call, how to dress for success, and so on. You can't assume, however, that your Vietnamese staff will know the same things. You have to teach and train them. This won't mean telling them once, or showing them a picture in a book. You will have to spend some time in order to put what you teach into practice. For example, Stewart Stemple conducts phone practice with his staff secretaries. Not just once, but periodically, he has them answer mock calls, take messages, and write down phone numbers. Refrain from losing your temper. When a staff person takes down a number incorrectly or misspells a name, the worst thing you can do is start yelling. Foreign managers who see something misspelled and get abusive often find that once their staff members are trained, they leave for more money down the road. Stewart Stemple, as a consultant for BBI Investment Group, puts a premium on the discussion of mistakes in a mild-mannered way such that change can happen. For example, don't tell your new secretary to "send a fax to so-and-so in Hue and tell him you're going to be a day late," and expect that the fax will go out accurately without your careful coaching and review.

Training may not stick, either. A Singapore chef was brought into work at the first hotel set up by Singapore investors in Vietnam, where he spent 3 months training Vietnamese cooks until the food served was authentically Singaporean. Then he left and went home. Three months later, the food being cooked tasted entirely different. "The cooks would go to the market, and if they couldn't find the right seasoning, they would buy something else that *looked* the same and just replace it, not realizing that the *taste* would be totally changed," says a Singaporean executive in Hanoi close to the hotel's management. Stemple recently trained the staff of a state-owned hotel in Da Nang, which BBI had purchased to become part of its planned resort complex there. He had 2 months to train the staff. During the first 2 weeks, however, things looked ominous. There was pessimism and even some resentment. Then, suddenly, "the lights went on," says Stemple, "and they began to respond." The problem had been that, as state workers facing the fact that their hotel was being purchased by a foreign joint venture partner, they had assumed that they were going to be fired. The joint venture was a threat to them. It took Stemple's warm and soft-spoken communication skills to convince them that although there were to be big changes in the operation of the hotel, they were going to be changes that would affect the workers' lives in a positive manner. They were going to learn English. They were going to work in a renovated hotel. And they weren't going to be working 24-hour shifts any longer and sleeping on the café tables. They weren't going to go on without a worker's lounge. They were going to get tips! Stemple successfully convinced them that the foreign partners truly cared about the workers. That they were, indeed, lucky to be workers at the hotel. By the time a gaggle of international surfers came to stay in the hotel during a contest in Da Nang, it had become an entirely different place. The workers were speaking phrases of English, providing unheard-of-before customer service, and dressing for success. Not only were they now meeting with officials and traveling within their country for the first time, some were invited to participate in meetings over drinks at the Metropole! Stemple claims that the trained people who are provided with these kinds of transforming experiences are going to remain loyal to his company, and less vulnerable to poaching by other foreign firms, which is rampant in Vietnam. Stemple doesn't think his secretarial staff would leave if offered ten times the money, because of the extensive training he has provided them and commitment he has shown to them. And he might be right. Expats are constantly telling him how fantastic his staff members are: they take notes, they're friendly, they're computer literate, and they translate huge documents for him.

So train your workers, and if you are not a Human Resource Trainer or don't have the time, hire a trainer to come in and do so. At least one foreign company in Hanoi provides this service.

COMMUNICATING

AND NEGOTIATING

*I*n December 1994, the National Administration Academy in Hanoi started up a program of required English classes for Vietnam's top government officials, in response to Prime Minister Vo Van Kiet's order that high cadres speak at least one foreign language. Meanwhile, 80 percent of young people in the country are learning to speak English in an estimated 200 English-language instruction centers. Even Vietnamese children watch Muzzy on television, the green extraterrestrial who instructs in English with a British accent, an import from the BBC. To the consternation of the French, who want to promote their language in France's former colony, English is fast becoming the *lingua franca* of business in the country. Unfortunately, that day is not quite here yet and in the meantime, you will have to speak with Vietnamese partners and officials through an interpreter.

COMMUNICATING THROUGH AN INTERPRETER

An interpreter acts as a transmitter of your words, ideas, humor, intelligence, and personality. Though all that has been said about building relationships in Vietnam may have sounded easy to do solely through an interpreter, in fact, this makes the endeavor hardly a simple proposition. Most Westerners who experience problems "getting through" to the Vietnamese blame their interpreters; in fact, a better approach is to *take responsibility* for getting your message better interpreted.

What are the secrets of being interpreted well?

First, limit your sentences to seven to twelve words, max. This may seem like a lot of words, but it's not. Try it and you'll see how tough it is to speak in such short sentences. The shorter your sentences, the less likely your audience will lose your train of thought and become fatigued. Second, be redundant. Given that a large share of your message will normally fail to pass through an interpreter to the audience, and that much of that will be comprehended only hazily because your words will have been denuded of their cultural context, it doesn't hurt for you to reiterate important points and check for nods of comprehension. You should also prepare to present seminal points of your presentation in more than one way.

Third, find and train a good interpreter. The best way to find an interpreter is through referral. Call your business colleagues and ask whether they know of an interpreter, one they have used before. If that doesn't work, call the American Translators' Association (ATA) in Alexandria, Virginia at (703) 683-6100. This organization represents hundreds of certified interpreters and translators for all languages, many with special expertise. They can refer you to a chapter of the organization located in your area or overseas, and send you a personnel directory. When I say "train" your interpreter, I mean rehearse your presentation with them well before you depart for Vietnam. No interpreter will be able to translate all of your technical terms without opening a dictionary; this should be done at home and not in front of your Vietnamese audience. Moreover, if there is any humor, irony, or special verbal twist in your presentation, make sure the interpreter has rehearsed it, found just the right nuance to translate it, and knows the body and facial language in which to deliver it, so that your audience gets your message clearly and responds favorably. Some marketers work with their interpreters for 2 or 3 weeks before negotiations start. Westerners often forget, especially when things get heated during a negotiation, that anything they say that is not heard by their interpreter will not be understood at all on the other side. They often get angry and cut in before their interpreter has finished their last sentence. Do not speak until your interpreter has finished. Another tip: when speaking through an interpreter, look at the person to whom you are speaking and not at your interpreter, which can be more comfortable than looking at a listener who cannot understand your language. Rehearse doing this as part of your pre-trip training. Lastly, don't use your interpreter to merely "summarize" what you have said or what your counterpart has said. Again, allow the interpreter to translate what you say in sound bites, and if you can get your counterpart to do likewise, all the better.

Do the Vietnamese communicate in ways different from the typical Westerner?

To some degree, yes. Vietnam's ministry officials vary widely in style, background, and knowledge level. Southerners tend to lean toward you more when they talk to you. They're more "in-your-face" than Northerners. People in the South tend to be jollier and more affable than Northerners. In the North, the communication style can be deadpan and direct; if someone doesn't like you, they might just say so in straight blunt monotone: "I don't like you." Researchers and scientific people, on the other hand, tend to be forthcoming, frank, extremely well informed, and dynamic. You can get them to talk about politics, corruption, their work, Vietnam history—they just love to talk and they offer the foreigner a valuable source of information. You are more likely to glean sensitive information from a lower level, perhaps technical, person. Officials will always know more than they tell you, so don't get upset when you know that they know something they're not telling you.

Begin the discussion by being general rather than particular. Be willing to retreat if your inquiry runs up against exposed nerves. After you have made general comments and asked general questions, *slowly* focus in on your target area. You'll notice a change of tone and gesture when you cross the line. Pull back and take another tack. Don't keep poking at a sensitive spot until the Party line gets played. Realize going in that you are not going to exit the meeting with everything you set out to accomplish. "They won't give you black or white," says Jason Phua of CTS International. "They always give you grey. They keep you wondering. So it's very difficult to get confirmation of anything. They won't say 'yes'; they say 'maybe,' and let you wonder." Moreover, nods of comprehension are just that and not to be taken as agreement with you. The Vietnamese smile constantly, but this may not mean that they are pleased or happy. It could mean that they feel fear or embarrassment, or even that they strongly disagree with you.

What gestures might be offensive to a Vietnamese person?

I only wish to mention a few taboos having to do with what communications specialists call your "nonverbals." First, as in all Buddhist cultures, try to refrain from touching people, especially children, on the head, which is considered a spiritual center. Second, try not to sit with your legs crossed in a formal meeting, or sit with the soles of your feet pointing at someone, even though the gesture will not elicit the reaction it might in Thailand. Third, to summon somebody, use the traditional method of cupping your hand downward and waving into your body, rather than waving at the person or wiggling your finger. Vietnamese who have come to America have become angered when people beckon them with a single finger, which is the way one summons an animal in Vietnam. Finally, opposite-sex touching is minimized among business people. Do not pat people on the back or tap someone on the arm to show affection or emphasize a remark. Two women might hold hands, however, while walking down the street and two men may also, without there being anything romantic between them.

Where do negotiations take place—in an office or a meeting room—and who will the players be?

The Vietnamese don't typically negotiate as individuals. They do so as a group. As companies are state-owned, any number of

ministries will be involved in any negotiation. Thus, multiple players will be present in a typical meeting, including enterprise managers and ministry directors. For example, the Ministry of
Construction would participate if a building is to be renovated
before installation of a factory. Ultimately, however, two-to-four
persons on the Vietnamese side will comprise the group with
whom you will actually negotiate a deal. On a team representing
a state enterprise or government body (but not a private company) there will also be a "Party person," or secret police type, who
is charged with making sure that whatever the Vietnamese side
says is pasteurized politically. "You need to find out who the Party
person is," recommends the chief representative of a French
investment bank who lives in Hanoi. "And who is the highest-
ranking Party member on the team, which may not turn out to be
the person who is conducting the highest level of the negotiation."
In any given state factory, there is one person who is making the
decisions—and only one person—and you've got to find out who
that person is. When meeting with someone for the purpose of
negotiating or just exchanging information, start out by discerning
the person's position in the Party. Knowing where a person is in
the Party hierarchy tells you much about their position in the government hierarchy. The managers of state-owned enterprises are,
by and large, Party people, but there are exceptions. You may, in
fact, be negotiating or going into partnership with a person who
is not in the Party. He may have an assistant who is, by title,
beneath him, but who is a Party member and thus is likely to wield
the real power. Negotiate with that person if possible.

DURING THE FIRST MEETING. At the very beginning of a business
meeting, the Vietnamese may ask you a number of questions
about your family and background. Some of these questions might
be of a personal nature, for example, whether or not you are married, how many kids you have, and so forth. Do not fail to ask
such questions of your Vietnamese counterpart before jumping
into business topics. Be patient, sip the green tea, and eat the mandarins. Wait for them to initiate business. Next, each side will give
an introductory speech. In terms of your presentation, the more
bells and whistles the better. "They love high-tech and multimedia," says Fred Burke of Baker & McKenzie. "To the extent that
firms can do that, it's always encouraged."

How do the Vietnamese negotiate—what is their bargaining style—and how should the foreigner respond?

Here again, let me reiterate that the Vietnamese are a prideful people, if not overly prideful. Any negotiation is, in a real way, a replaying of past conflicts with foreign parties in which the Vietnamese emerge as victors. "They are going to prevail, they are going to win, they are going to outwit you," says a Swiss expat who didn't want his name used. In all of their textbooks and their upbringing they have been trained to beat the foreigner. When they enter into any kind of relationship or a negotiation with a foreign party, it's played out as a war, and they assume that they will defeat you. If you're going to deal with them, don't go in worrying about raising your voice a little, despite many cultural commentaries that would advise otherwise. You're going to have to *push* to win a deal worth doing. Take Al DeMatteis. He's a brazen, in-your-face New Yorker who often swears and screams and hollers and has to leave the negotiating room because he gets so angry. He breaks the rules articulated in the business books that admonish the Westerner not to become unglued and offend Vietnamese in a public setting. When confronted by an official who informs you that "we can't do that for this reason," you need to be tougher than nails. The best tactic is always to stand your ground and firmly explain why you have taken your position and why you must continue to hold it. As long as such explanations are delivered in a sincere, composed, respectful manner, they should be received well. Often, the Vietnamese do not understand why a Western firm must do something a certain way; they may not be familiar with a standard international business practice. You need to make them see your rationale clearly. In one case, the Architectural Department of a government planning agency had only dealt with Korean firms, so when an American construction firm submitted their drawings, the Department asked that the company redraw them to conform to the Korean style of drawing, thinking that this represented the international standard. The Vietnamese are having to get accustomed to Western standards all at once, and you may take a few knocks as part of the process.

Don't reveal what you want up front in a negotiation. You will be negotiating with midlevel people at the outset, rather than the highest-level people. Midlevel drones have to prove to their superiors that they won something from you...that they maneuvered the foreigner out of something of tangible value. You must account for this need on their part in the beginning and not give up too many concessions along the way. Wait until the last minute. Then make a *sacrifice*—give them something in order to clinch the deal. Make them think that they won.

Lastly, the Vietnamese use patience as a tactic during negotiation. They will delay and delay and delay to win concessions. "They delay because they can afford to delay," says Jason Phua of CTS International. "They know that most foreigners come to Vietnam on a very short trip," and realize that most foreign reps need to return with confirmation of a deal, so they push for concessions at the last minute. And don't assume that their willingness to draw up a preliminary agreement means a final decision has been made to go with you. "They don't negotiate with one supplier," says Mark Mitchell of VATICO. "They'll negotiate with ten different suppliers at once and take the best deal that they can get. Letters of Understanding don't mean anything. They send them to all ten suppliers."

What role do lawyers play in negotiating a deal?

Unlike some other Asian groups, Vietnamese negotiators do not object to, nor will they be offended by, lawyers being present at business meetings, though it's not standard practice by any means. There are few established local lawyers in Vietnam. Traditionally, the legal bar in the South has been a criminal one, with few lawyers involved in commercial business. Overall, Vietnamese lawyers leave much to be desired. "They're either trained in the former system of law before 1975, and haven't learned the socialist system," says Fred Burke of Baker & McKenzie, "or they're just not interested in writing contracts in a very detailed fashion, checking laws and provisions, and building a database." Notaries play a bigger role than lawyers in Vietnam for many business purposes. While in the West, legal opinions are often obtained to decide whether a certain legality might be enforceable; under Vietnamese law the city notary office, which is staffed by lawyers, carries out this task. Lawyers per se are not used for this purpose. The system is similar to the French civil code system. Your task is to make sure that your contract conforms to the local code. (See the sample contractual agreements in the appendix.)

ESSENTIAL

ETIQUETTE

AND PROTOCOL

*H*aving experienced 1,000 years of Chinese, 100 years of French, and 30 years of American occupation, Vietnamese culture has been inundated with foreign influences. Because of this, the sensitivity to cultural protocol is much subdued relative to the more closed societies of China and Japan. Should you commit constant blunders or exhibit coarse and crass behavior, the tolerant Vietnamese will inwardly acknowledge that you are a barbaric foreigner, though will never exhibit any negative reaction for you to see. This alone should pique your interest in knowing the most basic rules of proper manners and etiquette before you arrive.

How should a foreigner greet a Vietnamese person?

The Vietnamese don't bow like the Japanese, *wai* like the Thai, or *salaam* like the Malays. They shake hands Western-style, though the hand grasp is less firm. The shaking of the hands might be accompanied by a slight bow of the head. Some Vietnamese might clasp your hand between both of theirs. Greet senior Vietnamese first and introduce senior people before less senior in descending order of rank.

The word for "hello" in Vietnamese is *chào,* but to use only *chào* as a greeting would be impolite. The Vietnamese qualify a "hello" with an appropriate pronoun, indicating the relationship between the two people conversing. Thus, when meeting a man of your age or older, who you want to greet formally, say *Chào ông,* which roughly translates to Hello, Mister. To greet a woman formally for the first time, say *Chào bà,* meaning Hello, Mrs. When greeting a man whom you know well, say, *Chào anh,* or Hello, older brother. For greeting a woman you know well, use *Chào chi.* An unmarried woman or female teacher is addressed, *Chào cô.* You can greet a child, boy or girl, with *Chào em.* Moreover, *Chào* is also the Vietnamese word for "goodbye," and requires the same use of a qualifying pronoun. The Vietnamese do not use the Western greeting expressions like "Good morning" or "Good night," but typically use either "What are you doing?" (*Anh dang làm gì do?*) or "Where are you going" (*Anh dang di dâu dó?*).

When you meet people in Vietnam they will probably ask you your age and whether or not you are married because they want to judge your status. (Married people have more status than unmarried.) Position and title in your company comes next. Knowing these things helps Vietnamese determine their status relative to yours.

BUSINESS CARDS. Vietnamese business people expect you to exchange business cards at a first meeting. Make sure you bring along 100–200 of your business cards to Vietnam, as running out midtrip can put a damper on all subsequent meetings. Provide a card to each member of the group with whom you meet, and exchange cards using both hands to be formal and polite. Take the time to have your card translated into Vietnamese, which is done phonetically, rather than with ideographic characters as is Chinese. Most expats have their company name and title translated and leave their name in English, as depicted on the card on the next page.

Red River Oil Company

Mel Jackson
Administration Manager

78 Mai Hac De Street, Hanoi, Socialist Republic of Vietnam
Tel: 84-4-258005 Fax: 84-4-258139

Cong ty Dau Khi Song Hong

Mel Jackson
Giam doc Hanh chinh

78 Mai Hac De, Hanoi, Viet Nam
Tel: 84-4-258005 Fax: 84-4-258139

VIETNAMESE NAMES. Because there are so few family names used in Vietnam, people address each other using their given names. However, on a person's business card the family name will come first, followed by a middle name, and then a given name. Take the name, Nguyen Xuan Oahn. His family name—Nguyen—comes first on his business card. If I wrote him a letter, I would start with: Dear Dr. Nguyen. In addressing him in conversation, however, I would use Dr. Oahn, his given name. The middle name is usually ornamental or refers to a social role or clan.

What is appropriate business attire for doing business in the country?

Business attire in Vietnam is quite simple. For formal business meetings men should wear a suit and tie. On hot days the jacket can be left at home. Women should wear work suits or loose-fitting blouses and skirts. Some Vietnamese women will wear the traditional *ao dai* at a meeting, though increasingly women are wearing Western-style suits and skirts. Vietnamese society winces at public displays of affection and sexual suggestiveness, and thus shorts are *verboten*, except for recreational sports. For working men and women, hats are in order. In the North, you will see men wearing the green tropical helmet, and in the countryside women can be seen wearing the cone-shaped straw hat. Men and women attending business meetings will, of course, not be donning such head gear.

What is Vietnamese food like, and what are the most important points of dining etiquette?

Most Vietnamese companies lack the facilities to hold large banquets on site, thus dinner out in a nice restaurant (rather than a person's home) is always part of a negotiation in Vietnam. The banquet will probably take place at a well-known local restaurant, of which there is a growing selection serving Chinese, French, Italian, Japanese, and Vietnamese cuisine. At an elegant restaurant the meal begins with water, almost always a bottle of mineral water. You pour the water into your glass yourself. Same goes if you order a bottle of beer. Unlike in Japan or Korea you don't have to worry about pouring for your neighbor and they won't make a ritual out of keeping your glass full for you, either.

The Vietnamese will often order beer with lunch or dinner, so it's okay to order alcohol without feeling you might be looked upon as a drinker. The Vietnamese may toast one another during a meal, but the ritual is not formal as in China or done throughout the meal. You can say "cheers" in Vietnamese by saying, "*trucsuque.*" They toast, but don't worry about making a formal toast at the start of the meal. Small quantities of whiskey and brandy and wine (the French influence) are served as beverages. Also, there is a traditional liqueur made from rice, often stored in an old bottle and served in a tiny porcelain shot glass. Note that a really big deal might involve "heavy drinking of cognac out of water glasses," says an experienced expat.

The banquet table will likely be rectangular rather than the traditionally round table in China. The table setting is normally Western style, with plate, fork, napkin, and glass. Chopsticks will be included as well, and if not, you can ask that they be brought.

Chopsticks are not reversed when the Vietnamese eat from similar plates. If you order a steak, then a knife will come with the fork. If you eat at one of the outdoor streetside eateries, consider bringing along your own chopsticks or try to wipe down the set provided as best that you can. A dish of vinegar and one of chili sauce will accompany a bowl used for rice or noodles, along with slices of lime. At these places, which are comprised of tiny tables and chairs set about under a tarpaulin with a gas stove to the side, you pick out what you want to eat at a table of raw foods, they cook it up and bring it to your table, and then you eat communally from a common dish set in the center of your table. Dish rice into your bowl with the large spoon and use your chopsticks to mix other food with the rice for eating. Unlike in Japan, you mix food with the rice for eating. Incidentally, noodles are as popular as rice in Vietnam. At the outdoor restaurants the food is delicious but the sanitation might be lacking.

Some dishes are eaten communally and some are not. If you are in a Western restaurant, a waiter will take your order individually and you will eat from your own plate and bowl. At a Vietnamese restaurant, your host will probably order a number of dishes and an assortment of appetizers such as spring rolls, and you will eat communally from the various plates set in the center of the table. The Vietnamese enjoy steak dishes and these are served individually, often from a heated cast-iron plate set on a piece of wood, the meat sizzling until done while on the table. The coffee is very good but very strong and often overly sweetened with a viscous cream-colored syrup claimed to be condensed milk. Many places will bring coffee with the condensed milk added unless you ask that it not be. The cream on the table will normally be thick and dun-colored condensed milk.

The Vietnamese diet consists of much meat—beef, chicken, pork, and fish. Duck, frog, and assorted species of seafood round out a light, but fulfilling cuisine. Don't worry about your Vietnamese host making you eat dogmeat at one of the dogmeat restaurants on the outskirts of Hanoi. Dog is considered a delicacy but no one is going to force it upon you as a must-eat local dish, or trick you into eating it without your knowledge...unless, or course, they know you really well and are playing a joke. The word for dogmeat is *thitcha*, a combination of the word for dog (*cha*), and the word for meat (*thit*), which reminds me of a funny story. A dear friend of mine was coming in from the airport into downtown Hanoi with a Vietnamese interpreter when she noticed a passing sign on a building that read: THITHOUSE. She said to her interpreter, "There's the *thit* house." The interpreter said, "Don't you mean *meat* house?" And my friend said, "Well, call it what you will."

Do the Vietnamese drink alcohol as part of business entertaining?

Liquor drinking with business associates takes place in restaurants rather than while bar hopping, as in the case of Japan or Korea. There just aren't many bars to hop to that are not strictly the domain of raucous tourists. Many Vietnamese business people drink hard and will want you to join them in the "bottom's up" toast: "*tram phan tram,*" which means "100 percent," or finish everything in your glass. Sometimes everyone present will stand up together and offer you a toast. When drinking, maintain control and composure. Getting tipsy is okay but lurid jokes or heavy pats on the back will quickly rob you of credibility. They won't tell you directly that you are an ugly American, but Vietnam's business community is small and tight-knit. Word gets around like electricity.

Singing in a *karaoke* establishment might be another site for business entertaining. *Karoake* means "empty orchestra" in Japanese and in English it means, "awful singing experience." In Vietnam *karaoke* is merged not so much with drinking bars as elsewhere in Asia, but with small coffee shops and juice bars where family and friends often meet at night to sing Vietnamese and Chinese songs accompanied by pirated music videotapes. Karaoke is a special rapport-building activity, singing being a universal camaraderie-enhancer. I highly recommend that you learn to belt out a short song list: "Feelings," "Yesterday," and "Tie a Yellow Ribbon 'Round the Old Oak Tree." Go over with those three ready to croon and you're going to do just fine.

Should the foreign visitor bring gifts for a Vietnamese business partner? Are there tabooed gifts?

The Vietnamese won't necessarily do anything for you unless they expect to receive something tangible in return. Like China, it's a give-and-take society built on bonds of reciprocity and obligation. Even though the Vietnamese are friendly and sincere, unless they know you well, don't expect them to go completely out of their way to do something for you without expecting something in return. (To do so would be naive.) "Gift giving is very, very important in Vietnam," says Jason Phua of CTS in Hanoi. "Every festival and celebration you give gifts—you cannot forget to do this." You don't have to give a gift at the first meeting, though if you do, logo gifts are fine—diaries, calendars, clocks, or books. A company pen given at a first meeting will always be received well. For future meetings you should bring gifts from the States to give to your counterpart, his or her spouse, and to his or her children. Taboos are few. Any item that says "Made In America" works as a gift. Make-up is expensive in Vietnam, so bring some as gifts for women. Young men like baseball caps of American teams.

Business gifts should either address the receiver's hobbies and tastes, or reflect your business relationship. "Our gifts are legal materials," says an American lawyer in Saigon. "We give a lot of laws and regulations from all sorts of countries. That goes a long way for us because it's valuable to [Vietnamese officials] who are working on laws."

An extravagant gesture, made often, is to invite counterparts overseas and call it training. . . when actually the purpose is to allow them to go shop for their friends back in Vietnam, and bring them a television or a stereo. An American oilman explains: "Last year we took four guys to Singapore for three days and gave them some pocket money. We told them Singapore is more expensive than Hanoi— 'you'll need this just to get around for a few days.' It was like 500 U.S. dollars each. After we toured the relevant oil facilities, they were free from around 4:30 P.M. to dinnertime to go shopping. When we came back, they each had two suitcases filled with stuff to bring back to Hanoi. It was unbelievable."

Will a foreigner be asked to participate in holiday celebrations?

To the Vietnamese, the first day of the first lunar month of the year (falling in late January or early February) is the beginning of Tet, the traditional New Year as celebrated throughout Asia. Tet is the most important cultural event of the year in Vietnam—and some say soon to be as commercialized as Christmas in the West— when people mark the end of one chapter of life and the start of a new one. It's also a time to ponder one's roots by remembering ancestors, to settle the past year's debts, to clean up lingering personal affairs, and to forgive past indiscretions. People visit relatives and friends, and hold family banquets with festive food and drink. Your Vietnamese friends may invite you to their homes at this time to participate. It's considered an honor to be invited to go to someone's house on the first, second, or third day of the New Year. You cross over the threshold of their house at this event, which symbolizes (in a not-so-corny way) that you are crossing the threshold into a new phase of your relationship with the host. The Vietnamese believe that the first person to cross over the threshold into the house on the first day of the new year must be an auspicious person. "I was highly honored," says Mel Jackson, "when a few people asked me to come to their house at 8 A.M. on the first day to be the first person in. They thought that maybe having a foreigner come in first would bring them good luck for the year or something." It's also considered lucky for the person who happens to be the first unexpected guest to cross over the threshold. Tet is the biggest gift-giving holiday of the year; prepare both to give alcohol-related gifts, and also, give red envelopes of crisp new money to adolescent or younger children, but not to adults.

Inside the home, women take great care in preparing the traditional "sticky rice cakes," called *Ban Chung*, which are given as gifts. According to legend, the three household kitchen gods make their reports on the family to the Jade King; thus, all must be in order. Families festoon the ancestral altar and burn joss sticks to welcome the departed back into the household. Firecrackers would normally be heard throughout the day, culminating in a final barrage at midnight and producing an acrid mist over the cities, but now the government has outlawed fireworks due to the high number of yearly injuries and deaths.

Tet lasts for 5 days while people eat and drink and visit one another's homes. Somehow people keep a complicated calender in their heads about whose home they need to visit next throughout the entire week. Your host will want you to remain at their home all New Year's Day; thus, gracefully obtaining leave is an art. The Vietnamese are masterful at politely excusing themselves to leave a home and move on to the next. After you attend Tet at a person's home, your relationship with them deepens. The formal pronoun they use to address you might change. You may find yourself from then on being addressed, literally, as "brother" or "sister." During Tet you are expected to give gifts to your business counterparts and to bring them to people's homes if you are to visit them during the

New Year. The Hanoi International Women's Club advises, "whiskey is a good choice, Red and Black label being the most popular. The bottle should be boxed and the more beautifully wrapped the better. After you have signed the card, everything goes into a plastic bag before it is delivered." During the *Tet Trung Thu* mid-autumn festival, children are the theme and you should give your counterpart and employees toys for them to give to their children.

LUCKY AND UNLUCKY DAYS. According to the lunar calendar, your Vietnamese counterpart may find that certain days are better than others, or more auspicious than others, for starting a venture or a project ribbon-cutting. The seventh, seventeenth, and twenty-seventh of any given month are not good days to begin a trip in the minds of many Vietnamese, just as the third, the thirteenth, and the twenty-third are not auspicious days to return. As Al DeMatteis told conference participants in Washington DC in 1994, "the Vietnamese rely on fortune tellers to [tell them] when to sign a contract, when to have a ceremony, and when to start construction." You might want to obtain a lunar calendar to find the dates to make sure you don't offend the superstitious sensibilities of your counterpart.

OFFICIAL HOLIDAYS

January 1	New Year's Day (TET)
February 3	Anniversary of the Founding of the Vietnamese Communist Party in 1930
April 30	Liberation Day, celebrating the liberation of Saigon by the North Vietnamese Army in 1975
May 1	International Worker's Day
May 19	Ho Chi Minh's Birthday
	Buddha's Birthday, which falls on the 8th day of the 4th moon, usually in June
September 2	National Day. Commemorates the founding of the Democratic Republic of Vietnam by Ho Chi Minh in 1945
September 3	Anniversary of Ho Chi Minh's death (1969)
December 25	Christmas Day

What should you be aware of before visiting a Vietnamese person at home?

Rarely will the foreign business person be invited to the Vietnamese person's home, except perhaps during Tet celebrations. Most Vietnamese live in small, rather drab apartments that are not suitable for entertaining. Inside the home, you may notice that people do not sit with their backs facing the household altar, which is the most sacred place in the household. Remember during such a visit not to praise a baby too openly as this is considered an ill omen. When visiting a home, bring along a nicely wrapped food gift. If you are to attend a wedding or funeral, bring new money placed inside an envelope.

CHAPTER
16

TRAVELING

AND LIVING

IN THE COUNTRY

You still have to register your passport number at the hotel, but you are no longer required to obtain a pass before being permitted to leave for your next destination in the country. The foreign traveler can now travel freely virtually anywhere in the country, with the exception of some areas in the far North, where conflicts with indigenous ethnic groups persist. According to the Vietnamese, tourists are allowed to venture into these areas, but one researcher we spoke to recently was turned away because she was entering the region to conduct linguistic research, which for some reason was a reason to keep her away.

What documents are needed to visit Vietnam?

To visit Vietnam, you will need a passport and a visa to enter the country, and to travel anywhere in the country. You can travel to Vietnam on a tourist visa and just keep quiet about the business you're doing—especially if you're only going to be there a few days. However, if you want to meet with a large number of people for the purpose of business, it's best to go over on a business visa. To obtain a business visa you must request that a Vietnamese sponsor apply to the Ministry of the Interior to formally invite you to the country. It's not difficult finding a Vietnamese entity willing to sponsor you; just contact the Vietnam Chamber of Commerce and Industry and they will arrange a business visa for you, and even set up meetings for you. (See the appendix for the address.) You will be asked to supply your sponsor with a letter stating your full name, date and place of birth, passport number with place of issue and expiration, nationality, and the date of entry into Vietnam as well as city of arrival. Presumably, the ministry will forward an approved visa to Vietnam's liaison office in Washington, DC, which has just recently opened as of this writing. Otherwise, you must work in conjunction with an international visa service, which will have the visa officially approved in Canada or Mexico and then sent to the United States. Either way you will be required to submit four passport photos and an official application form. Fees for visas run as follows: a single entry/exit/transit visa runs $25; a multiple entry/exit visa runs for 6 months and is $50. The total cost of hiring an international service to obtain a visa for you as a U.S. citizen costs about $120. Should you intend to visit more than one city, be sure you list the other cities on your visa application form.

Upon arrival in Vietnam, you will be asked to present two copies of your entry declaration form and to declare all consumer electronics, lap tops, and so on, with serial numbers. Try not to lose your copy of the Customs entry declaration, as there is a fine for doing so.

How does the visitor arrange for accommodations, and how much do hotels charge?

Don't bother looking for the expected booths at the airport manned by touts for the major hotels who can make hotel reservations. This familiar institution hasn't yet come to Vietnam. Make hotel arrangements by phone. (Hotel phone numbers are listed in the appendix.) Don't expect a hotel to fax you a confirmation either, as a one-page fax sent to the United States costs the hotel

$10. A good method is to arrive in Saigon without a reservation, and find a hotel room, which won't be a problem. Then telephone a hotel in Hanoi to make a reservation there when you decide to head north. The call will only cost you a couple of dollars and the reservation can be confirmed. Most travel guides recommend making reservations well before arrival because "hotels are always full." This isn't really the case unless you want to stay at the Metropole in Hanoi, which is usually packed because it's the only five-star hotel in town. A decent room elsewhere can be found, however, even on short notice.

Vietnam Tourism, the government-owned monopoly that controls the industry, can be of help in finding accommodations too. They have offices everywhere; try the one inside the Saigon Hotel. International hotels range in price from $70 a night at the very comfortable Chains First Hotel near the Saigon airport (featuring buffet breakfast, lighted tennis court, disco, and Swedish massage) to around $160 at the Rex and the Continental downtown. I suggest staying outside town where it's quieter and cheaper, while dining and meeting for drinks in town. The Sofitel Metropole has a virtual monopoly on first-class accommodations for foreigners intending to stay in central Hanoi. The room rates are criminal (though what the market will bear) at $300 a night and soaring. The Old Government Guest House around the corner is only $55 a night, with cavernous rooms loaded with Stalinesque furnishings and views of the Governor's Palace (built by the French) just across the courtyard. A range of very small budget minihotels also exist for nonbusiness travelers in both Saigon and Hanoi where you can pay as little as $25 a night for something survivable.

What are the problems of traveling in Vietnam by air, road, and train?

Business travel in Vietnam is done mainly by air, as long-distance journeying by rail or road is time-consuming and often perilous. Arranging flights and changing flights on Vietnam Airlines is surprisingly easy. You do, however, need to make arrangements by visiting a local office. There is a small surcharge for using traveler's checks or credit cards to purchase tickets—Visa and Mastercard only, as of this writing. Traveling by bus is hardly for the faint of heart, with frequent breakdowns, bad roads, and no air-conditioning, though the train ride between Hue and Da Nang is eye-popping—you come around a mountain and look down on a sloping valley filled with paddies of every shade of green, a couple of farmers working their oxen, behind them a line of palm trees, white beach, and crystal blue water. A sleeper from Hanoi to Da Nang costs the foreigner $40. Common modes of city transportation are motorbike, motorcycle, bicycle, cyclo, shuttle van, and the Toyota Land Cruiser— the vehicle of choice among those of the diplomatic corps. However, with cars, motorbikes, bicycles, cyclos, diesel tractors as well as ox carts fighting to get across town, city streets can be said to be unsafe at any hour. Only 25 of Hanoi's 250 intersections have traffic lights. Death-defying rush hours start in the very early morning because the banks and other government offices open at 7:30 A.M., and again in the evening around 4:30 to 6:00 P.M. Unfinished construction projects everywhere make traffic matters worse. Expats walking the streets of Hanoi and Saigon late weekend nights often encounter a sudden swarm of screaming motorbikes rounding a corner—illegal racers.

Whether you are in a peddle-driven cyclo, the back of a motorbike, or in a car, there is always the chance you could become involved in an accident. In that case, I offer the advice of a seasoned resident of Hanoi. "If you are in an accident," says the American student, "get up no matter how badly you're hurt and walk over to the other guy and help him up, and then tell him that it was his fault. And make sure that everyone else has heard you and understands that it's not your fault."

Why? "Because you are a foreigner and the police are going to arrive and try to make you pay a lot of money. Even if it clearly wasn't your fault, they are going to try to make you pay." It's not like Mexico where you are guilty in an accident until proven innocent; in Vietnam you are a foreigner and have more money, and thus it's felt that you should give money to the person with whom you are involved in an accident. There are exceptions to this rule, but most Vietnamese policemen are corrupt and will ask for money even if you are lying in the street with a broken leg and your assailant is standing next to his undamaged bike. Damages will likely be calculated right then and there, with the policeman as arbitrator. So blame the other first ("You were driving too fast!"), and then negotiate.

Traffic cops don't drive around on motorcycles. They stand on street corners or on umbrella-covered pedestals in the center of traffic circles. Rule: keep to the right of the umbrella and don't try to take a shortcut closer to the center of the traffic circle by going inside, or to its left. They'll stop you and ask for your license, and then extort you by charging you to get it back. Three U.S. dollars will normally retrieve the license. Don't go above $10 for a minor infraction.

What health and safety risks should the visitor to Vietnam be aware of?

There are no required vaccinations for entering Vietnam, but doctors do recommend vaccinations against diphtheria, tetanus, meningitis, gamma globulin (hepatitis A), and polio, with the hepatitis shot being the only "must" on the list. You might also take along malaria pills if you plan to travel outside Hanoi and Saigon, as about 1 million Vietnamese were afflicted in 1991. Encephalitis is present outside the city as well, though the three different shots necessary to protect yourself against it are only marginally effective.

A few precautions are in order. Water-born bacteria and viruses can only be avoided by drinking boiled coffee or tea or bottled beverages. Avoid the ice except at the top hotels where the water is purified before freezing. Most times you will find a thermos of hot water waiting for you in your hotel room, as well as (expensive) bottled water in the room refrigerator. If there isn't a thermos, request one and it will be brought at no charge. You'll be tempted to eat the fresh fruit and to drink the wonderful lemonade and other juice drinks during long humid afternoons, but don't unless you have been in the country for some time and your system has acclimated to the local germ army. Lastly, foreigners in Vietnam often suffer dehydration due to the humidity and lack of clean tap water. As small bottles of mineral water out of the hotel room refrigerator cost about $3, consider walking to a local market and buying three or four large bottles of water to stock in your hotel room much more cheaply.

TRAVELER'S INFORMATION

MONEY MATTERS. Vietnam's internationally nonconvertible currency unit is called the *dong*. Bills come in denominations of: 100; 200; 500; 1,000; 2,000; 5,000; 10,000; 20,000; and 50,000. The exchange rate as of this writing is 11,000 *dong* to 1 U.S. dollar. Exchange your dollars for *dong* at the VietcomBank where the exchange rate is better than on the street or in a restaurant. Traders on the street may accost you as well, but the black market rate is hardly better than the official rate, especially those outside the central post office. Travelers checks can only be cashed at a bank. Remember to arrive with an amount of U.S. dollars in small denominations, especially if arriving on a weekend when banks are closed. The government encourages shops to quote prices in *dong*, but you can pay with U.S. dollars or *dong* at all establishments. I suggest that you pay in *dong*, not dollars, because many proprietors will round off the amount in their favor; the restaurant or hotel will likely use a rate of 10,000 *dong* to the dollar instead of 11,000 because "it makes it easier for their accountant." They all say that. All major credit cards are now accepted in Vietnam, including Visa, Mastercard, American Express, and Diner's Club, though not all hotels and restaurants accept credit cards so one is advised to call ahead. (See appendix for restaurant phone numbers.)

TIPPING. Waiters and taxi drivers don't expect foreigners to conscientiously tip, though a 10 percent gratuity is well appreciated. Bellhops expect a few thousand *dong*, or a dollar. A VAT tax is not added to your hotel or restaurant bill.

TWO-TIER PRICING. While a ticket from Saigon to Hanoi costs the foreigner $150, the price for a local Vietnamese is about half that. The local pays $.25 per kilometer to ride a cyclo, while the foreigner pays approximately $1.00 per kilometer. Soon after arriving in Vietnam, you'll start asking why. When a foreigner living in Vietnam talks about so-called two-tier pricing, their faces get flushed and their breathing gets erratic. Institutionalized two-tier pricing is a fancy way of saying you pay more for services than the locals do because you come from the capitalist West. The only solution is to learn as much of the language as possible before you visit or relocate to the country. If you speak Vietnamese, prices for just about everything drop dramatically.

PHONE CALLS AND FAXES. The cheapest option for calling home is to go down to the post office (addresses in the appendix) and use the phone booth, though the heat and noise and radio signals that snarl your connection may be too much for you. A one-page fax sent from the general post office in Hanoi or Saigon runs about $7–8. The same fax sent from your hotel can run you between $11–18. E-mail is said to be "officially unavailable in Vietnam," yet some companies (with deep pockets) are managing to set up their own e-mail facilities.

WORKING HOURS. The Vietnamese work 6 days a week, 8:00 A.M. to 4:30 P.M. Most shops close at noon for an hour, though some close for 2 hours, but stay open later in the evening. Government workers start work at 7:30 A.M., take a 2-hour lunch, and end the day at around 4:30 P.M. People take their lunch from 11:30 to 1:30 or noon to 2:00. Thus, an appropriate time for setting up meetings, if early morning is not available, is around 2:30 in the afternoon.

ENTERTAINMENT AND SHOPPING. As of this writing, there exist few places to entertain business guests in Vietnam besides restaurants, which are listed in the appendix. You apply certain criteria in deciding where to eat out. Does the place serve non-Vietnamese food, which you might have become too acquainted with during a long stay. And two, is it air conditioned—an absolute must even in "winter." A *karoake* night club or a golf outing are other possibilities. Expats relax together at any number of bars. The Sunset Bar is perhaps the most popular hangout for expats, vying with the totally incongruous neomodern interior of the Q-Bar located alongside the Opera House. The Brits, Aussies, and Kiwis hang out at the Gold Cock. The Tin-Tin is a long thin and somewhat shady bar where the foreign backpackers, Rastafarian-style twenty-something's, and diplomats' kids (who are thought by other expats to be socially abnormal) kick back and get high. This one's not for business types unless they're incognito.

For bargain hunters, shops catering to high-class tourists and business travelers cluster near the Rex Hotel in central Saigon and near the Metropole in Hanoi, and sell gold jewelry, oil paintings,

lacquerware, cameras, and handicrafts fashioned out of the car-
casses of turtles and other endangered species.

CRIME, PANHANDLERS, AND PROSTITUTION. Unlike in Russia, no local
mafia controls retail distribution, and no *triads,* as in Hong Kong
and South China, operate an organized crime syndicate, though
loosely organized crime does control much of the prostitution
business in the South, illegal gambling, and the legion of child sellers of trinkets and postcards who pester tourists while they eat in
restaurants. I sat in Restaurant #19 and couldn't get rid of three
toddlers hawking $3 fake Swiss Army knives. I learned later that
organized crime gangs trade in "protection services" for eating
establishments, and in exchange the owners permit child peddlers
to sell to dining tourists. The limbless beggars of Saigon are said
to be controlled by mob elements too, and most of the money that
they receive ends up in the hands of gangsters. In Hanoi, one
should note, the children who sell phrasebooks, maps, and postcards are more likely to be working with an official organization
that uses the money they earn to run the orphanages where these
children live. Some carry identification cards carrying the name of
their orphanage; others work for illegitimate organizations.

Murder and rape against foreigners is virtually unknown, but
economic crimes such as burglary and pickpocketing are prevalent
in the South. In short, the country is safe—very safe—relative to
the United States. Pickpockets and purse snatchers are multiplying
though, so a money belt is advised.

With *doi moi,* prostitution has returned, which many
remember un-fondly from the wartime days. Prostitution is quite
open in the South and it is not uncommon to see a Western man
walking about or showing up at a party with a lady of the evening.
The boldest of the breed seek out their prey on motorcycles, even
driving up on the sidewalk to accost a potential client! The government has created a special department to crack down on prostitution, gambling, and the drug trade, but because the government owns many of these establishments, little is done to close
them. The National Committee Against AIDS (NCAA) has estimated that 2,280 Vietnamese are HIV positive as of February 1995.

POLICE. Local Vietnamese complain about the police as much as
expats do. Cops tend to be uneducated, underpaid, and power-

hungry men in uniform who feel they can extort money from any-body for no reason. Visitors should avoid them as much as possible.

POSTAL SERVICES. The time it takes mail to be delivered from the United States to Vietnam or from Vietnam to the United States varies widely, between 1-3 weeks. Often letters don't arrive at all; thus, all business correspondence should be sent via overnight delivery (which takes 3–5 days to Vietnam from the United States depending on the carrier), or via fax.

TIME ZONE. Vietnam's time zone is 16 hours ahead of Los Angeles, 13 hours ahead of New York.

AIRPORT DEPARTURE TAX. Prepare to pay an $8 departure tax when leaving via Vietnam's international airports.

ELECTRICITY/VOLTAGE. The power sockets in your hotel room may be either 110 or 240 volts, so you'll have to inquire. The sockets are of the two-prong type found in Western Europe.

PHOTOGRAPHY AND PHOTOCOPYING. If you plan to transport photographic film and computer disks, make sure you either store them in the appropriate lead bag or have them checked by hand because X-ray machines in Vietnam are not film-safe. Two of the many bargains in Vietnam are photo-finishing and photocopying. The cost for having film developed is about $2.80 per roll of 36 exposures. Professional-quality copying and binding is available everywhere and costs a few pennies per page.

WHAT TO BRING. Don't forget to bring along the following items, as they may be difficult to find in Vietnam at the level of quality to which you are accustomed.

Antibiotic

Coffee filters

Earplugs

First-aid kit

Insect repellant

Razor blades

Sewing kit

Shampoo/conditioner

Suntan lotion

Tampons

Toothpaste

Umbrella

Voltage converter

Washing detergent

Water purification tablets

RECREATION. Soccer is the most popular sport, followed by bad-minton, tai quan tow, tennis, golf, and water-skiing on the Saigon River. "They've got these old boards from the war," says an expat in Saigon. "You head out to some little islands an hour from down-town. You don't want to have any open cuts, of course."

LIVING IN VIETNAM AS AN EXPAT

Vietnam is a hardship duty post for expats. Too little to do, inad-equate housing and schools, and no entertainment. "Everybody tries to get out of here at least once every 2 months," says William Howell of IBM. Going outside the country to shop is essential. Many foods Westerners eat on a daily basis are still unavailable, such as baking goods, canned goods, and dressings. Two mini-marts in Ho Chi Minh City have smoothed this problem somewhat, but still, a constant question among expats is "Who's going out?" That is, who will buy a needed item not available in Vietnam dur-ing their weekend trip to Singapore or Hong Kong.

What is the American expat community like, and how supportive of newcomers?

By all accounts, the American expat community in Vietnam is tight-knit, low-profile, and rather too hard-working. Expats divide into two broad groups. The first, for example, is the middle-aged male living there with his family enjoying a cushy expat package. Fortune 500 companies tend to send such a smart and experienced person to Vietnam, say, somebody who has worked in China, is a little older, and seasoned. The other breed is the young woman or man, 26–34 years old, who came to Vietnam early in their careers, is unmarried, and works extremely hard 6 or 7 days a week. Few are having any fun, but they're independently running small- and medium-sized firms, gaining valuable experience, and are finding themselves being poached by larger firms to run their operations in the country. Most expats from both groups are quite frank about the fact that no one knows exactly what they are doing and that they are making it up as they go along. It's a pioneering experience for everyone.

Generally, the expat crowd is a well bonded and highly supportive one. "We're trying to get a lot of sporting activities together," says Mel Jackson of Red River Oil Company. "Al DeMatteis is the self-proclaimed commissioner of the softball league of Hanoi, which consists of one team. And we're trying to get a soccer team together so we can challenge the Saigon team, which is an expat soccer team down in Saigon called the Raiders. So we put together our own little team called the Capitalists." The American Chamber of Commerce has two chapters, one in Hanoi and one in Ho Chi Minh City. "We have our monthly meetings," says Al DeMatteis, President of the Hanoi Chapter. "We're here to help each other. I stress this over and over at all the meetings that I go to because Americans are a little funny about this—they like to hold everything to their chest and so forth. They walk into the Metropole with their three-piece suits on and they think that they're God."

DeMatteis recently formed a consortium of American companies to go after a particular project in Vietnam. "We tried—we tried—to keep them all close together." But obviously, self-interests threatened the cohesiveness of the U.S. group.

The week I arrived, a new bar called the Pear Tree was the site of a Friday night 8-ball expat pool tournament. "People ask me if I miss home," says Jackson, "and I say, 'yeah, I miss family and friends,' but I'll tell you, I've got *more* friends here in Hanoi, who are Americans age 25 to 35. We travel together. We drink beer together. It's great."

How does an expat go about renting a house in Vietnam?

Expats often have to live for months in a hotel before finding an apartment or house to rent in Vietnam. Residential housing
is only now coming online. As Vietnam moves to accommodate
foreign business and investment, the government has issued regulations pertaining to foreigners renting residential property, and
the rules differ from location to location. Most of these regulations
affect the landlord directly, and you as a renter only indirectly. In
order for a landowner to rent property, he is required to: (1)
obtain a permit allowing him to lease the property to foreigners;
(2) register with the police who will then investigate the landowner's past record; (3) check with the local Architect's Office to be
certain the house fits in with the city's overall masterplan, and is
not slated for rezoning; and (4) obtain final permit approval from
the Department of Land Use. The landlord must also ensure that
when the house was remodeled or built for rental purposes, that
it had been issued a construction permit, suitable for foreign
rentals.

As the foreign renter, you will be required to meet one of the
three following conditions. You must either possess a
Representative Office license for a JVE, FOE, BCC or other accept-
able entity, issued by the SCCI, an investment license from the
Ministry of Trade, or a letter of introduction from the People's
Committee.

So-called Service Companies in Vietnam act much like real
estate agents in helping you find a place to rent. (Four of them
are listed in the appendix.) As well as acting as agents, Service
Companies will ensure that all necessary contractual conditions
are met by the landlord before the contract is signed. They also
make sure that the landlord abides by the contract after signing
it.

Regardless of how you find a place, negotiations about price,
deposit, advance payment, payment method, and so on are done
between you and the landlord. Be aware of the minimum rent set
by the state, which your agent can update you about. As the
renter, you sign a contract with the Service Company. You will pay
rental deposits, advance payments, and your monthly rent to the
Service Company in U.S. dollars, which will in turn pay the landlord in *dong*.

Can foreigners purchase residential real estate property in Vietnam?

Though foreign individuals are not permitted to own land outright, under regulations issued in 1991 some provisions are made for limited ownership rights of residential property. The regulations (Decree 60-cp) specifically state that "foreign individuals residing long term in Vietnam are entitled to own houses for themselves and their family members, during their stay in Vietnam." They may buy houses from state-run companies or build their own houses, but they are not permitted to buy houses from other entities, such as joint ventures or Vietnamese individuals. Investing in real estate may not be wise, however, because the foreign owner must actually live in the house purchased; should he or she not live in it for longer than 90 days, the property rights can be withdrawn—just a slight catch still in place, as of this writing.

Are Vietnam's cities "party towns" like others in Asia, or more staid?

At least for American expats in Vietnam, being discreet is the watchword, especially about romantic relations with Vietnamese, as well as with other expats. This seems wise in a place where everyone still knows everyone, reputation can make or break a deal, and secrets are hard to keep. Unlike in other Asian climes, male expats in Vietnam find that an ascetic way of life is somewhat enforced. As one male expat noted, "You have to register a woman to live with you, and you can't take a woman into a hotel room without registering her." Moreover, while the typical Vietnamese male (as opposed to an official or businessman) can be an unsavory cretin of base morals, and typical Vietnamese women can be elegant, charming, and well dressed (which gives the foreign male in Vietnam an edge), the guy who believes home plate is two dates away in Vietnam is in for a big surprise. Romance moves glacially in Vietnam, especially when a foreigner is involved. A handsome American twenty-something I spoke to conceded: "I've dated three girls since I arrived here and I got to first base with one of them after nine months of dating. I think they think we're Martians." Vietnamese women tend to be wise and pragmatic, perhaps a bit prudish. "You're going to have to court a Vietnamese woman for a very long time," said a Vietnamese woman friend to Tamara Richardson. Consultant Mark Gillin, who lives and works in Saigon, told me the same thing, (Guys mutter this lament constantly in Vietnam.) "In the rest of Asia, you're either a player or a payer; but in Vietnam, you're either a payer or you're a very good liar." The meaning is that Vietnamese women, no matter how hard Hollywood or Broadway tries to stereotype them otherwise, are tough customers in romance who demand total devotion, loyalty, and commitment. Thus, the male expat population in Vietnam works the longest hours of perhaps any population of Americans. As a group they are an impeccably moral bunch compared to their brethren in Taiwan or Hong Kong or Bangkok; they are clearer-headed and more motivated in their jobs. In a few short years when they look back on their terrific success in Vietnam, I hope they will remember how much they owe to Vietnamese women and their sobering decorum.

APPENDICES

USEFUL BUSINESS ADDRESSES[*]

Government Offices—Hanoi

Ministry of Light Industry
7 Trang Thi Street
Tel: 253831,253832,253833

Ministry of Heavy Duty
54 Hai Ba Trung Street
Tel: 258311,267842,267873

Ministry of Transportation
80 Tran Jung Dao Street
Tel: 254012,254015,255417

Ministry of Aquatic Products
57 Ngoc Khanh Street
Tel: 256396,254714

---

[*] Please be advised that addresses and telephone numbers are subject to frequent change in Vietnam.

Ministry of Trade and Tourism
31 Tran Tien Street
Tel: 254950,264038,263227

Ministry of Forestry
123 Lo Duc Street
Tel: 253236,253237,211145

Ministry of Labour, Invalid and Social Affairs
2 Dinh Le Street
Tel: 255870,254728,269521

Ministry of Energy
18 Tran Nguyen Han Street
Tel: 257644,263725,253813

Ministry of Foreign Affairs
1 Ton That Dam Street
Tel: 258201,258322,252084

Ministry of Food Industry and Agriculture
Bach Thao Street
Tel: 268161,252113,234650

Ministry of Finance
8 Phan Huy Chu
Tel: 264872,262061,262773

Ministry of Construction
37 Le Dai Hanh Street
Tel: 268271,266732

Petro Vietnam
80 Nguyen Du Street
Tel: 257004,258423,258424

General Post Office
18 Nguyen Du Street
Tel: 257004,258423,258424

Vietnam Tourism
30A Ly Thuong Kiet Street
Tel: 264319,269130,257571

Vietnam Insurance General Company
7 Ly Thuong Kiet Street
Tel: 262632,262623

Customs Office
51 Nguyen Van Cu Street
Tel: 263951,263918,265256

The State Bank of Vietnam
7 Le Lai Street
Tel: 258388,252831,265589

Vietnam Chamber of Industry and Commerce
33 Ba Trieu Street
Tel: 252961,252962,260854

Government Offices—Ho Chi Minh City

Chamber of Commerce and Industry
171 vo thi Sau Street, District 3
Tel: 230301

City Customs Office
21 Ton Duc Thang Street, District 1
Tel: 290912

City Planning Committee
30-32 Le Thanh Ton Street, District 1
Tel: 290904

City Post Office
125 Hai Ba Trung Street, District 1
Tel: 293310

The Economic Institute
175 Hai Ba Trung Street, District 3
Tel: 286590

Office of Economic Relations
86 Le Thanh Ton Street, District 1
Tel: 290048

Export Development Centre
92-96 Nguyen Hue Boulevard, District 1
Tel: 290072

Office of External Relations
6 Thai Van Lung Street, District 1
Tel: 224128

Office of Finance
140 Xo viet nghe Tinh Street, District 3
Tel: 292141

Foreign Investment Services Company (FISC)
12 Nam Ky Khoi Nghia Street, District 1
Tel: 293616

Foreign Trade and Investment Development
Centre (FDTC)
92-96 Nguyen Hue Street, District 1
Tel: 222982

Office of Industry
101 Hai Ba Trung Street, District 3
Tel: 298018,296322

Office of Labour
159 Nguyen Thi Minh Khai Street, District 3
Tel: 291302

The People's Committee
86 Le Thanh Ton Street, District 1
Tel: 291054

Services of Foreign Economic Relations
45-47 en Chuong Duong Street, District 1
Tel: 298116

Banks (Foreign and Domestic)

ANZ Bank
14 Le Thai To
Hanoi, Vietnam
Tel: (84-4) 258190

Cathay Trust Bank
55 Quang Trung
Hanoi, Vietnam
Tel: (84-4) 250555

Deutsche Bank
(Rep Office)
25, Tran Binh Trong
Hanoi, Vietnam
Tel: (84-4) 268554

HongKong Bank
(Rep Office)
Unit 6
Hanoi, Vietnam
Tel: (84-4) 269994

VID Public Bank (JV Bank)
194 Tran Quang Khai
Hanoi, Vietnam
Tel: (84-4) 266953

Credit Lyonnais
10 Trang Thi
Hanoi, Vietnam
Tel: (84-4) 260157

Banque Nationale de Paris
8 Trang Hung Dao 602
Hanoi, Vietnam
Tel: (84-4) 253175

Indovina Bank
88 Hai Ba Trung
Hanoi, Vietnam
Tel: (84-4) 265516

Societe Generale
40 Tang Bat Ho
Hanoi, Vietnam
Tel: (84-4) 259822

Banque National De Paris
1 Ton That Dam
2nd Floor, State Bank Building, D1
Ho Chi Minh City, Vietnam
Tel: (84-8) 299504

Banque Francaise du Commerce
Exterieur
11 Me Linh Square
Ho Chi Minh City, Vietnam
Tel: (84-8) 294144

Deutsche Bank (Rep Office)
1174 Nguyen Dinh Chieu, D3
Ho Chi Minh City, Vietnam
Tel: (84-8) 22747

Indovina Bank (JV Bank)
36 Ton That Dam D1
Ho Chi Minh City, Vietnam
Tel: (84-8) 224995

Hong Kong Bank (Rep Office)
4th Floor, Textimex Building
10 Nguyen Hue Boulevard, Q1
Ho Chi Minh City, Vietnam
Tel: (84-8) 251226

Firstvina Bank (JV Bank)
69 Bui Thi Xuan D1
Ho Chi Minh City, Vietnam
Tel: (84-8) 391050

ING Bank (Rep Office)
136, Nam Ky Khoi Nghia, D1
Ho Chi Minh City, Vietnam
Tel: (84-8) 241500

Credit Lyonnais
17 Ton Duc Thang, D1
Ho Chi Minh City, Vietnam
Tel: (84-8) 299226

The Export Import Bank of Korea
Suite A, 5th Floor, OSIC
8 Nguyen Hue, D1
Ho Chi Minh City, Vietnam
Tel: (84-8) 224237

VID Public Bank (JV Bank)
15 Ben Chuong Duong, D1
Ho Chi Minh City, Vietnam
Tel: (84-8) 223583

The Thai Military Bank, Ltd.
11 Ben Chuong Duong Street, D1
Ho Chi Minh City, Vietnam
Tel: (84-8) 222218

Bangkok Bank Limited
117 Nguyen Hue Street, Q1
Ho Chi Minh City, Vietnam
Tel: (84-8) 223416

Essential Contacts in Da Nang

University of Da Nang
357 Ngo Quyen
Tel: (0151) 36169
Fax: (0151) 36225

People's Committee of Quangnam Da Nang
Foreign Economic Relations Dept.
452 Ong Ich Kiehm
Tel: (0151) 22759
Fax: (0151) 25853

People's Committee Main Office
42 Bach Dang
Tel: (0151) 21050
Fax: (0151) 25321

Port of Da Nang (Port Authority)
24 Bach Dang
Tel: (0151) 22517/2114
Fax: (0151) 22565

EPZ Massda
6B Tran Quy Cap
Tel: (0151) 26839
Fax: (0151) 26840

Country Embassies—Hanoi

Algeria
15, Phan Chu Trin Street
Tel: 253865

Australia
66, Ly Thuong Kiet Street
Tel: 252763

Bangladesh
101-104 A1 Van Phuc
Tel: 231625

Belgium
48-50, Nguyen Thai Hoc Street
Tel: 252263

Britain
16, Ly Thuong Kiet Street
Tel: 252510

Bulgaria
358 Van Phuc Street
Tel: 252908

Cambodia
71A, Tran Hung Dao Street
Tel: 253788

Canada
389, Nguyen Dinh Chieu Street
Tel: 265840

China
46, Hoang Dieu Street
Tel: 253736

Czech
13, Chu Van An Street
Tel: 254131

Denmark
BT 6, Van Phuc 3
Tel: 231888

Egypt
85, Ly Thuong Kiet Street
Tel: 252944

Finland
B3b, Giang vo Quarter 1-2
Tel: 256754

France
57, Tran Hung Dao Street
Tel: 252719

Germany
29, Tran Phu Street
Tel: 253836

Hungary
43-47, Dien Bien Phu Street
Tel: 252858

India
58-60, Tran Hung Dao Street
Tel: 253409

Indonesia
50, Ngo Quyen Street
Tel: 253353

Iran
54, Tran Phu Street
Tel: 232068

Iraq
66, Tran Hung Dao Street
Tel: 254141

Israel
Hotel Sofitel-Metropole
Tel: 266919

Italy
9, Le Phung Hieu Street
Tel: 256246

Japan
61, Trung Chinh Street
Tel: 692600

Korea (DPRK)
25, Cao Ba Quat Street
Tel: 253008

Korea (ROK)
29, Nguyen Dinh Chieu Street
Tel: 226677

Laos
22, Tran Binh Trong Street
Tel: 254576

Libya
A3, Van Phuc
Tel: 253379

Malaysia
A3, Van Phuc
Tel: 253371

Mongolia
39, Tran Phuc Street
Tel: 253009

Myanmar
A3, Van Phuc
Tel: 253269

Netherlands
Dan Chu Hotel
Tel: 253323

Palestine
E 4B, Trung Tu Quarter
Tel: 524013

Philippines
27 B, Tran Hung Dao Street
Tel: 257948

Poland
3, Chua Mot Cot Street
Tel: 252027

Romania
5, Le Hong Phong Street
Tel: 252014

Russia
58, Tran Phu Street
Tel: 254631

Singapore
41-43 Tran Phu Street
Tel: 233965

Slovak
6, Le Hong Phong Street
Tel: 254335

Sweden
2, 358 Street
Tel: 254824

Switzerland
77B, Kim Ma, Torserco Building
Tel: 232019

Thailand
63-65, Hoang Dieu Street
Tel: 235092

Yugoslavia
47, Tran Phu Street
Tel: 252343

European Economic Union
2, Dinh Le Street
Tel: 267367

Office Support Entities
(Rental agents and labor services)

Ho Chi Minh City Investment and Trading of Property
Company
Tel: 230256/299391

FOSCO
Ho Chi Minh City
Tel: 299763/297351

Petro Service Company
Ho Chi Minh City
Tel: 296702/291867

Housing Management and Trading Company
Ho Chi Minh City
Tel: 225232/222451

International Organizations—Hanoi

U.N.D.P.
27-29, Phan Boi Chau Street
Tel: 257495

UNIDO
27-29, Phan Boi Chau Street
Tel: 257495

UNFPA
B 36, Giang Vo Quarters, 3-4
Tel: 254763

FAO
3, Nguyen Gia Thieu
Tel: 257239

IMF
12, Tran Thi Street
Tel: 251927

WFP
28, Van Phuc
Tel: 263896

WHO
2A, Van Phuc
Tel: 257901

World Bank
Suite 301, Binh Minh Hotel
27, Ly Thai To Street
Tel: 244077

UNICEF
72, Ly Thuong Kiet Street
Tel: 261170

UNHCR
60, Nguyen Thai Hoc Street
Tel: 256785

Schools Accepting Foreigners

United Nations International School
Hanoi-Amsterdam School, Giang Vo, Hanoi
Tel: 263635
Fax: 263635

École Française International De Hanoi
Hanoi-Amsterdam School, Giang Vo, Hanoi
Tel: 232023
Fax: 232023

The Russian School
56/58 Pho Nguyen Thai Hoc, Hanoi
Tel: 252170

The Finnish School
Hanoi Water Supply Project
Mai Dich, Hanoi
Tel: 344039

Centre Cultural 'Alliance Française' de Hanoi
42 Yet Kieu Street, Hanoi
Tel: 266970-71

Hanoi School of Fine Arts
Yet Kieu Street, Hanoi
Tel: 226859

Hanoi University
Tel: 581419

Hanoi Polytechnic University
Tel: 692222

Hanoi University for Teachers
Tel: 343423

Hanoi University for Foreign Language Teachers
Tel: 343269,346056

Hanoi Foreign Language College
Tel: 244338

Hanoi Foreign Trade College
Tel: 343495/343605

Hanoi Conservatory
Tel: 254969

DIRECTORY OF TRADE CONTACTS

Light Industrial Companies in Vietnam Interested in Doing Business with Foreign Companies:

TEXTILES

Fideco
46 Truong Dinh Street
3rd District
Ho Chi Minh City
Tel: 291107
Fax: 84-8-225241

General Export-Import and Service Company
226 A Pasteur Street
District 3
Ho Chi Minh City
Tel: 299219
Fax: 84-8-298130

Legamex State Company
15 Truong Son Street
Ho Chi Minh City
Tel: 84-8-640523
Fax: 861265

Thanh Cong Textile Company
8, Quoc Lo I
Tan Binh District
Ho Chi Minh City
Tel: 641168
Fax: 84-8-550979

Vietnam National Textile Corporation
10 Nguyen Hue Street
District 1
Ho Chi Minh City
Tel: 84-8-293578
Fax: 292349

Mulberry Silkworm and Silks United Company
38 Quang Trung Street
Da Nang City
Tel: 22372
Fax: 84-51-23891

Union Of Textile PDTN and I/E Corporation
25 Ba Trieu Street
Hanoi
Tel: 257700
Fax: 84-42-62268

Hong Quan Textile Company Ltd.
Km 3, Highway No. 10
Quang Trung Quarter
Thai Binh Province
Tel: 84-36-31918
Fax: 84-36-31918

Wool Embroidery and Carpet Export Company
146 (4/F) Nguyen Cong Tru Street
District 1
Ho Chi Minh City
Tel: 222174/238079
Fax: 84-8-296581

Generalimex
66 Pho Duc Chinh Street
District 1
Ho Chi Minh City
Tel: 293925-298614
Fax: 292968

Textaco
05 Dien Bien Phu
Hanoi
Tel: 84-42-32098
Fax: 84-42-32318

Meko Leather Factory
Tra Noc Indl Zone
Can Tho City
Tel: 71-24590
Fax: 84-71-21431

GARMENTS

Saigon Union Producing and Trading For Import-Export
71-79 Dong Khoi Street
District 1
Ho Chi Minh City
Tel: 296406
Fax: 84-8-222941

Minh Phung Production Team
241 Lac Long Quan
11th District
Ho Chi Minh City
Tel: 650392/650671
Fax: 84-8-650304

Trihaco Imp. Exp. Garments Co. Ltd.
360 Le Van Sy Street
3rd District
Ho Chi Minh City
Tel: 441-273-4421-212
Fax: 84-8-442-2267

Vico Ltd.
61, Tran Quang Dieu Street
District 3
Ho Chi Minh City
Tel: 441438
Fax: 298540

Secoin Co Ltd.
40 Ba Triev Street
Hanoi
Tel: 262750/265756
Fax: 84-4-262750

Van Xuan Investment and Commercial Company
18B, Ho Xuan Huong
Hanoi
Tel: 346070
Fax: 84-4-255212

Van Xuan Trading and Investment Company
Lang Thuong
Dong Da
Hanoi
Tel: 246070
Fax: 84-4-255282

Artex Thang Long
164, Ton Duc Thang Street
Hanoi
Tel: 257973
Fax: 84-2-56730

Manolis and Company Asia Ltd.
51, Ly Thai To Street
Hanoi
Tel: 84-42-66122
Fax: 84-42-66031

Legamex Company
63-65 Ngo Gia Tu Street
Ho Chi Minh City
Tel: 51727-553682
Fax: 84-8-554124

Govimex
280 Nguyen Van Nghi Street
Go Vap District
Ho Chi Minh City
Tel: 941869/941307
Fax: 84-8-943847

Industrial Export Import Corporation
275B Pham Ngu Lao Street
District 1
Ho Chi Minh City
Tel: 394480
Fax: 84-8-99413

ELECTRONIC PRODUCTS

Vung Tau Intourco (Branch Office)
30, Nguyen Van Troi Street
Phu Nhuan District
Ho Chi Minh City
Tel: 447467,447948
Fax: 84-8-447162

The Company for Finan-Promo-Techno
25 Ly Thuong Kiet Street
Hanoi
Tel: 2-67312, 2-67313
Fax: 84-42-67706

Sapina Holding Saigon Company Ltd.
Sapina Building, 2 Hoang Van Thu Street
Ward 9 Phu Nhuan District
Ho Chi Minh City
Tel: 848-442-608
Fax: 848-444-431

V.E.I.C.
29F Hai Ba Trung
Hanoi
Tel: 84-4-265460
Fax: 84-4-259595

Phuc Loi Trading Company, Ltd.
153 Bis Nguyen Dinh Chinh Street
Phu Nhuan District
Ho Chi Minh City
Tel: 443680
Fax: 444290

Duyen Hai Commercial Company
342, Ly Thuong Kiet Street
Hanoi
Tel: 31848
Fax: 84-36-31222

IMET (Institute for Micro-Electronics)
39-40, Ly Thuong Kiet Street
Hanoi
Tel: 250767
Fax: 844-267645

Ha Nam Electronic Company (Haneco)
National Road, Number 1A
Minh Khai Area
Tel: 35-51088
Fax: 84-35-51227

Viettronics Thu Duc
15C, Nguyen Van Troi Street
Phu Nhuan District
Ho Chi Minh City
Tel: 447928,904354
Fax: 84-8-444829

Sao Mai Electronic Corporation (MSC)
Nghia Do, Tu Liem
Hanoi
Tel: 3-45589
Fax: 84-4-344263

Viettronics Binh Hoa Company
204, No Trang Long Street
Binh Thanh District
Ho Chi Minh City
Tel: 43300,941300
Fax: 84-8-942926

TOYS

Manolis and Company Asia Ltd.
51, Ly Thai To Street
Hanoi
Tel: 84-42-66122
Fax: 84-42-66031

Technology Development Supporting Corporation
(DETECH C.)
65, Nguyen Du Street
Hanoi
Tel: 265612
Fax: 84-4-268842

Binh-Tien Imex Corporation, PTE., Ltd.
01, Thuy Khue
Ba Dinh District
Hanoi
Tel: 2-33736
Fax: 84-4-234038

Hai Hung Export-Import Corporation
11, Nguyen Du Street
Hai Duong Town
Hai Hung Province
Tel: 84-32-53950
Fax: 84-32-53559

Phuc Hung Toy Ltd.
67B, Cua Bac Street
Hanoi
Tel: 512124
Fax: 844-253172

Quyet Co-Operative
201 A Nguyen Thi M. Kjai
1st District
Ho Chi Minh City
Tel: 558983/396024
Fax: 84-8-322298

VIF Vietnam Computer Company
54 Giang Vo Street
Ba Dinh District
Hanoi
Tel: 84-4-244542
Fax: 84-4-268561

Viettronimex Hanoi Branch
19 Nha Tho Street
Hanoi
Tel: 256789
Fax: 84-4-264225

FOOTWEAR

Saigon Shoe FTY
419 Le Hong Phong Street
10th District
Ho Chi Minh City
Tel: 557117/553820
Fax: 84-8-299217

INEXIM
275B Pham Ngu Lao Street
1st District
Ho Chi Minh City
Tel: 394480/324512
Fax: 84-8-399413

Secoin Company Ltd.
40 Ba Triev Street
Hanoi
Tel: 262750/265756
Fax: 84-4-262750

Minh Phung Production Team
241 Lac Long Quan
11th District
Ho Chi Minh City
Tel: 650392/650670
Fax: 84-8-650304

Fuplarubex Phu Nhuan Export Plastic and Rubber
FTY, Industrial Sector
Ward Number 9 Phu Nhuan District
Ho Chi Minh City
Tel: 446145
Fax: 84-8-443563

Leather Goods, GMT, Textile E-I Company
63-65 Ngo Gia Tu Street
District 10
Ho Chi Minh City
Tel: 51727
Fax: 84-8-55124

Binh Tien Rubber Co-Operative
129B Ly Chieu Hoang Street
District 6
Ho Chi Minh City
Tel: 755701/756563
Fax: 84-8-553443

Union of Nghe An Import-Export Company
Vinh City
Nghe An Province
Tel: 4842-2429-3173
Fax: 84-01-38-2682

An Lac Footwear Factory
92 Avenue 1 An Lac Town
Binh Chanh District
Ho Chi Minh City
Tel: 259299/558107
Fax: 848-58107

Cholimex Company
631, 633, Nguyen Trai Street
District 5
Ho Chi Minh City
Tel: 558576
Fax: 555682

HOUSEHOLD PRODUCTS

Generalimex
46 Ngo Quyen Street
Hanoi
Tel: 84-42-64009
Fax: 84-42-59894

Vietnam National Gen. Export-Import Corporation
Marketing Department
46 Ngo Quyen Street
Hanoi
Tel: 64009
Fax: 84-42-59894

Cuulong Agricultural Sea-Products Company
78 vo Thi Sau Street
District 1
Ho Chi Minh City
Tel: 299417
Fax: 299417

Phi Hung Trading and Service Company Ltd.
312 Lanh Binh Thang, Ward 8
District 11
Ho Chi Minh City
Tel: 84-8-553442
Fax: 84-8-290282

Vung Tau-Con Dao Import-Export Company
36A Avenue 1
Vung Tau
Tel: 97129 7403 7414

Datviet Import-Export Company
259 Tay Son Street
Dong Da District
Hanoi
Tel: 264647
Fax: 253172

Import-Export and Investment for Development
Company Cangio
57-59 Le Loi Street
District 1
Ho Chi Minh City
Tel: 297583
Fax: 225513

Tian Trading & Tour PTE Enterprise
98B Ly Thai To Street
District 10
Ho Chi Minh City
Tel: 84-8-350009
Fax: 84-8-350009

Tran Thi Tinh
265, Tran Jung Dao Street
District 1
Ho Chi Minh City
Tel: 394533
Fax: 84-8-330038

Artex Thang Long
164, Ton Duc Thang Street
Hanoi
Tel: 2-57973
Fax: 84-2-56731

Vinh Hoang Trading Company
378E, Dien Bien Phu Street
District 10
Ho Chi Minh City
Tel: 391395/332674
Fax: 322073

Sao Mai Tourist Service Company
16,18, Thong Phong Alley
Ton Duc Thang Street
Hanoi
Tel: 2-55827
Fax: 844-233887

WATCHES AND CLOCKS

Cong Ty Compact
16 Dao Tan Q5, T P
Ho Chi Minh City
Tel: 551352

Meko Leather FTY
2 Le Hong Phong Street
Cantho City
Haugiang Province
Tel: 21583

Saigon Trading Tech. Service Center
84, Nguyen Hue Street
District 1
Ho Chi Minh City
Tel: 294729

Sakyno Company (Import-Export and Investment)
101, Hai Ba Trung Street
District 1
Ho Chi Minh City
Tel: 84-8-296416
Fax: 84-8-251161

Tran Nam Phu
Cantho City, S R
Tel: 20201

Dofyco Company, Ltd.
476, Hoa Hao Street
District 10
Ho Chi Minh City
Tel: 559856/555990

SAMPLE CONTRACTUAL AGREEMENTS*

Form 1
INVESTMENT APPLICATION FOR LICENSING
A BUSINESS COOPERATION CONTRACT

Date:_____

To: The State Committee for Cooperation and Investment

An investment application under the Foreign Investment Law of Vietnam is herewith being submitted by the undersigned to the Socialist Republic of Vietnam through the State Committee for Cooperation and Investment.

Particulars regarding the proposed Business Cooperation as well as the requested Investment Incentives and related Data/Documentation are described herein and or submitted herewith:

Name of Parties, comprising:

Vietnamese party(ies) (the name of the company(ies):

Foreign party(-ies) (the name of the company or individual(s):

Wish to apply for a Business License in order to implement the Business Co-operation Contract signed on _____.

We wish to apply for the following Investment Incentives:

-
-
-

The documents enclosed with this Application comprise:

---

*The sample contracts which follow are adapted from: "Guidance on Preparation of Documents for Foreign Direct Investment Projects in Vietnam" Hanoi: Statistical Publishing House, Office of the State Committee for Cooperation and Investment, 1993.

Certification concerning juridical person status, as well as the Company's certified Annual General Report and/or Banker's reference from an internationally acceptable Financial Institution;

Legalized Power(s) of Attorney for signing this Application and the Business Cooperation Contract;

Business Cooperation Contract;

The economic and technical feasibility studies;

The surveyor's inspection report regarding used or second hand equipment (if such equipment are intended for use/importation into the Socialist Republic of Vietnam).

VIETNAMESE PARTY(IES):   **FOREIGN PARTY(IES):**
(Signature,seal)   (Signature,seal)

Form 2
GUIDANCE FOR A BUSINESS COOPERATION CONTRACT

Business on the Foreign Investment Law of Vietnam and relevant legal documents, the parties mentioned hereinafter wish to implement investment activities in the Socialist Republic of Vietnam as outlined in the scope of this business cooperation contract.

A—The Vietnamese party(ies):

1. Company name:
2. Delegated representative:
   Title:
3. Head Office:
   Telephone:
   Telex:
   Fax:
4. The main business line:
5. License number for the already established Vietnamese company:
   Registered at: Date:
   Registered capital:
   Company account opened at:
   Account number:

B—The Foreign party(ies):

1. Name of the company or individuals:
2. Delegated representative:
   Title:
   Nationality:
   Resident Address:
3. Head Office:
   Telephone:
   Telex:
   Fax:
4. The main business line:

5. License number for the already established Foreign
company:

    Registered at: Date:

    Financial situation (registered capital):

    Company account opened at:

    Account number:

(Note: If either contracting party comprises more than one
member, then each member shall describe all the aforesaid details.
Each party needs to appoint its own delegated representative.)

Agree to sign this business cooperation contract with the following terms and conditions:

Article 1:

Objectives of the Business Cooperation:

(State in detail a clear description of the intended scope of
the Business Cooperation.)

Article 2:

1. Location:

    Common (Ward)/District (Precinct)/Province(City)

2. Production capacity:

    (List goods/services, quantity of units, and maximum
    designed production capacity.)

3. The product(s) of the Business cooperation contract shall
be marketed as follows:

   - To the Vietnamese market: (the quantity or product
     percentage projected to be sold annually and its antic-
     ipated value expressed in U.S.$ valued at current
     exchange rates.)

Article 3:

Quantify the Specific Responsibilities of each Party in implementing this Business Cooperation Contract:

(Include responsibilities of each party, value of contribution,
and date of completion.)

At the time when the actual financial contribution is made, if the projected values shown above differ when compared with the actual contributed values, the two parties must agree to these differences and report same to the State Committee for Cooperation and Investment for consideration and approval.

In case either party is unable to carry out his/her responsibilities as agreed upon, this party must inform the other party within ... days of the reasons for his/her inability to carry out such responsibilities as well as the measures taken to remedy the situation. Actual and true losses caused by the delay or inability of one party to carry out its responsibility(ies) must be compensated for accordingly.

Article 4:

Duration of this Contract is for .... years from the date of granting the business license. Any changes to the duration of this contract shall have to be agreed upon by the contracting parties and reported to the State Committee for Cooperation and Investment for consideration and final approval.

Either contracting party wishing to extend the agreed duration of this contract, must so inform the other party at least ... days before the expiry of the contract. If the parties agree to the extension of the contract, they must submit a relevant application for consideration by SCCI, at least six (6) months before the expiry of the contract.

If all condition for termination of the contract cannot be implemented, the contract shall remain in effect provided that contract continuation is approved by SCCI.

Article 5:

The schedule for implementing this contract after the date on which the Investment License by SCCI has been issued, is as follows:

1. a.) Importation (if applicable) of building materials for the main production area/plant or the office:

   from month ... to month ...

b.) Construction of the main production area/plant or the office:

from month ... to month ...

2. Importation of equipment and machinery related to the actual production:

from month ... to month ...

3. Production/trial operation:

from month ... to month ...

4. Official production:

from month ...

Article 6:

1. This business cooperation contract uses the monetary unit of ... (state the specific currency) for all financial matters. Any and all currency conversions for the purpose of accounting administration or making payments, shall be made in accordance with the official rates made public by the State Bank of Vietnam at the time each financial transaction is actually made.

2. The contracting parties must implement all payments envisioned in the Contract, through an account in Vietnamese currency and/or a foreign currency opened at ... (state the name of the Bank, its address in the Socialist Republic of Vietnam, etc.)

(Selection of any Bank among the Foreign Trade Banks of Vietnam, a foreign bank branch in Vietnam, a joint venture bank between a Vietnamese Bank and a foreign bank is allowed.)

Article 7:

1. The accounting system for implementing this contract is ... (the name of the system agreed upon by the parties). The system is set up in conformity with international practices, is approved by the Ministry of Finance and falls within the control of a Vietnamese authorized financial agency.

2. The rates of depreciation of the fixed assets belonging to this Business Cooperation are as follows:

- Workshop:.......percent/year
- Equipment:......percent/year
- Other fixed assets:......percent/year

Article 8

1. The Foreign party(ies) must fully carry out its/their financial obligations toward the State of Vietnam as stipulated in the Business License and shall pay taxes in accordance with the following method:

   (Clearly state the method of paying profit tax and withholding tax of the foreign party; whether, for example, via direct payment, or perhaps via the Vietnamese party by deducting part of the shared profits, etc.)

2. The Vietnamese party(ies) undertake to fully carry out its/their financial obligation toward the State of Vietnam in accordance with current laws and provisions of the financial obligations as described in the Business License.

Article 9:

The contracting parties agree to share products and/or profits or losses through the implementation of the contract as follows:

- The Vietnam Party(ies) (Do clearly state each party if necessary.)
- The Foreign Party(ies): (Do clearly state each party if necessary.)

Article 10:

Disputes among the parties, related to or arising from the contract, must first of all be resolved through negotiation. In case of continued disagreement, the disputes shall be brought to ... (clearly state the name of the arbitration organization and address.)

Decision of ... (the name of the above-said organization) is final and shall be observed by both parties.

Article 11:

This Business Cooperation contract may be terminated ahead of schedule and/or in the following cases:

a) Where force majeure such as natural disasters, war, etc..., renders the investment activities inoperable provided of course that this force majeure is indeed the actual cause of obstruction to or unacceptable delay in the implementation/continuation of the contract and that the parties have already applied all possible measures to overcome the impact of force majeure disasters but without success. In such case, it is anticipated that the party in whose area the force majeure has occurred shall have immediately informed the other party(-ies) a written statement concerning the measures taken as well as details of the force majeure events certified by the local authority(ies). In addition, the contracting parties shall immediately inform the State Committee for Cooperation and Investment about all measures taken to overcome the situation (albeit unsuccessful).

b) In case the business entity is unable to continue its operations due to serious losses or breach of contract terms, leading to serious economic losses and this has been approved by the SCCI.

c) As a result of a decision by the State Committee for Cooperation and Investment, to withdraw the investment license.

Article 12:

Upon contract expiration, the parties agree to apportion the Business cooperation assets in relation to their share-holding capacity and responsibility as follows:
(Describe in detail conditions in relation to each party's approved rights, responsibilities, assets, etc.)

Article 13:

All other terms relating to the business cooperation agreement but not specifically provided for in the Business Cooperation

Contract, shall be implemented by the Party(ies) in accordance with the current stipulations of the Foreign Investment Law of Vietnam and other stipulations in the Business License issued for this investment by SCCI.

Article 14:

The Business Cooperation Contract may be added to and/or amended after a written agreement between the Parties and with approval of SCCI.

Article 15:

This Contract shall take effect from the date of approval of the Application for Investment by SCCI.

Article 16:

This Business Cooperation Contract is signed in (location) on (date)......in the Vietnamese version and in (a widely used foreign language). These two versions are of equal legal validity.

THE FOREIGN PARTY	THE VIETNAMESE PARTY
(Signature, title, and seal, if any)	(Signature, title, and seal, if any)
In case there are several foreign parties, state the name of each party and affix appropriate seal (if any)	In case there are several Vietnamese parties, state the name of each party and affix appropriate seal (if any)

Form 3
INVESTMENT APPLICATION
FOR LICENSING A JOINT VENTURE

Date:_____

To: The State Committee for Cooperation and Investment

An investment application under the Foreign Investment Law of Vietnam is herewith being submitted by the undersigned to the Socialist Republic of Vietnam through the State Committee for Cooperation and Investment.

Particulars regarding the proposed Joint Venture as well as requested Investment Incentives and related Data/Documentation are described herein and are submitted herewith:

I. Name of Parties, comprising:

* The Vietnamese Party(ies) (the name of the Company(ies):

* The Foreign Party(ies) (the name of the Company(ies) or individual(s):

Wish to apply for the following Investment Incentives:

*

*

*

III. The documents enclosed with this Application comprise:

* The Joint Venture Contract;
* The Joint Venture Charter/Articles of Association;
* Certification concerning juridical person status, as well as the Company's certified Annual General Report and/or Banker's reference from an internationally acceptable Financial Institution;

- Legalized Power(s) of Attorney for signing this Application and the JV Contract;
- The economic and technical feasibility studies;
- The appointed surveyor's inspection report regarding used or second-hand equipment (if such equipment is intended for use/importation into the Socialist Republic of Vietnam).

VIETNAMESE PARTY(IES)   **FOREIGN PARTY(IES)**
(Signature and seal)   (Signature and seal)

Form 4
GUIDANCE FOR A JOINT VENTURE CONTRACT

Based of the Foreign Investment Law of Vietnam and relevant legal documents, the Parties mentioned hereinafter have signed a Joint Venture Contract to establish in the Socialist Republic of Vietnam, a Joint Venture Company as follows:

A—Participating member(s) of the Vietnamese Party

    1. Name of the company:

    2. Delegated representative:

       Title:

    3. Head office:

       Telephone:

       Telex:

       Fax:

    4. Main business line:

    5. Certificate of Incorporation No.:

       Registered at: Date:

       Registered capital:

       Account opened at the bank:

       Account number:

B—Participating member(s) of the Foreign Party

    1. Name of the company or individuals:

    2. Delegated representative:

       Title:

       Nationality:

       Resident address:

    3. Head Office:

       Telephone:

       Telex:

       Fax:

4. Main business:

5. Incorporation No.:

Registered at: Date:

Registered capital:

Account opened at the bank:

Account number:

(Note: If one or both joint venture Parties comprise more than one member, then each member shall describe all the above details. In the case of two-party Joint Ventures each party needs to appoint its own delegated representative.)

Article 1:

1. The Parties agree to establish the JV Company in the Socialist Republic of Vietnam with purposes of (state in detail the objective of the JV Company):

2. a) The name of the JV Company is:

   b) The transaction name of the JVC under which it intends to conduct its business affairs is (if different from 2a above):........

Article 2:

1. Address of the JV Company:
   - Head Office:
   - Main production factory/workshop:
   - Branch(es):
   - Representative office(s):

2. Production capabilities:

   (List goods and/or services to be produced, unit output, and maximum designed production potential; divide list into main and auxiliary products (if applicable)

3. Products of the JV Company will be marketed as follows:
   - At the Vietnamese market: (quantity or percentage if products anticipated to be sold annually, and expected value).

- At Foreign markets (quantity or percentage if products anticipated to be sold annually, and expected value).

Article 3:

1. Total invested capital of the JVC:

2. Legal capital of the JVC is ....., to which:

   a) The Vietnamese party contributes ..... (value, accounting for ... percent of the legal capital), comprising:

      - Cash (Vietnamese currency with equivalent value);
      - Equipment, machinery: .... (value);
      - The transfer of technology (if any, value, royalties, copyright fees, etc.);
      - Workshops, land sites, or other contribution in accordance with the Foreign Investment Law .... (value).

   b) The Foreign Party contributes .... (value, accounting for .... percent of the legal capital), comprising:

      - Foreign currency .... (value);
      - Equipment, machinery .... (value);
      - The transfer of technology (if any, value);
      - Other contributions, copyright fees, ... (if any).

   (In case this is a "multiparty joint venture," describe in detail the legal capital and capital contribution percentages by each party.) Details in product quantity, technical specifications, equipment, unit price, etc., are presented in Annex No. .... of the JV Contract.

   The value contributed by the transfer of technology (if any) as agreed upon by both Parties, appears in a separate annex attached to the JV Contract.

3. In addition to its legal capital, the JV company may acquire loans or credits in order to increase its capital for business purposes.

   (Note: If the JV company needs any loan, list the party responsible for loan arrangement and its conditions.)

Article 4:

The two parties undertake to contribute their respective capital fully and on time, as follows:

- The party(ies) of Vietnam: (State clearly the value contributed and the schedule for capital contribution of the Vietnamese Party(ies) after being granted the JV Investment License.)
- The foreign party(ies): (State clearly the value contributed and the schedule for capital contribution of the Foreign Party(ies) after being granted the JV Investment License.)

Note: At the time when the actual financial contribution is made, if the projected values shown above differ when compared with the actual contributed values, the two parties must agree to these differences and report same to the State Committee for Cooperation and Investment for consideration and approval.

Article 5:

Any party unable to complete the payment schedule as agreed upon above, shall have to inform the other party stating the reasons why and the measures to be taken by this party, in order to resolve the situation before .... (the date). The delinquent party agrees to provide compensation to the other party for losses (if any, such as for example, delays in the supply of equipment, machines, and materials caused by its inability to contribute funds according to the schedule of payments).

Article 6:

The program for gradual increase of capital contribution of the Vietnamese Party(ies) (commencing with the first production year) shall be stated as below, for instance:
(For example:
within first 3 or 5 years: ..... percent capital contribution;
within the second 3 or 5 years: .... percent capital contribution;
following years ....: ..... percent capital contribution).

Article 7:

The term of this JV Contract is .... years, commencing from the date of the issuing of the JV Investment License. Any changes to this term shall have to be agreed upon by all parties concerned and reported to SCCI for approval.

Article 8:

The schedule for implementing this contract after the date on which the Investment License by SCCI has been issued, is as follows:

1. a) Importation (if applicable) of building materials for the main production area/plant of the office:

      from month .... to month ....

   b) Construction of the main production area/plant or the office:

      from month .... to month ....

2. Importation of equipment and machinery related to the actual production:

   from month .... to month ....

3. Production/trial operation:

   from month .... to month ....

4. Official production:

   from month ....

Article 9:

Other responsibilities of the joint venture parties are stipulated as follows:

a) The Vietnamese Party(ies): ....

   (State clearly such responsibilities as: supply of equipment, expertise, technology, finance, loans and credits, building materials, sources of market, training, technical management, etc.)

b) The Foreign Party(ies):

   (State clearly such responsibilities as: supply of equipment, expertise, technology, finance, loans and credits, building materials, sources of market, training, technical management, etc.)

Article 10:

After fulfilling all financial obligations toward the State of Vietnam and establishing the Reserve Fund, the Welfare Fund, and other appropriate funds, the remaining net profits of the JV Company are shared as follows:.....

(State clearly the rates of profits shared for each JV party.)

The structure of operation, as well as the scope and principle of using each fund, shall be decided by the Board of Management in conformity with the Laws of Socialist Republic of Vietnam.

Article 11:

Any dispute between the Parties arising in respect of the implementation of the Contract, must be resolved through negotiations. In cases where the parties in dispute cannot agree with each other, the disputes shall be brought to ... (state clearly the name of the arbitration organization and address). The decision of .... (the above organization) is final and the JV parties or the company must abide by it.

Article 12:

The Joint Venture company may be dissolved ahead of schedule or terminated as stipulated in Article 18 of the JV Charter.

Article 13:

This Business Cooperation Contract may be terminated ahead of schedule in the following cases:

a) Where force majeure such as natural disasters, war, etc.

renders the investment activities inoperable, provided of course that this force majeure is indeed the actual cause of obstruction to or unacceptable delay in the implementation/continuation of the contract and that the parties have already applied all possible measures to overcome the impact of force majeure disasters but without success.

In such cases, it is anticipated that the party in whose area the force majeure has occurred shall have immediately informed the other party(ies) about the above state of affairs, and shall have within 20 days, sent the other Party(ies) a written statement concerning the measures taken as well as details of the force majeure events certified by the local authority(ies). In addition, the contracting parties shall immediately inform the State Committee for Cooperation and Investment about all measures taken to overcome the situation (albeit unsuccessful).

b) In case the business activity is unable to continue its operations due to serious losses or due to breach of contract terms leading to serious economic losses and this has been approved by SCCI.

c) As a result of a decision by the State Committee for Cooperation and Investment, to withdraw the investment license.

Article 14:

All other terms relating to the activities of the JV company but not stipulated in the JV Charter, shall be implemented by the parties in accordance with current provisions of the Foreign Investment Law of Vietnam and the stipulations (if any) in the JV Investment License granted by the SCCI.

Article 15:

The JV contract may be added and/or amended after a unanimous decision of the Board of Management of the JVC and following approval of SCCI.

Article 16:

This contract shall take effect immediately after the Investment Application is approved by SCCI.

Article 17:

The JV Contract is signed in (location) .... on (date) in the Vietnamese version and in the .... version (a widely used foreign language). The two versions are of equal validity.

THE FOREIGN PARTY

(Signature, title, and
seal, if any)

In case there are several
foreign parties, state
the name of each party
and affix appropriate seal
(if any)

THE VIETNAMESE PARTY

(Signature, title, and
seal, if any)

In case there are several
Vietnamese parties, state
the name of each party
and affix appropriate seal
(if any)

Form 5
INVESTMENT APPLICATION FOR LICENSING AN ENTERPRISE WITH 100 PERCENT FOREIGN-OWNED CAPITAL

Date:_____

To: The State Committee for Cooperation and Investment

An investment application under the Foreign Investment Law in Vietnam is herewith being submitted by the undersigned to the Socialist Republic of Vietnam through the State Committee for Cooperation and Investment.

Particulars regarding the proposed Business Cooperation as well as the requested Investment Incentives and related Data/Documentation are described herein and or submitted herewith:

I. Company .....(The name of the Company/Enterprise) wishes to be issued with an investment license in order to establish in Vietnam an Enterprise with 100 percent foreign-owned capital in accordance with the Charter attached herewith.

II. We wish to apply for the following Investment Incentives:

•

•

III. The Documents enclosed with this Application comprise:

• The Charter of the Enterprise with 100 percent foreign-owned capital.

• Certification concerning juridical person status, as well as the Company's certified Annual General Report and/or Banker's reference from an internationally acceptable Financial Institution;

- Legalized Power(s) of Attorney for signing this application and the Charter of the Proposed Enterprise;

- The economic and technical feasibility studies;

- The appointed surveyor's inspection report concerning used or second-hand equipment (if such equipment is intended for use-importation into the Socialist Republic of Vietnam).

THE INVESTOR
(or the Authorized Representative)
(Signature and Seal)

VISITOR INFORMATION

Airlines Offices in Hanoi and Ho Chi Minh City

Cathay Pacific
27 Ly Thai To Street
Hanoi
Tel: 269232

Cathay Pacific
49 Le Thanh Tong Street, District 1
Ho Chi Minh City
Tel: 223203

China Airlines
116 Nguyen Hue Street, District 1
Ho Chi Minh City
Tel: 251387

China Southern Airlines
27 Ly Thai To Street
Hanoi
Tel: 267232

China Southern Airlines
52B Pham Hong Thai, District 1
Ho Chi Minh City
Tel: 291172

Museums—Hanoi

The Museum of History
1 Trang Tien Street
Closed Mondays

The Museum of the Revolution
25, Tong Dan Street
Closed Mondays

The Museum of Fine Arts
66, Nguyen Thai Hoc Street
Closed Mondays

The Army Museum
28A Dien Bien Phu Avenue
Closed Mondays

The Air Force Museum
Truong Chinh Street in the Dong Da District
Open Thursday and Sunday

Ho Chi Minh's Mausoleum
Closed Mondays and Fridays

The Ho Chi Minh Museum
Behind the One Pillar Pagoda near Ho's Mausoleum

Ho Chi Minh's Wooden House
Closed Mondays

Hotels—Hanoi

Metropole
15 Ngo Quyen, Central
Tel: (84-4) 266919

Heritage Hotel
80 Giang Vo
Tel: (84-4) 351414

Thang Loi Hotel
Yen Phu, West Lake
Tel: (84-4) 268211, 268215

Orient (Phuong Dong) Hotel
16 Lang Ha, Ba Dinh
Tel: (84-4) 345397, 345398

Hai Dang Hotel
49 Hong Bong
Tel: (84-4) 260843, 250962

Saigon Hotel
80 Ly Thuong Kiet
Tel: (84-4) 268499, 268505

Hanoi Hotel
D8 Giang Vo
Tel: (84-4) 452240

Hotels—Ho Chi Minh City

Rex Hotel
141 Nguyen Hue
Tel: (84-8) 292185

The Saigon Floating Hotel
1 A Me Linh Square, D1
Tel: (84-8) 290783

Century Saigon Hotel
68A Nguyen Hue Boulevard, D1
Tel: (84-8) 231818

Hotel Majestic Saigon
01 Dong Khoi, D1
Tel: (84-8) 295510

Caravelle (Doc Lap)
19-23 Lam Son Square, D1
Tel: (84-8) 293704

Continental
132 Dong Khoi, D1
Tel: (84-8) 294456

Omni Saigon Hotel
251 Nguyen Van Troi
Phu Nhuan District
Tel: (84-8) 449222

Hotels—Vung Tau, Da Nang, and Hai Phong

Hai Au Hotel
100 Ha Long
Vung Tau, Vietnam
Tel: (84-6) 452278

Rex Hotel
1 Duy Tan
Vung Tau, Vietnam
Tel: (84-6) 452165

Hoa Binh Hotel
104 Luong Khanh Thien
Hai Phong, Vietnam
Tel: (84-3) 146907

Dien Bien Hotel
67 Dien Bien Phu
Hai Phong, Vietnam
Tel: (84-3) 142573

Hong Bang Hotel
64 Dien Bien Phu
Hai Phong, Vietnam
Tel: (84-3) 142229

Non Nuoc Hotel (on the beach)
Da Nang, Vietnam
Tel: (84-5) 136216

Phuong Dong Hotel
93 Phan Chu Trinh
Da Nang, Vietnam
Tel: (84-5) 121266

Dien Luc Hotel
37 Hai Phong
Da Nang, Vietnam
Tel: (84-5) 121864

Van Hai Hotel
Bai Chay Road (on the beach)
Ha Long Bay, Vietnam
Tel: (84-3) 346403

Restaurants—Hanoi

A Little Italian
81 Tho Nhoum
Hanoi
Tel: (84-4) 258167

Le Beaulieu
Metropole
15 Ngo Quyen
Hanoi
Tel: (84-4) 266919

Piano Restaurant and Bar
50 Hang Vai
Hanoi
Tel: (84-4) 232423

Restaurant 22
22 Hang Can
Hanoi
Tel: (84-4) 267160

Restaurant 75
75 Tran Quoc Toan
Hanoi
Tel: (84-4) 265619

Restaurant 202
202A Hue
Hanoi
Tel: (84-4) 269487

Mekki-Lan Anh Restaurant
9A Da Tuong
Hanoi
Tel: (84-4) 267552

Saigon Pull
217 Doi Can
Hanoi
Tel: (84-4) 246181

Gala International Restaurant
33 Nghi Tam
Hanoi
Tel: (84-4) 234290

Sunset Pub
On top of Dong Do Hotel
Giang Vo Street
Hanoi
Tel: (84-4) 351382

Restaurants—Ho Chi Minh City

Vietnam House
93, 95 Dong Khoi, D1
Tel: (84-8) 291623

Oscar's Grill
Century Saigon Hotel
68A Nguyen Hue, D5
Tel: (84-8) 231818

Cung Dinh
41 Pasteur
Tel: (84-8) 296042

Huong Xuan
123 Le Loi
Tel: (84-8) 290930

German Beer
34 Dong Khoi
Tel: (84-8) 223623

Cay Dua
154 Le Lai
Tel: (84-8) 398467

Nihon Bashi
Rex Hotel
46 Le Loi, D1
Tel: (84-8) 292186

Garden Court Restaurant
Saigon Century Hotel
68 Nguyen Hue, D1
Tel: (84-8) 231818

Seoul Restaurant
37 Ngo Duc Ke, D1
Tel: (84-8) 294297

The Oriental Court
1A Me Linh Square, D1
Tel: (84-8) 290783

Rex Garden Restaurant
86 Le Thanh Ton, D1
Tel: (84-8) 292186, ext. 7768

Jacky Restaurant
5 Kong Truong Me Linh, D1
Tel: (84-8) 294476

Sky View
Mondial Hotel
109 Dong Khoi, D1
Tel: (84-8) 296291

Orient Dancing Restaurant
104 Hai Ba Trung, D1
Tel: (84-8) 225478

Dong Que Restaurant
905 Hau Giang, D6

Givral
169 Dong Khoi, D1
Tel: (84-8) 292747

Liberty Restaurant
80 Dong Khoi, D1
Tel: (84-8) 299820

Maxims Theatre Restaurant
17 Dong Khoi, D1
Tel: (84-8) 296676

Huong Uyen Garden Palace
1051 Xo Viet Nghe Tinh
Tel: (84-8) 994000

Phuc Lam Mon Restaurant
1A Trinh Van Can, D1
Tel: (84-8) 223681

The Thanh
5-9 Nguyen Trung, D1
Tel: (84-8) 291214

City Bar and Grill
63 Dong Khoi, D1
Tel: (84-8) 298006

Ngan Dinh Harbour View Restaurant
2A ton Duc Thang, D1
Tel: (84-8) 299137

Siren Floating Restaurant
Bach Dang Quay, D1
Tel: (84-8) 225402

Restaurants—Da Nang

The Tu Do
172 Tran Phu
Tel: (0151) 21869

Christie's
On The Waterfront
9 Bach Dang

Nightclubs and Discotheques—Hanoi

Royal Hotel Disco
20 Hang Tre Street
Tel: (84-4) 244233

VIP Club
62 Nguyen Du
Tel: (84-4) 269167

Top Disco Club
Thuyen Quang Lake
Tel: (84-4) 226641

ATC Musical Restaurant
39-41 Hang Giay
Tel: (84-4) 225611

Thang Loi Dancing Hall
Thanh Loi Hotel, West Lake
Tel: (84-4) 268211

Sunset Pub
Giang Vo
Tel: (84-4) 351382

Apocalypse Now
44 Hang Vai

The Emerald Pub
53 Hang Luoc
Tel: (84-4) 259258

Saigon Pull
217 Doi Can
Tel: (84-4) 346181

Nightclubs and Discotheques—Ho Chi Minh City

Lakeview Club
28 Thanh Nien

Starlight Night Club
68A Nguyen Hue, D1
Tel: (84-8) 231818

Superstar Disco
431/A/2 Hoang Van Thu
Tel: (84-8) 440242

VIP Club
2D Pham Ngoc Thach, D1
Tel: (84-8) 229860

Queen Bee
104 Nguyen Hue, D1
Tel: (84-8) 298839

Shangri La Complex
1196, 3/2, D11
Tel: (84-8) 556831

Cheers Music and KTV
Vien Dong Hotel
275A Pham Ngu Lao,D1
Tel: (84-8) 392055

The Down Under Disco
1A Me Linh Square, D1
Tel: (84-8) 290783

Orient Dancing Restaurant
104 Hai Ba Trung, D1
Tel: (84-8) 225478

Pub International Restaurant/Disco
32 Ngo Duc Ke Street, D1
Tel: (84-8) 295427

Gartenstadt, German Bar
34 Dong Khoi Street, D1
Tel: (84-8) 223623

The Lobby Bar
1A Me Linh Square, D1
Tel: (84-8) 290783

Q Bar
7 Lam Son Square, D1
Tel: (84-8) 291299

Superstar Disco
431/A Hoang Van Thu Street
Tan Binh District
Tel: (84-8) 440242

Cheers Disco
First Floor of Vien Dong Hotel
Pham Ngu Lao
Tel: (84-8) 392052

River Bar
Ho Huan Nghiep Street

Tiger Tavern
227 Dong Khoi Street
Tel: (84-8) 222738

International Tourist Club Saigon
76 Le Lai Street, D1
Tel: (84-8) 295134

Orient Restaurant
104 Hai Ba Trung, D1
Tel: (84-8) 225478

Linda's Bar
Hai Ba Trung, near Q Bar

Casino Bar
Between Dong Khoi and Nguyen Hue Street

Shakes Pub
16/32 Phan Van Dat
Tel: (84-8) 231624

BIBLIOGRAPHIC

SOURCES

"A Summary of Recent Legal Developments in Indochina," *Indochina Law Quarterly: Cambodia, Laos, Vietnam.* Baker & McKenzie. June, 1994, Volume 2, No. 2.

"A Summary of Recent Legal Developments in Indochina," *Indochina Law Quarterly: Cambodia, Laos, Vietnam.* Baker & McKenzie. June, 1994, Volume 3, Nos. 1 & 2.

"Billboard Red Tape Incites Agency Protests Over 'Ambiguous' Rules," *Vietnam Investment Review,* April 25-May 1, 1994, pg. 5.

"Command Economy Confronts the Free Market on the Shop Floor," *Vietnam Today,* Vol. 3, Issue 1, 1994, pg. 11.

"Distribution: An Official View," *Vietnam Economic Times,* July, 1994, pg. 24.

"Entering the Vietnamese Market?" *Vietnam Today,* Vol. 3, Issue 1, 1994, pg. 36.

"Fact File: A Guide to Business in Vietnam for First Time Visitors," *Vietnam Today,* Vol. 3, Issue 1, 1994, pg. 10.

"Guide to Renting Property," *Vietnam Economic Times,* June, 1994, pg. 19.

"Legal Protection for Software Companies Key to Major Growth," *Vietnam Investment Review,* May 2-8, 1994, pg. 12.

"Licensing of Trademarks," *Vietnam Economic Times,* July, 1994, pg. 28.

"Organizers Claim Success with US Expo," *Vietnam Investment Review,* April 25-May 1, 1994, pg. 1.

"Owning a House in Vietnam: What the Regulations Mean," *Vietnam Investment Review,* August 1-7, 1994, pg. 12.

"Regulations on Import/Export in Vietnam," *Vietnam Economic Times,* June, 1994, pg. 28.

"The Complete Business Guide," *Vietnam Economic Times,* Issue 3, June 3, 1994.

"The Long and Winding Road," *Vietnam Investment Review,* July 11-17, 1994, pg. 6.

"The First Step," *Vietnam Today,* Vol. 3, Issue 1, 1994, pg. 27.

"Vietnam in 1993 Trade and Investment Review," *The Indochina Project.* Washington, D.C. 1993.

"Vietnam: A Guide to the Legal Framework," Published by Clifford Chance law firm, 1994.

An, Kieu "The Linh Trung EPZ: Demand Surpasses Supply," *The Saigon Times,* July 15-21, 1993, pg. 10.

An, Nguyen "Charting Equitization through Difficult Waters," *Vietnam Investment Review,* May 23-29, 1994, pg. 18.

Anh, Haoi "Towards Most-Favored-Nation Status," *Vietnam Investment Review,* May 23-29, 1994, pg. 14.

Jan Annerstedt and Tim Sturgeon, "Electronics and Information Technology in Vietnam," published by UNIDO/UNDP for the Ministry of Science, Technology and Environment, Hanoi, April, 1994.

David Dollar et al., "Vietnam: Transition to the Market," The World Bank, Country Operations Division, September, 1993.

Christopher F. Bruton and Mathilde L. Genovese, "Vietnam: An Investor's Appraisal," Hong Kong: Business International Asia/Pacific Ltd., 1990.

Kelvin Chia, "Steps to Prevent Trademark 'Ripoff'," *Vietnam Investment Review*, July 4-10, 1994, pg. 8.

Chia, Kelvin "Project Evaluation Process Depends on Sector and Size" *Vietnam Investment Review,* July 25-31, 1994, pg. 12.

Michael Collins, "Exhibitors Disappointed By Showing," *Vietnam Investment Review*, April 25-May 1, 1994, pg. 14.

Ho Tien Dung, "Reaching the End User," *Vietnam Economic Times,* July, 1994, pg 15.

Nguyen Tri Dung, "'We're Listening,' says SCCI Chief," *Vietnam Investment Review*, May 16-22, 1994, pg. 1.

Adam Fforde, "Vietnam: Economic Commentary and Analysis," ADUKI Pty. Ltd., Issue no 4., Dec., 1993.

Jeremy Grant, "Hedging in Danang," *Vietnam Economic Times,* June, 1994, pg. 23.

Hanoi International Women's Club. Hanoi Guide. Hanoi: Hanoi Publishing House, 1994.

Hong Kong Trade and Development Council. Trade and Investment Opportunities in Vietnam. Hong Kong: Research Department, Hong Kong Trade Development Council, 1994.

Tran Viet Hung, "Trademark Protection Beginning to Take Hold," *Vietnam Investment Review*, June 27-July 3, 1994, pg. 19.

International Labour Office. "Employment, Enterprise Development and Training in Vietnam," Bangkok Area Office, Bangkok, January, 1994.

Sam Korsmoe, "The Price of Saigon," *Vietnam Economic Times*, June, 1994, pg. 12.

Nguyen Van Mihn, "The Facts Behind a Fax," *Vietnam Economic Times*, June, 1994, pg. 7.

Thai Nhu, "Billboards Sign of a New Era," *Vietnam Investment Review,* June 13-19, 1994, pg. 16.

Marita van Oldenborgh, "Vietnam's Transport Swamp," *International Business,* May, 1994, pg. 40.

Vu Tien Phuc, "Portrait of Five E.P.Zs in Vietnam," *Vietnam Economic News,* No. 9, March 8, 1994, pg. 11.

Le Minh Quan, "Danang: The Bubbles Gets Bigger, Business Surges," *Vietnam Investment Review,* May 2-8, 1994, pg. 16.

Michael Shapiro, "Pioneer Financier Eugene Matthews," *The New York Times Magazine,* August 28, 1994, pg. 35.

Andy Soloman, "Now It's Hanoi's Turn," *Vietnam Economic Times,* June, 1994, pg. 20.

Andy Soloman, "Walkman Wishes & Video Dreams," *Vietnam Today,* Vol. 3, Issue 1, 1994, pg. 17.

Vu Manh Son, "Look Before You Leap," *Vietnam Economic Times,* September, 1994, pg. 19.

Robert Storey, "Vietnam: A Travel Survival Kit," Berkeley, CA: Lonely Planet, 1993.

Nguyen Chi Thanh, "Fakes Leave Buyers Flat," *Vietnam Investment Review,* June 6-12, 1994, pg. 17.

The Economist Intelligence Unit. Vietnam Outlook, 3rd quarter, 1994.

Hoang Minh Tuan, "Choosing the Right Way to Enter Vietnam," *Vietnam Economic Times,* August, 1994, pg. 14.

Hoang Minh Tuan, "Danang: Rising Star?" *Vietnam Economic Times,* October, 1994, pg. 16.

Vietnam Investment Review, March 14, 1994, "Accountants Celebrate Anniversary," Thuy Huong.

Thuy Huong, "Accountants Celebrate Anniversary," *Vietnam Investment Review.* March 14, 1994.

Nguyen Tri Dung, "New Masterplan Foists Tourism into 'Doi Moi' Limelight," *Vietnam Investment Review.* October 3, 1994.

Vietnam: A Country Study. Federal Research Division, Library of Congress. Published by Department of the Army. Washington D.C., 1989.

Vu Duc Thi, "Information Technology Lagging in Vietnam," *Vietnam Investment Review,* March 28-April 3, 1994, p. 21.

INDEX

W